War, Human Dignity and Nation Building

War, Human Dignity and Nation Building: Theological Perspectives on Canada's Role in Afghanistan

Edited by

Gary D. Badcock and Darren C. Marks

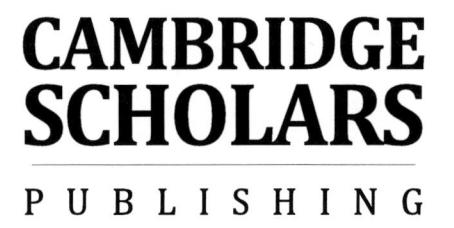

CAMBRIDGE SCHOLARS
PUBLISHING

War, Human Dignity and Nation Building:
Theological Perspectives on Canada's Role in Afghanistan,
Edited by Gary D. Badcock and Darren C. Marks

This book first published 2010

Cambridge Scholars Publishing

12 Back Chapman Street, Newcastle upon Tyne, NE6 2XX, UK

British Library Cataloguing in Publication Data
A catalogue record for this book is available from the British Library

Copyright © 2010 by Gary D. Badcock and Darren C. Marks and contributors

All rights for this book reserved. No part of this book may be reproduced, stored in a retrieval system, or transmitted, in any form or by any means, electronic, mechanical, photocopying, recording or otherwise, without the prior permission of the copyright owner.

ISBN (10): 1-4438-2381-3, ISBN (13): 978-1-4438-2381-4

TABLE OF CONTENTS

Acknowledgements vii

Introduction 1
Gary D. Badcock and Darren C. Marks

Warfighting, Counterinsurgency and Peacekeeping in Afghanistan:
Three Strategies Examined in the Light of Just War Theory 16
A. Walter Dorn

The NATO Club and Afghanistan: Northern, Rich, and White Nations
Defend the Imperial Palace 71
Erika Simpson

Muslim Opposition to the War in Afghanistan:
The Case(s) of Bangladesh and Turkey 91
Rashed Chowdhury

Afghanistan's Villages and Districts: Notes on A Forgotten Priority 113
Remmelt C. Hummelen

Inculturation and Intervention in Afghanistan: Perspectives
from Contextual Theology 118
Christopher Hrynkow

Death, Interpretation and Prophecy 141
Howard Adelman

No Choice but to Confront Afghanistan: Theological Reflections
on the Impasse Between Policy and Theology 171
Darren C. Marks

Reason, the Moral Order and Inter-Religious Dialogue: Pope Benedict
XVI's Regensburg Lecture 198
Craig A. Carter

Christian Realism and Its Limits 212
Gary D. Badcock

Reconciliation and the "War" on Terror: Canadian Churches Respond
to 9/11 and the War in Afghanistan 231
Ernie Regehr

Many Faiths, One Planet: The Perils and Possibilities of Religion
in a Fragile World 253
John Douglas Hall

Contributors 267

ACKNOWLEDGEMENTS

This volume is based on the May, 2009 Conference of the Centre for Public Theology at Huron University College, London, Ontario. Financial support for this Conference and for the Centre for Public Theology's research was provided under the Aids to Small Universities program of the Social Sciences and Humanities Research Council of Canada.

INTRODUCTION

GARY D. BADCOCK AND DARREN C. MARKS

In his Foreword to the 2008 report to the Canadian Parliament of the Independent Panel on the Future of Canada's Role in Afghanistan, the distinguished Canadian politician John Manley wrote as Panel Chair of how Canada finds itself, as a NATO member and a sizable contributor to ISAF, the International Security Assistance Force in Afghanistan, "in a land that is far from us, little known by us and where our interests do not seem self-evident…whose recent history has been one long, unending tragedy, and whose prospects still appear bleak."[1] It was a fitting summary of the general problem faced, not only by Canada, by all the Western nations involved in the Afghanistan war. And yet, despite the fact that the Panel's Report made wide-ranging recommendations on the basis of an informed and realistic assessment of the prevailing situation on the ground, it was almost wholly silent on one of the central issues underlying and helping to sustain the conflict: religion. For it is religious factors, or, at the very least, cultural factors deeply interwoven with religion, that help both to make Afghanistan such an incomprehensible land to the average Westerner, and that equally help to make the presence of Western troops, diplomats and development agencies so ambiguous a blessing to the average Afghan citizen. But if Western governments, as represented by the Report of this Panel appointed by the Parliament of Canada, are silent on the question of religion's significance in the Afghanistan conflict, it is also true that religious traditions, particularly those of the Abrahamic family, have largely been silent on the conflict as well. Given the fact that Afghanistan is the longest running war in Canadian history and that Canadian casualties have been so heavy, and given the immense financial commitment made to the conflict since 2002, this is an astonishing oversight.

To say this, it must immediately be acknowledged, is not to deny that

---

[1] *Independent Panel on Canada's Future Role in Afghanistan* (The Queen's Printer, No. FR5-20/1-2008), http://dsp-psd.pwgsc.gc.ca/collection_2008/dfait-maeci/FR5-20-1-2008E.pdf, p. 3.

the Afghanistan crisis involves a great deal more than religion, as well as much that is not authentically related to it. Much of the conflict, for instance, is driven by lawless elements in the society, including criminals involved in the drugs trade. Such people have distinct and very different reasons than does the Taliban to want no viable central government to emerge, for their future is contingent on the failure of any campaign for the "rule of law," whether Islamic or secular. Yet such diverse players are all perfectly prepared to use religious language in order to buttress their cause within the population. Sheer poverty is also a massive factor: where Taliban pay is much better even than that available in the employ of the Afghan National Army, never mind what can be earned from working on the land or in some trade, and where families go hungry, there must always be a ready supply of recruits to the insurgent cause. Corruption in government and in the security and police apparatus of the state is also a huge issue, helping to sustain hostility to the regime in marginal populations, and serving as an impetus to armed resistance against the regime. The tragic recent history of Afghanistan also feeds ethnic rivalries and provides a super-abundance of "scores" that must be settled according to the honour codes by which people live and die. To confuse such factors with religion per se would obviously be a mistake.

Nevertheless, though more than religion is obviously in question, the conflict also involves nothing less than religion. At its epicentre presently is a loose alliance of Sunni Muslims, drawn largely from the ethnic Pashtuns of Afghanistan and Pakistan, and reinforced by a steady stream of international jihadists allied sometimes closely, sometimes more loosely with the al-Qaeda cause, for whom the war is an overwhelmingly religious concern. Their fundamental loyalties lie either with a rigorist interpretation of Islamic law as formed by and enforced within longstanding tribal codes in the region, or else with the eschatological dream of a global Islamic Caliphate, bringing peace and justice to the earth by the enforcement of divine law (Sharia).

The former, as the case of Pakistan in recent months and years amply demonstrates, constitutes a power in the world of the sort that has long-since been forgotten in the West, but that in the borderlands of Afghanistan and Pakistan is capable of marshalling formidably determined foes. It can compete in the sphere of "hearts and minds" in the region very effectively against the ideals of "freedom," "human rights," or even "development" on offer from Western democracies. Indeed, even beyond the immediate region, such Western ideals are as often as not understood to be religiously undesirable, related as they are to social change and grounding as they do the availability of pornography and the like.

The dream of a global Islamic Caliphate, for its part, though clearly vague and incapable of realization, is just for this reason the sort of apocalyptic vision suited to inspire rebellion among disaffected youth born to a culture that has learned, often for good reason, to be suspicious of and resentful towards Western influence. The whole movement to resist the West in its policy in Afghanistan, finally, though financed in part from the drugs trade (as noted, for instance, by Erika Simpson in what follows in this volume), and sustained by a flourishing black market, is also supported financially by extremely well-heeled private individuals in the Gulf states and beyond, who have overtly religious as well as economic and political reasons for hostility to Western influence in the Muslim world—and who are perfectly prepared, it would seem, to tolerate the suffering of millions in order to see the West fail in its present Afghan venture.

There is, of course, a reason to explain why it is that the Independent Panel on the Future of Canada's Role in Afghanistan, among a multitude of other agencies internationally, resisted any substantial reference to the religious dimension. The reason can be very simply stated: the Western political process is strictly incapable of engaging it. Given the particular history of relations between politics and religion in the Western world in the context of modernity, it is able to address the question of religious identity only to the extent that religion has already been rendered purely "private," and thus apolitical, something precisely not fundamental to the common weal. And yet such is what is at stake for those who at this moment stand against American and ISAF forces in Afghanistan; indeed, one of the central things resisted is just this marginalization of religious obligation in the political sphere of human life.

What a nation such as Canada faces in Afghanistan is, therefore, something profoundly foreign not only to its base values but also to its available political conceptuality, so that it is difficult to see how it can ever come to understand what it fights against. "Islamofascism" is a neologism much used by the Bush regime after the attacks of 11 September, 2001, as well as by a range of political scholarship, to define the enemy faced. It has prominent intellectual defenders (such as Christopher Hitchens, who credits the Scottish Islamic Studies scholar Malise Ruthven, writing in the British newspaper, *The Independent*, with its invention on September 8, 1990).[2] From the standpoint of religion, however, it is a poor word to use, ill-adapted to the motives of Taliban and jihadist alike, and thus prone to

---

[2] Christopher Hitchens, "Defending *Islamofascism*," *Slate*, October 22, 2007, http://www.slate.com/id/2176389/. A more detailed treatment was provided by William Safire, "Islamofascism," *New York Times Magazine*, October 1, 2006, 6.20.

badly misrepresent the underlying views of the enemy. Ruthven's original reference in the article, in fact, was to the disturbing strain of authoritarianism evident in Islamic politics in nations such as Pakistan and Morocco—administrations which the Taliban and the jihadists uniformly detest—and so was basically an ad hominem use of language intended for a predominantly Western audience. It nevertheless caught on, perhaps because, as projection onto the "other" by the West, it made a kind of sense. The term "Islamofascism" succeeds, in short, to the extent that it makes the "other" something made in our image, and so comprehensible in our own terms. The fact of the matter is, however, that the Taliban themselves have as little interest in Fascism, which in its main twentieth century representations was an anti-religious political philosophy in which talk of freedom and modernization featured prominently, as they do in the Liberalism that in the twentieth century triumphed over it. Their political goal is something else altogether, and that has nothing to do with the Fascist vision. The goal is a sacred Islamic state living under divine law, and it is to this extent a political order that resists and rejects the political claim of modernity (whether Liberal, Fascist or Communist) altogether.

In a certain sense, then, the problem of Afghanistan represents not just a crisis for the military strategist, the diplomat or the aid worker, but a crisis that places in question a whole set of assumptions foundational to modern Western politics itself. For in its politics, modernity is the universal claim of a practical reason that has abstracted itself from religious commitment in order to further a purely human good. The wars of modernity hitherto have concerned, for the most part, the details of that project. What has dominated is whether the aim of this or that modern state is the more human, and whether within the state it is Fascism, Liberalism or Communism that makes the more rational claim, thus (axiomatically, it seems) securing human freedom. Short of simply imposing a political vision on the world though military and economic means, as in the era of grand imperial ambition, or by attacking religion as praeparatio for the happy dawn of the secularist ideal, modernity in its political outlook has very little idea how to deal with a culture that rejects those broad assumptions altogether.

Since some are already calling the conflict that we face—with our children, on some accounts—"World War IV,"[3] we might do better in our own context to address the religious question anew. Rather than continuing to pretend that, like all things religious in modern democratic liberalism, the religious question in Afghanistan too is a political

---

[3] Norman Podhoretz, World War IV: The Long Struggle Against Islamofascism (New York: Vintage Books, 2008).

irrelevance, perhaps it is time we asked some basic questions concerning the wisdom of the modern political stance. For religion is patently no irrelevance in the Afghanistan war. While an approach which takes the public dimension of religion seriously could obviously not resolve the conflict, the roots of which are tangled together with all manner of motives and grievances, it might at least help us to understand the sources of the conflict better, and to communicate more effectively concerning both means and ends.

Not the least of the potential shifts needed, for instance, is an abandonment on the part of Western politicians and pundits of the language of "Islamofascism," which almost wholly obscures rather than illuminates the problem and the potential alike of politics in the Islamic world. However, the conceptual shift needed extends well beyond this, to such things as what the West instinctively wants to think and say and do in connection with that distinctively modern conception termed "human rights," and to the kind of political ideals that not only can but actually ought to be embraced in a nation such as Afghanistan now and in the future.

No doubt most of the labour and pain required for any movement beyond the present impasse must take place in Afghanistan itself, as in the Muslim areas of South Asia generally. The problem that has to be faced emerges on two fronts, and it would be well for a moment to ponder the potential significance of each. The first concerns what can already been seen in Islamic religion and civilization today, and the second, what we are beginning to see in it, particularly in the Iranian setting, but which also must happen elsewhere as well if the first is allowed to continue. Nearly twenty-five years ago, the foremost non-Muslim interpreter of Islam in the West of his day, W. Montgomery Watt, observed the following in a essay written toward the end of his long academic career:

> It is hardly too much to say that the conservative traditionalist ulema [the jurists at the centre of Islamic religion] are shutting themselves and the masses who follow them into a ghetto of their own where they are not open to what is happening in the rest of the world. In the long run this state of affairs must lead to disaster. There are so many weaknesses and contradictions…in the traditionalist Islamic self-image that sooner or later there is bound to be a great revulsion of feeling against those who are maintaining the image….It is almost certain, however, that only after much struggle and suffering will the medieval self-image be replaced by a

truer one and the power of the conservative ulema broken.[4]

The judgment thus expressed was based not on any antipathy towards the history and glories of Islam as such, concerning which Watt was regarded by Muslim scholars themselves as a trusted dialogue partner, but on an exceptionally well-informed sense of the recent character of Islamic religious sensibility, in which the self-image is, as he put it, "the product more of imagination than of reason."[5] Its profound deficiency can most readily be evidenced in the abandonment of any serious attempt at historical criticism within Islamic thought in the modern context. Watt traced the same deficiency, however, through a range of further themes: from the prominence of the view that Islam is totally self-sufficient and has nothing to learn from other religions and cultures; to the view that Islam has the final truth for all humanity from now until the end of time—which is not only an infantile idea but a profoundly unworkable one in a world of constant development and change (and is eerily similar to evangelical Christianity's grotesque "creation science"); to its inability to adapt Islamic law to modern conditions. Watt observed: "It should be noted that the movement of Islamic resurgence has shown little interest in the adaptation of [Islamic law] to the world of today. Its main emphasis has been on those practices which distinguish Muslims from Westerners, in order to strengthen the sense of Muslim identity...."[6] The trouble with such a strategy, of course, is that saying "No" in such a constantly reactionary mode turns out in the end to be a poor route to self-definition, and, quite literally, the pathway to a peculiar form of nihilism.

Watt's observations help to inform our understanding of the religious situation not only in Afghanistan, but also in neighbouring countries such as Iran and Pakistan—indeed, in the Muslim world generally. However, what his view also reveals is a rather prescient grasp of a second source of present and future contention, which is the crisis that must face Islamic civilization in the broadest sense if the religious situation does not improve. Watt said this, not of "secular" political systems such as obtained at the time in Syria, Iraq or Morocco, but specifically of Iran in the aftermath of the Islamic Revolution. What may happen in Iranian religion, given "the great revulsion of feeling" that we are presently witnessing against the traditionalist *ulema* which seized power in 1979, is one of the great questions of the moment. It is so fundamental a question for Iran,

---

[4] W. Montgomery Watt, "The Muslim Tradition in Today's World," in Frank Whaling, ed., *Religion in Today's World* (Edinburgh: T & T Clark, 1987), 248-9.
[5] Ibid., 245.
[6] Ibid., 247.

indeed, that it can be doubted whether the Iranian *ulema* will survive it intact. What the future holds is uncertain, as again the capacity of the Iranian *ulema* to change is doubtful, but what has become all-too-clear is that further struggle and suffering are likely.

Afghanistan cannot be compared directly with Iran, for a host of reasons which include major differences in religious outlook, economics, educational standards, social development, tribal loyalties, and history generally. And yet, at the same time, many of the same dynamics that have shaped the history of Iran since 1979 and that have emerged so powerfully at the present moment are at the very least *echoed* in Afghanistan: from the genuinely popular desire for a more Islamic system of government; to the assumption that only an Islamic system can lead to a resolution of the troubles faced (both the Russian and Western-liberal alternatives being widely understood to be futile); to the existence of a powerful and highly conservative *ulema* which stands to gain from such a system of government; to the inevitability of failure in view of the inner self-contradictions and false self-image that its religious outlook represents; to the prospect of massive civil unrest and (especially in the Afghan context) the virtual certainty of curbed but continued violence. In this setting, it ought to be said here at the outset, the idea that the sending of a hundred thousand troops or even ten times that number to Afghanistan can resolve the problem is clearly a fiction. A surgical operation such deployment may be; a solution for Afghanistan's sorrows it is not. The bitter truth is that the path ahead will almost certainly lead through more sorrows—and this for the very reasons upon which Montgomery Watt put his finger a quarter century ago.

It would, however, obviously be short-sighted to treat the religious dimension of the conflict only in terms of the need for an in-house conversation within global Islam on the question of accommodating modernity, or even to see the underlying issue as that of a coming of age within Islam with respect to the political dangers of theocracy (as has been suggested by Jonathan Sacks, the Chief Rabbi of Great Britain).[7] For the fact is that there has for the most part been a failure of theological responsibility on all sides. To speak plainly, the editors of this volume in setting the Conference on which it is based had reason to anticipate, within the Canadian Christian fold, that the peace churches would align themselves with the theme of protest against violence; that the more established traditions such as the Anglican would move to respond pastorally to soldiers and their families and thereby mainly avoid politics

---

[7] Jonathan Sacks, "Islam Must Separate Religion from Power," *The Sunday Times*, 6 November, 2009.

and criticism; and that evangelicals might be more politically realist at best or at worst selective in discussion of Islam. Such expectations were sometimes realized, but what was too often clear was the lack of theological foundation upon which the standard responses represented were built. The one possible exception to this was the peace churches, who did speak with a John Howard Yoder-esque inflection. With rare and laudable exceptions, however (and even these have been under-resourced and have gone largely unheard by the average pew-sitter, such as those examined by Ernie Regehr in this volume), there has mostly been silence on the war in Afghanistan within Canadian faith communities, both in those classically associated with *de facto* establishment, and in those more clearly on the margins.

The Canadian Muslim response was something of an unknown quantity at the outset, though it was perhaps to be expected that Muslims, who are overwhelmingly relatively recent immigrants, would for the most part want to keep heads beneath the parapet on the question of the Afghanistan war. Some, however, did join the debate to make highly constructive contributions concerning, for instance, the importance of the strand of religious tolerance that can be identified in Islamic tradition at its source in the lifetime of the Prophet, or concerning the widespread perception of many women in parts of Afghanistan today that things were *better*, not worse, for them under the Taliban, in view of the present danger of sexual assault. However, at this point it is also imperative that we be as honest about the deficiencies of Canadian Islam as we have been about those of Canadian Christianity. David Goldberg, a former University of Toronto professor and now an independent analyst, points out that the three largest national Muslim organizations in Canada have increasingly become more "extreme" in terms of dialogue with Jews, civil action, and Afghanistan.[8] These organizations, he notes, undermine more moderate and likely more representative groups at the grassroots, who work in closer proximity to the other Abrahamic faiths and are likely more disposed to favour inter-religious dialogue. It may be, as Goldberg suggests, that moderates make up the majority, but the truth of the matter is that these are not the ones informing public opinion at large, or who are most visibly securing the "hearts and minds" of the average citizen. In Goldberg's rather depressing estimation, in other words, too much of Canadian Muslim-Christian-Jewish dialogue in the public sphere has become

---

[8] David Goldberg, "Jewish-Muslim Interaction in Canada," (interview by Manfred Gerstenfeld) *Institute for Global Jewish Affairs* 57 (2010), http://www.jcpa.org/JCPA/Templates/ShowPage.asp?DRIT=4&DBID=1&LNGID=1&TMID=111&FID=614&PID=0&IID=3934&TTL=Jewish-Muslim_Interaction_in_Canada.

uncomfortably extremist in character.

Thus the failure in the Canadian political context to take the religious dimension of the conflict sufficiently seriously is also broadly mirrored in a theological reluctance or even paralysis in undertaking responsible conversation about Afghanistan—indeed, the two failures are surely related. For Christians, whether in mainstream churches or smaller sectarian denominations, the issue is perhaps equally their misgivings concerning the "relevance" of such engagement within a culture that officially only permits "private spirituality" on the one side, and a paradoxically related inability to separate between religious values and those of the wider culture on the other. If religion is conceived to be something purely private, in short, then one has a religious duty to keep it so. Canadian Jews for the most part are naturally worried about Muslim extremism nationally and internationally, and increasingly about the clear tendency of many Canadian Christians to avoid so much as hinting that this might just be a defining issue; in the public space thus left vacant, knee-jerk reactions in support of the state of Israel's every gesture are only to be expected. The wider debate concerning Afghanistan has not, for the most part, been something that Canadian Jewry has much joined.

Happily, however, there are also instances of more developed theological reflection and criticism, and the papers represented in this volume reflect hope for the possibility of a deeper theological engagement with questions of realism, peace, and the spectrum in-between, as well as with the conduct of the Afghanistan war specifically. Though, in many of the churches, response to date has largely been driven by cultural cues, parroted theologies or indeed no theology at all, there is growing awareness that both criticism and support ought rather to derive from theological foundations—else the community in question clearly fails to take seriously its own religious dimensions. As terrible as it might seem to the Western mind, at least the Taliban has the wisdom to know that there is a connection between theology and human life as social reality. Ought we not to demand of the Judeo-Christian traditions in the West a similar commitment themselves to reflect seriously on these themes, and thus on how we might serve as co-agents in the mending of the world according to God's will? And could Islam be expected ever actually to listen to what we have to say and to take it seriously if we have not first taken this crucial step?

It cannot be underscored enough that were faith communities deeply to engage with Afghanistan and with one another on Afghanistan, and then with their governments, the issue of the war might well seem less bleak than it appears at present. But as John Douglas Hall maintains in his sage and sane contribution to this volume, such engagement might also have other, more unexpected benefits—not only for inter-religious understanding, or relations with secularists and secular government, or for future policy in Afghanistan—but also for each of the faith traditions themselves. Real dialogue among the traditions entails that each will be driven to discover why it is that it advocates what it does, and indeed, what that might and might not mean (the meaning of religious words being inherently subject to hermeneutical gloss). What passes for dialogue between faith traditions is too often only a kind of "dinner-club" friendship rather than serious engagement about serious issues, drawing as deeply as possible upon the resources of each faith. In any inter-religious dialogue of substance, however, it should for instance be possible for Judaism and Christianity to ask deep questions of Islam—and *vice versa*, let us say in the context of Christianity's collusion with colonialism. In fact, the truth is that such real dialogue among the traditions scarcely ever happens. We ought not to be surprised, therefore, that what we do have tends to yield superficial results, or that in the absence of meaningful critique from within or without, more radical and entrepreneurial groups are so able to further their particular agendas in the name of religion. Multiple sources influence such things, of course, not the least of which is the history of modernity itself (e.g., in connection with colonialism). In the present context, however, we are driven to say that the lack of theological responsibility has the effect of yielding the field to theological *irresponsibility*, so that, at one and the same time—and for some of the same reasons—we get the kind of chauvinistic, right-wing religious rhetoric that helped sustain the Bush administration's policies in Afghanistan, the distorted religious outlook of radical Islam, and the commonplace Islamophobia of the media and of many Western populations.

The end result is an incipiently weak theological voice, the utterances of which are steadily becoming more and more irrelevant to the cultural and moral fabric of society. Thus, as this Introduction is being written, the Canadian Parliament is challenged by the failure to meet a basic human— and, dare it be said, divine—mandate in the probable torture of combatants arrested, detained and given over to local officials in Afghanistan by Canadian soldiers. The official stance at least suspected by opposition parties (who, of course, would have done the same thing if in power—and indeed did do so even more egregiously in the case of the Liberals in the early years of the war) is that state security in the post 9/11 world must on occasion preclude the protection of basic human worth. However, all three of the Abrahamic traditions would surely be of a single mind that state security must be measured against a deeper awareness of what kind of state is permissible under God. After all, a state which abhorred due democratic process, which obstructed Parliamentary access to state documents, and which permitted its military leaders to sign "treaty" documents without Parliamentary scrutiny, and then sought to remain unaccountable afterwards for the outcome, is something that has been experienced before, even in living memory. There has, however, been a deafening silence on this question to date from the faith communities of Canada. This silence, unfortunately, amounts to a failure to name the particular folly of the state for what it is: human sin. Chief Rabbi Sacks, in the article mentioned earlier, argues that this is a lesson that has been learned in the crucible of history by Jews and Christians, and, of course, he references Nazism and the Holocaust in this connection. But it would appear that, amid the absence of a deep theological conversation by all involved, the lesson has been only very poorly learned in Canada.

One important voice, however, is largely left out in general conversation on Afghanistan in our daily politics, and this voice is a voice found in the Abrahamic faiths in thundering cascades. This is the voice of those without power, and without privilege, but of whom God surely knows and whose cry God surely hears. In the context of Afghanistan, this means the most vulnerable socially and economically, and in particular the women and children, the disabled, the dispossessed and the refugee. Advocacy, protest, and, not least, the provision of actual support for these people ought to be the concern of the faith traditions involved—yet our voice is largely silent, our actions are fragmentary, and both voice and action would have all the more power were it to be raised together. It is to the shame of the Abrahamic traditions that the extraordinary suffering of the disempowered and impoverished people of Afghanistan is left largely unmentioned in the midst of the political posturing taking place in the media and Parliament. While their discussion could not be included in this volume, it was enlightening to have Afghan women at our Conference speak on the on-going blight of the Afghanistan conflict, by which the most marginalized seem to pay the dearest price. It was also hugely hopeful to hear the voices of active NGOs whose experience in Afghanistan, working with actual human beings, seems so vastly different than what we hear constantly in the news. Remmelt Hummelen's essay is just such a voice—a voice that offers an elegant solution to many of the Afghan people's needs in so simple a project as reforestation.

With the exception of the contribution of John Douglas Hall, all the essays collected in this volume represent versions of papers presented at the inaugural Conference of the Centre for Public Theology at Huron

University College, University of Western Ontario, in May of 2009.[9] Each offers a separate reflection on the Afghanistan conflict, drawing on disciplines from political science to military studies, philosophy, conflict resolution strategies and theology, each illumined in one way or another by reference to questions of religious faith. The contributors draw upon resources in Judaism, Christianity and Islam, together making a twofold case. In the first place, what becomes clear is that, religiously, something more than the view of the Taliban seems immediately problematic; as Rashed Chowdhury argues in "Muslim Opposition to the War in Afghanistan: The Case(s) of Bangladesh and Turkey," even moderate Muslims globally are broadly opposed to the military policies of the U.S.A. and ISAF, the reason being that Western policy in general is perceived to be so morally tainted. Because there is little trust across a broad range of issues, there is an instinctive suspicion of motives in relation to Afghanistan in particular. Such suspicion has been profoundly reinforced by the death of civilians, particularly as a result of aerial bombings undertaken by (mainly) American forces.

What emerges from essays by Walter Dorn, Erika Simpson, and others is closely related: that while there is concentration in the West on the problem of extremist Islam, the reality is that the West itself needs to come clean concerning what is perceived to be its own extremism globally. It needs to realize that, to the more theologically and politically seamed Muslim world, our politics and the question of religion frequently appear to be one and the same. In more simple terms, the West's motivations for war are neither understood nor received as something secular, but as stemming from a kind of relation to questions of religious significance that much of the Islamic world rejects a priori. On the opposite side of the spectrum, though to much the same practical effect, the Jewish philosopher Howard Adelman's essay, "Death, Interpretation and Prophecy," argues that the children and widows of the military's dead need good reason for their loss, and that ultimately, none can be forthcoming. Adelman sees the war as futile, and maintains (against what he sees as a mistaken tendency within Christian civilization to think that the dawn always follows the darkest hour) that a very Jewish realism concerning evil in face of the inescapable prospect of suffering is what is needed. If this is so,

---

[9] John Douglas Hall was, however, present and did address the Conference. Hall's essay, "Many Faiths, One Planet: The Perils and Possibilities of Religion in a Fragile World," is a version of a more developed paper delivered in a previous speaking engagement, the content of which represents a longstanding theme in his more occasional writings. The essay has had very limited circulation, and has been lightly adapted for use in this volume.

Adelman's essay can be taken to suggest, then the priority in military planning and in the political discussions surrounding it should be an early withdrawal.

There are also alternative voices to Adelman's represented in this volume. Theologians such as Gary D. Badcock and Darren Marks find themselves advocating continued presence, although for different reasons than merely stabilization or contribution to the war on terror. Both theologians argue that the war cannot be sustained if the goal is conceived purely in terms of geo-political stabilization or security. Instead, Marks asks whether such ideas may in fact be idols, and develops a theological response according to which the long term commitment to Afghanistan that is necessary—with its costs, both human and financial—must be rooted in responsibility to actual Afghan human beings and thereby also to God, whose command it is that we treat them with respect. Likewise, Badcock asks his own Christian context whether it is capable of detaching itself from civil religion for the sake of something theologically deeper, in order to sustain what will in all likelihood be decades of commitment, and suggests that both Islam and Christianity have a common stake in the outcome of such reflection. A vision of commitment rooted in God's own life that makes responsibility to Afghanistan a central theme thus emerges.

As a quasi-representative of the peace churches (working from their voice and for one of their institutions), interestingly, the young Canadian scholar Christopher Hrynkow argues for the importance, not necessarily of military detachment, but of much more widespread and better-funded grass-roots engagement. Bombing missions undertaken several hundred or even several thousand feet above ground, and military convoys which roar through villages in order to avoid contact with the local population, are absolutely no substitute for building trust with people, person by person and community by community, or to assisting them to establish good governance in ways attuned to the local culture. In Hrynkow's view, this is far more than a matter of the "battle for hearts and minds" as espoused in official counter-insurgency doctrine, but one of prophetic principle, which is what a Christian theological perspective is able to contribute to the process. The starting point again, therefore, must be respect for the goodness and dignity of the Afghan people themselves, which requires that humility be learned by the West as much as it does the offering of economic, political or military assistance. Evangelical theologian Craig Carter finds himself in agreement with Pope Benedict XVI, not so much in advocating for a theological renewal within Islam as in advocating the need for the kind of theological renewal within Christian civilization that alone can allow it to respond with wisdom to the challenges of our time.

Just as Islam must look within in order to find resources to answer extremist claims, so the Christian tradition as represented in its old heartlands also must rediscover the resources to critique its own deficiencies and excesses.

No attempt is made in this brief Introduction, however, to offer a full survey of the essays here collected. Nor is a synthesis of the arguments developed possible. The varied writers, rather, must be left to speak for themselves. What emerges is a contribution to the theological and political debate concerning the Afghanistan war, in which no single view is defended, but in which a series of positions occasionally standing in tension can be identified. The collection, therefore, offers no final or definitive treatment of its theme, but as a step in that direction, it can hopefully serve as a resource for others who may be able to take its question further: for politicians, for example, or even social scientists, who need a rationale to escape modernity's one-dimensional and reductionist view that religion is irrelevant to these issues; for representatives of non-governmental organizations and government-sponsored aid agencies, who must at all points engage with the question of religion as inescapable in their work in the non-western world; for religious leaders who wonder about the silence of the quietist stance or the equally passive alternative of mere civil religion; for students and teachers of politics and ethics; and for soldiers and those families of soldiers who must one day wonder for what cause their sacrifices were made. Public theology has something to say to each of these groups, and while it is too much to expect that a little volume of this sort can have a great impact, it is not too much to hope that, inshallah, here or there and for some people it might.

One final point, however, can be made by way of transition to what follows, which is to re-emphasize that it is not only the religious situation in Afghanistan that requires discussion or that may be problematic. The greater number of the contributions to this volume insist, to the contrary, that it is Western (and very often, therefore, Christian or post-Christian) attitudes that require the closer examination, both in light of the profound moral issues raised by war, and in connection with the clearly religious and inter-religious dimension of the Afghanistan conflict. Though generally denied by NATO members, the religious dimension of the war in Afghanistan is in fact inescapable, precisely because it is so often through the lens of religion that the "mission" of nations such as Canada in Afghanistan is read and received by large sections of the Afghan population, and by hundreds of millions of Muslims globally. To fail to see this ourselves is to fail to perceive the importance of religion in the world generally; to fail to be self-critical about it, therefore, is to miss opportunity both for self-understanding, and for communication with and to the people of Afghanistan—that "land that is far from us, little known by us and where our interests do not seem self-evident."

WARFIGHTING, COUNTERINSURGENCY AND PEACEKEEPING IN AFGHANISTAN: THREE STRATEGIES EXAMINED IN THE LIGHT OF JUST WAR THEORY

A. WALTER DORN[1]

Just War theory is an ethical framework, refined over many centuries, used to assess whether war or a particular use of force in war is justified.[2] The theory can be considered in general or applied to specific cases, either actual or contemplated. It offers a set of important principles (typically five to seven) that cumulatively suggest the degree of moral justification for the application of armed force. These principles have proven so useful and meaningful that they have been incorporated into international law.[3] Furthermore, the UN-endorsed "Responsibility to Protect" criteria for military intervention were based on them.[4]

---

[1] The research work for this paper was funded, in part, by Defence Research and Development Canada and the Technology Investment Fund Project on Adversarial Intent. The views expressed are those of the author and do not necessarily represent the views of the Government of Canada. The author thanks Courtney Hood for research assistance and for feedback on earlier drafts.

[2] A standard modern work on Just War theory is Michael Walzer, *Just and Unjust Wars* 4th ed. (New York: Basic Books, 1977, 2006). Original texts with commentary, showing the evolution of Just War theory, are provided in: Gregory M. Reichberg, Henrik Syse, Endre Begby, eds., *The Ethics of War: Classic and Contemporary Readings* (Oxford: Blackwell Publishers, 2005).

[3] See, for instance: Richard Falk, "Legality to Legitimacy: The Revival of the Just War Framework," *Harvard International Review* 26 (Spring 2004): 40-44.

[4] The "Responsibility to Protect" ("R2P" for short) concept was developed by the International Commission on Intervention and State Sovereignty, established by the government Canada in 2000. R2P adopts the following principles explicitly: "Just cause," "Right intention," "Last resort," "Proportional means," "Reasonable prospects of success," "Right Authority," and a series of "Operational Principles," including adherence to international humanitarian law. See: International Commission on Intervention and State Sovereignty, *The Responsibility to Protect* (Ottawa:

One of the enduring strengths of the Just War theory's principles is that they can provide relatively straightforward answers to some of the most basic questions concerning war. As these questions will be addressed in connection with the Afghanistan conflict later in this essay, they can at the outset be briefly enumerated as follows: Question 1: Why use force? Answer: Just War theory requires that there be just cause, right intent and a net benefit. Question 2: Who should authorize force? Answer: A legitimate authority should authorize the use of force. Question 3: When can force be used? Answer: Force can only justly be used as a last resort. Question 4: What type of force can be used? Answer: A proportional means of force can be used. Question 5: Where is it just to apply such proportional force? Answer: Proportional force may be applied to military, not civilian locations and targets. Question 6: How to apply force? Answer: Force must be used with right conduct.

Just War theory has often been used as a simple checklist to declare wars as either just or unjust. However, such applications are prone to oversimplification. For example, if each criterion is somewhat satisfied (as is often the case), a proponent might declare the entire war just. A more refined application takes the theory beyond simple binary evaluation of yes/no or just/unjust and recognizes that the criteria are almost always satisfied *to some degree*. To handle this, a novel measure, the "Just War Index," is introduced in what follows. The Just War Index gives scores to each criterion, and will be applied to the case at hand—the post-9/11 war in Afghanistan. The Index allows us to compare not only the justifications of different wars or conflicts but also the strengths and weaknesses of different strategies or operations within the same conflict.

Afghanistan provides an excellent test or "proving ground" for such an approach, since several international forces are in the country, struggling to achieve different ends through different means. The United States government heads the "Operation Enduring Freedom" (OEF) coalition, whose primary objective is to "defeat terrorists," especially al-Qaeda and more broadly the Taliban. The North Atlantic Treaty Organization (NATO) leads the International Security Assistance Force (ISAF), whose mission is to enhance security in the country. Over time, ISAF has fashioned itself as a counterinsurgency mission. Finally, the UN's peacekeeping department directs the United Nations Assistance Mission in Afghanistan (UNAMA) with the aim of creating conditions for a long-term peace. While these

---

International Development Research Centre), http://www.iciss.ca. Endorsement of R2P was made by a summit of world leaders in 2005. See: United Nations General Assembly, "2005 World Summit Outcome," UN Doc. A/60/L.1, 15 September 2005, para. 138-9.

missions overlap significantly, their methods differ considerably, including the degree and type of armed force applied. OEF uses primarily a warfighting strategy, while ISAF takes a counterinsurgency approach and UNAMA resembles a preliminary peacekeeping mission. OEF has to date shown considerably less restraint than ISAF. UNAMA, for its part, has at present only a small cadre of uniformed personnel in Afghanistan and very little ability to use force, but a more robust future peacekeeping operation can be envisioned with combat-capable forces, though undoubtedly with less firepower than either ISAF or OEF. Broadly speaking, these three missions can be classified as warfighting (OEF), counterinsurgency (ISAF) and quasi-peacekeeping (UNAMA).

Each of the three missions has a different origin, objective and strategy, arising out of different worldviews. Since the Just War theory provides an excellent prescriptive framework of factors that ought to be adhered to by each mission, it will be used in what follows to develop a moral assessment of the missions. In addition, the Just War Index offers a subjective measure of the degree of adherence to Just War criteria, permitting a contrast between the two missions employing force (OEF and ISAF) and an additional possible future mission involving robust peacekeeping (UNAMA II). Both the background below and the quantitative Just War Index assessment afterwards are intended to help intellectuals, planners and the public judge which activities are justified and worth pursuing.

Why Fight?

This fundamental question finds a natural answer in Just War theory: there must be a just cause coupled with the right intent to fight. In addition, there should be a net benefit arising from the fighting, so that the damage done does not exceed the good achieved. Different thinkers may define these three criteria differently but the general sense of the criteria remains clear. In the case of Afghanistan, the three missions are deployed for quite different reasons, which it would be helpful to parse out. While most of the reasoning summarized below is of American and international (UN) perspectives, the Canadian position is also presented and explored.

1. Warfighting (OEF)

The Bush administration formally launched Operation Enduring Freedom in October 2001 as the operational (military) arm of its "Global War on Terror." The goal of this war, in the view of President Bush, was to defeat "the terrorists." OEF was, to this extent, a direct response to the terrorist attacks of 11 September, 2001. Speaking hours after the attack, Bush told the world he had ordered a search "for those who are behind these evil acts." He also vowed to make "no distinction between the terrorists who committed these acts and those who harbour them."[5] On 16 September 2001, President Bush vowed to "hunt down and smoke out" the terrorists who were believed to be in Afghanistan.[6] Bush made a more assertive and encompassing statement of this policy (sometimes called the Bush Doctrine) in his 20 September 2001 address to the U.S. Congress:

> We will pursue nations that provide aid or safe haven to terrorism. Every nation, in every region, now has a decision to make. Either you are with us, or you are with the terrorists. From this day forward, any nation that continues to harbor or support terrorism will be regarded by the United States as a hostile regime.[7]

This doctrine became the justification for the October-November, 2001 "regime change" in Afghanistan, since the Taliban government was known to harbour al-Qaeda. From the beginning, the cause behind OEF was clearly stated (i.e., the defeat of terrorism), even if its logic and application to the Taliban might be questioned.

In contrast to its cause, the *intent* of OEF is harder to determine. Intention, like motivation, is often multifaceted and may not even be understood by the actors themselves. However, at least the overt intent of OEF was clearly stated by President Bush: "My administration has a job to do, and we're going to do it. We will rid the world of the evil-doers. We will call together freedom loving people to fight terrorism."[8] In this black and white world view, the "evildoers" were terrorists who "can't stand freedom" and "hate what America stands for."[9] America was again taking on

---

[5] The White House: President George W. Bush, "President's Address to the Nation," 11 September, 2001, http://www.georgewbush-whitehouse.archives.gov/news/releases/2001/09/20010911-16.html.

[6] The White House: President George W. Bush, "Remarks by the President Upon Arrival," 16 September 2001, at http://georgewbush-whitehouse.archives.gov/news/releases/2001/09/20010916-2.html. There is evidence the US administration was also contemplating regime change in Afghanistan at this point. See: Ian Traynor and Gary Yonge, "Secret memo reveals US plan to overthrow Taliban regime," *The Guardian*, September 21, 2001.

[7] The White House: President George W. Bush, "Address to a Joint Session of Congress and the American People," 20 September 2001, http://www.georgewbushwhitehouse.archives.gov/news/releases/2001/09/20010920-8.html.

[8] Bush, "Remarks by the President Upon Arrival."

[9] Ibid.

leadership of the "free world," as it had during the Cold War.[10] It was protecting its allies as well as itself.

Critics suggest that other factors, similar to those allegedly behind the 2003 Iraq invasion, were behind the Global War on Terror and the OEF-Afghanistan mission. These suspected motives include: self-promotion of a would-be war-president (along with the accompanying sharp increase in popularity);[11] a new global enemy on which to target governmental and military efforts (and divert attention from other matters such as the disputed election of 2000 and the economic challenges of 2001);[12] a new "lease on life" for the Pentagon over a decade after the end of the Cold War;[13] associated funding for the military-industrial complex (with annual defence expenditures increasing by well over $100 billion);[14] and control

---

[10] The White House: President George W. Bush, "President Bush's remarks on Afghanistan to the local business community Elizabeth, New Jersey," 16 June 2003, http://www.georgewbush-whitehouse.archives.gov/infocus/afghanistan/20040708.html.

[11] "Going the legal route won't boost the President's approval ratings the way a war does, nor will it make the world fear our military power. But at least we won't be fighting terrorism with more terrorism, and fuelling an escalating cycle of violence." Mark Weisbrot, "A War on Civilians?" *Counterpunch,* November 3, 2001, http://www.counterpunch.org/weisbrot1.html.

[12] "America was targeted for attack because we're the brightest beacon for freedom and opportunity in the world. And no one will keep that light from shining." The White House: President George W. Bush, "President's Address to the Nation," 11 September, 2001. See also: The White House: President George W. Bush, "Address to a Joint Session of Congress and the American People," 20 September 2001.

[13] "The Bush doctrine has been used to justify a new assertiveness abroad unprecedented since the early days of the Cold War—amounting nearly to the declaration of American hegemony—and it has redefined U.S. relationship around the world." Michael Hirsch, "Bush and the World," *Foreign Affairs*, 18, no. 5 (2002): 19, http://www.comw.org/qdr/fulltext/0209hirsh.pdf.

[14] A major critic of the Bush administration is Professor Paul Krugman (winner of the 2008 Nobel Prize in Economics, and New York Times columnist) who wrote in 2002: "It's true that the administration is using the terrorist threat to justify a huge military buildup....Second, the military buildup seems to have little to do with the actual threat, unless you think that Al Qaeda's next move will be a frontal assault by several heavy armored divisions....No politician hoping for re-election will dare to say it, but the administration's new motto seems to be 'Leave no defense contractor behind.'" Krugman, Paul, "Bush's Aggressive Accounting," *New York Times,* February 5, 2002, http://www.nytimes.com/2002/02/05/opinion/05KRUG.html.

over natural resources such as oil resources and future pipelines envisioned for the region.[15]

After assuming the Presidency in 2009, Barak Obama has continued OEF but he has generally avoided the black and white Bush outlook, with its U.S.-centred and jingoistic overtones. He has also dropped the term "Global War on Terror," saying it inflated the opponent and the nature of the conflict.[16] Nonetheless he has vowed to "disrupt, dismantle and defeat al Qaeda in Pakistan and Afghanistan, and to prevent their return to either country in the future,"[17] and has strongly defended the justice of the war. In keeping with these views, Obama increased the number of troops in Afghanistan by over 70,000 in his first two years of office, though some of these troops were placed under ISAF command and are not part of OEF.

Canada made its original military contribution to Afghanistan in 2001-02 through OEF, providing Special Forces to help search for al-Qaeda members, particularly its chief, Osama bin Laden, the alleged mastermind behind the 9/11 attacks. Prime Minister Jean Chrétien declared on 7 October 2001: "we are part of an unprecedented coalition of nations that has come together to fight the threat of terrorism."[18] In 2002, Canada provided

---

[15] "[T]he U.S. and U.K. ousted the Taliban and secured Afghanistan for the construction of an oil pipeline from Turkmenistan, south through Afghanistan, to the Arabian Sea." Marjorie Cohn, "Why Iraq and Afghanistan? It's About the Oil," *Counterpunch*, July 30, 2003, http://www.counterpunch.org/cohn07302003.html.

[16] The Obama administration did away with the Global War on Terror label using the following reasoning: "[D]escribing our efforts as a global war only plays into the warped narrative that al-Qaida propagates. …. And perhaps more dangerously, portraying this as a global war reinforces the very image that al-Qaida seeks to project of itself, that it is a highly organized, global entity capable of replacing sovereign nations with a global caliphate." Speech by John Brennan, Assistant to the President for Homeland Security and Counterterrorism at the Center for Strategic and Intelligence Studies, "A New Approach for Safeguarding Americans", Center for Strategic and Intelligence Studies, 6 August 2009, Washington, D.C., 8, http://csis.org/files/attachments/090806_brennan_transcript.pdf.

[17] "So I want the American people to understand that we have a clear and focused goal: to disrupt, dismantle and defeat al Qaeda in Pakistan and Afghanistan, and to prevent their return to either country in the future. That's the goal that must be achieved. That is a cause that could not be more just." The White House: President Barack Obama, Office of the Press Secretary, "Remarks by the President on a New Strategy for Afghanistan and Pakistan," 27 March, 2009, The White House, http://www.whitehouse.gov/the_press_office/Remarks-by-the-President-on-a-New-Strategy-for-Afghanistan-and-Pakistan/.

[18] "We are part of an unprecedented coalition of nations that has come together to fight the threat of terrorism." PM of Canada, Jean Chrétien, "An Address to the

over" 500 soldiers in the U.S.-led Operation Anaconda to scour the caves above the Shah-e-Kot valley, but the operation ended like the more famous Tora-Bora operation, without finding senior al-Qaeda leaders.

In 2003, Canada provided about 1,500 troops to ISAF, which was at the time confined to Kabul and its environs. In 2005 Canada went back to OEF, jumping from the "the frying pan into the fire" after accepting the leadership of the Provincial Reconstruction Team in Kandahar, the "homeland" of the Taliban insurgency. On his first trip abroad as Prime Minister, Stephen Harper visited Kandahar in March 2006, explaining to the soldiers the cause for which they were fighting: "You have put yourself on the line to defend our national interests; protect Canada and the world from terror; help the people of Afghanistan rebuild their country."[19] He clearly wanted Canada to be a leader internationally, not merely a follower, and boasted of the "Canadian-led security operation." In fact, the senior Canadian general (one star) in Regional Command (South) reported to a U.S. general (two star), even as the international operation in Kandahar transitioned from OEF to ISAF (NATO) leadership at the end of July, 2006. The U.S. two-star reported to Central Command in Tampa, Florida, which reported to the Pentagon, so Canadian "leadership" was really an insertion into a longer chain of American command.

2. Counterinsurgency (ISAF)

After the fall of the Taliban government and the creation of the Afghan Interim Authority, the UN Security Council established ISAF, in accordance with the Bonn proposals of December, 2001. The Bush Administration wanted to leave the envisioned "nation-building mission" to the United Nations after the overthrow of the Taliban government.[20] The UN-

---

Nation Concerning the International Campaign Against Terrorism," 7 October 2001, Archives Canada, http://epe.lac-bac.gc.ca/100/205/301/prime_minister-ef/jean_chretien/2003-12-08/stagingpm_3a8080/default.asp@language=e&page=newsroom&sub=speeches&doc=nationterrorism.20011007_e.htm.

[19] Later in the short speech PM Harper said: "Of course, standing up for these core Canadian values may not always be easy at times. It's never easy for the men and women on the front lines. And there may be some who want to cut and run. But cutting and running is not your way. It's not my way. And it's not the Canadian way." *CBC News Online*, "Text of Prime Minister Stephen Harper's address Monday to Canadian soldiers in Afghanistan," March 13, 2006, http://www.cbc.ca/news/background/afghanistan/pmspeech.html.

[20] In October, President Bush saw a role for the United Nations in stabilization and national-building after US operations completed their job: "It would be a useful function for the United Nations to take over the so-called 'nation-building.'" The

mandated military mission was to assist with the "maintenance of security" in Kabul and surrounding areas in order to allow Afghan authorities and UN personnel to "operate in a secure environment."[21] The Council also requested ISAF to help establish and train new Afghan security forces.

The leadership of ISAF initially transitioned from the United Kingdom to Turkey to a Dutch-German team until, in August of 2003, NATO agreed to take over the direction of the mission, while also dramatically increasing its size.[22] NATO did not have an organizational role in Afghanistan until then, even though it had invoked its collective security provision (Article 5 of its Charter) on 12 September, 2001 in response to the 9/11 attacks.[23] In Afghanistan, ISAF ran in parallel with OEF, though

---

White House: President George W. Bush, "President Holds Prime Time News Conference," 11 October 2001, The White House, Archives, http://georgewbushwhitehouse.archives.gov/news/releases/2001/10/20011011-7.html.

[21] Security Council Resolution 1386 (2001) of 20 December 2009, adopted unanimously, has an operational paragraph: "*Authorizes...* the establishment for 6 months of an International Security Assistance Force to assist the Afghan Interim Authority in the maintenance of security in Kabul and its surrounding areas, so that the Afghan Interim Authority as well as the personnel of the United Nations can operate in a secure environment." See: UN Press Release, SC/7248, UN News Service, http://www.un.org/News/Press/docs/2001/sc7248.doc.htm.

[22] When NATO took responsibility for ISAF on 11 August 2003, the total strength of the force was under 6,000 personnel, drawn from over 30 nations. Six years later, when it helped provide security for the August 2009 election, the number of troops was over ten times higher (65,000), drawn from 42 nations, including all 28 NATO member states, though most nations provide only a token contribution. Only seven nations provide over 2,000 military personnel: the United States (29,050), United Kingdom (9,000), Germany (4,050), France (3,160), Canada (2,800), Italy (2,795) and Poland (2,000). See: International Security Assistance Force (ISAF), "International Security Assistance Force and Afghan National Army Strength and Laydown," NATO, 23 July 2009,
http://www.nato.int/isaf/docu/epub/pdf/placemat.pdf.

[23] On 12 September 2001, NATO invoked the principle of Article 5 of its Charter (the Washington Treaty), stating that the attacks of 9/11 against the US constituted an attack on the alliance as a whole, provided that such actions had been conducted from abroad. When the latter was confirmed on 2 October 2001 by the NATO Secretary-General after an investigation, the Article 5 provision became fully operative. The investigation concluded that "the attacks belonged to the world-wide terrorist network of Al-Qaeda, headed by Osama bin Laden and protected by the Taliban regime in Afghanistan." NATO Update, "Invocation of Article 5 Confirmed," NATO http://www.nato.int/docu/update/2001/1001/e1002a.htm#FN1.

from 2008 onward both missions reported to the same commander (an American general).[24]

The ISAF mandate did not specify a role in fighting "terrorists" but the growing focus on the insurgency was natural for NATO, as this constituted the greatest threat to ISAF's and Afghan security. An ISAF spokesperson declared in 2004: "our intent is to make sure we can remove the capability of those people [terrorists] to perform those attacks no matter what form they take."[25] Like OEF and the press generally, ISAF often uses short form to characterize anti-government elements as the "Taliban," though in fact there are a number of different anti-government groups fighting for different reasons.[26] An additional oversimplification is to refer to the insurgents as "terrorists," as some groups target military forces only.

ISAF's goal under NATO continues to be to "assist the Afghan Government in exercising and extending its authority and influence across the country, paving the way for reconstruction and effective governance."[27] ISAF has accordingly gradually expanded its coverage from the Kabul region to the entire country. Its Provincial Reconstruction Teams support nation building, particularly by trying to secure areas so that national and international development agencies can operate safely. ISAF also strove to create a secure environment for the 2004, 2005 and 2009 national elections.[28] Over time, however, the anti-government insurgency gained con-

---

[24] Given that the US provides by far the largest contingent to ISAF, it will likely continue to be commanded by a US General (at the time of writing, Stanley McChrystal) for the foreseeable future. McChrystal currently also commands OEF.

[25] "We continue to work in support of the institution of the Afghan government to pre-empt them [insurgents], no matter what form they take.... Our intent is to make sure we can remove the capability of those people to perform those attacks no matter what form they take." ISAF, "Q&A: Norwegian Soldier killed during and RPG attack," 24 May 2004, NATO [spokesperson not identified], http://www.nato.int/ISAF/docu/speech/2004/sp040524b.htm.

[26] Besides al-Qaeda and the Taliban, other prominent anti-government forces fighting in Afghanistan or supporting from neighbouring Pakistan (and their leaders) are: Hizb-i-Islami (HIG) [Gulbuddin Hekmatyar], Hizb-i-Islami Khalis (HIK) [Malawi Khalis], Haqqani Faction [Jalaluddin Haqqani], Tehrik-e-Taliban Pakistan [Hakimullah Mahsud], Lashkar-e-Islami [Mangal Bagh Afridi], and Tehreek-e-Nafaz-e-Shariat-e-Mohammadi. In addition there are numerous local fundamentalist groups and tribe-based militia, drug lords and warlords, groups offering protectionist services and paid mercenaries, all claiming some reason to fighting against foreign forces.

[27] NATO, "NATO's role in Afghanistan," 17 August 2009, http://www.nato.int/cps/en/natolive/topics_8189.htm.

[28] Previously Karzai had been Chairman of the Transitional Administration (December 2001-June 2002) and Interim President (June 2002-December 04). "ISAF

siderable momentum. Suicide bombings and improvised explosive device attacks had devastating effects after being introduced by the insurgents, practices probably transferred from Iraq after 2003.[29] The number of ISAF soldiers killed annually increased significantly from 57 in 2003 to 294 in 2008.[30]

By the end of 2010, President Obama had increased the number of U.S. forces in ISAF by over 70,000, so that the U.S. provided three quarters of ISAF's total strength of 130,000.[31] The United Kingdom is the second largest of the 43 troop contributing nations with 9,500 troops. The U.K. has taken heavy casualties in Afghanistan, causing considerable debate about the mission domestically. Canada provided fewer troops (2,900) but has suffered the highest rate of casualties among ISAF contributors with a 2009 rate of 11 dead per 1,000 deployed.[32]

The greatest challenge to ISAF has been the insurgency, which caused most of the mission's 2,200 fatalities from 2001 through 2010. Over time, ISAF focused on a counterinsurgency strategy. After taking command in June 2009, General Stanley McChrystal emphasized, "it is most important to focus on almost classic counterinsurgency."[33] In 2009, he issued the "Commander ISAF's Counter Insurgency Guidance" and similar docu-

---

will continue to work toward ensuring a safe and secure environment conducive to free and fair elections and the spread of the rule of law." See: ISAF, "ISAF Spokesperson Speaking Notes Joint ISAF/CFC-A Press Conference," 5 May 2004, http://www.nato.int/ISAF/docu/speech/2004/sp-040505.htm.

[29] The number of suicide attacks in Afghanistan increased as follows: 0 (2002), 2 (2003), 3 (2004), 17 (2005), 123 (2006). Source: Abul Ahrar Ramizpoor, Human Rights Officer, UNAMA, personal communication, Bari, Italy, 23 October 2007.

[30] For ISAF and OEF combined, the annual number of fatalities increased annually: 58 (2003), 60(2004), 131 (2005), 191 (2006), 232 (2007), 295 (2008), to 521 (2009). See: "Coalition Military Fatalities by Year", icasualties.org: "Operation Enduring Freedom," http://www.icasualties.org/oef. The annual fatality rate (per 1,000 troops deployed) also increased from year to year.

[31] ISAF is responsible for 26 Provincial Reconstruction Teams, while OEF remains responsible for the remaining provinces, "International Security Assistance Force and Afghan National Army Strength & Laydown, as of 15 Nov 2010", http://www.nato.int/isaf/docu/epub/pdf/placemat.pdf.

[32] The annual fatality rates (per 1,000 troops deployed in Afghanistan) in 2008 were as follows: 11.9 (Canada), 6.6 (UK); 4.7 (U.S.A.); 3.3 (France). These calculations use fatality numbers found at http://www.icasualties.org and troop numbers supplied by ISAF.

[33] Total War Center, "Q&A with General Stanley McChrystal, Commander of ISAF," 29 July 2009, http://www.twcenter.net/forums/showthread.php?t=282029.

ments.[34] The goal was to "defeat the insurgency" by winning over the population as the primary means to success. But gaining the support of the population meant *supporting* the population, something quite "different from conventional combat." The Commander warned troops to avoid "the trap of winning tactical victories—but suffering strategic defeats—by causing civilian casualties or excessive damage and thus alienating the people."[35]

The stated intent behind NATO's mission in Afghanistan is to provide security in the country, which in turn should help prevent the spread of "terrorism" by removing Afghanistan as a potential base for the terrorist training (though in fact, the Taliban are certainly training their forces in terror tactics in Afghanistan still). More generally, NATO also seeks to serve as a collective alliance against common threats, and to maintain the trans-Atlantic partnership. Many members, particularly those from Eastern Europe, wanted to show the United States that they were good allies, and so sent forces to Afghanistan. For NATO in the new century, the Afghanistan mission continued its effort to justify the existence of its alliance, which was founded to meet a former no-longer-existent Soviet and Warsaw Pact menace.[36]

3. Peacekeeping and peacebuilding (UNAMA)

Like ISAF, UNAMA was established by the Security Council after the December 2001 Bonn Agreement, which put in place a transitional government for Afghanistan. Unlike ISAF, UNAMA is directly run by the United Nations, under the control of the UN Secretary-General. Its role is to promote peace and stability in Afghanistan. It supports a presumed peace process, though this has not attained the level of negotiations and cease-fires. In practice, UNAMA provides "political outreach" through its presence in provinces across the country, including the conflict-ridden south. It is mandated to offer "good offices in support of Afghan-led rec-

---

[34] Michael T. Hall and Stanley A. McChrystal, "ISAF Commander's Counterinsurgency Guidance," ISAF, August 2009. See also: NATO, "ISAF conducts counterinsurgency and relief operation," 23 May 2008,
http://www.nato.int/isaf/docu/news/2008/05-may/080523a.html.

[35] ISAF Commander Stanley McChrystal, "Tactical Directive," released 2 July 2009, portions made public on 6 July 2009.

[36] See: David Caprezza, comment on "NATO's One Priority: Afghanistan," New Atlanticist: Policy Analysis Blog, comment posted 6 February 2009,
http://www.acus.org/new_atlanticist/natos-one-priority-afghanistan.

onciliation programmes."[37] It could hold a future role as a mediator to assist discussions among the government, insurgents and the international community.

UNAMA is also mandated to strengthen the foundations of constitutional democracy in the country. It assisted with the drafting of a new constitution in 2003-04, and has played a major role in the 2004 and 2005 elections and in supporting and evaluating the 2009 Afghan-led elections. UNAMA also supports efforts to improve Afghan governance, to strengthen the rule of law and to combat corruption. The mission also sponsors a programme for human rights protection and promotion. In addition, it helps coordinate UN humanitarian aid, recovery, reconstruction and development activities.

UNAMA is primarily a political mission but it is directed and supported by the UN's Department of Peacekeeping Operations. It has some elements of a peacekeeping operation: it has, for instance, a political head (Special Representative of the Secretary-General or SRSG), along with branches dealing with military affairs, human rights and democracy. It also has field offices in many provinces of the country. UNAMA has approximately 1,500 staff in Afghanistan, the vast majority of whom (around 80%) are Afghan nationals. Only two dozen of the international staff are uniformed personnel, though this is likely to increase.[38] These lightly armed personnel provide military and police advice. ISAF is tasked to provide close protection for UN staff in Kabul and while travelling.[39] The United Nations contracts a private security firm to provide local security guards for UN premises.

Though it does not have the capacity to use force, one can envision a future operation (perhaps named UNAMA II) with the same guidelines found in modern robust UN peacekeeping missions, such as the United Nations Mission in the Democratic Republic of the Congo (MONUC). Such a mission could become a reality, especially if the situation becomes calmer, and a peace process gets underway. With the U.S. looking for a

---

[37] UNAMA, "Mandate," http://www.unama.unmissions.org/Default.aspx?tabid=1742.
[38] United Nations, "Security Council Endorses Establishment of a UN Assistance Mission in Afghanistan for Initial 12-month Period," 28 March 2002, http://www.un.org/News/Press/docs/2002/SC7345.doc.htm. Two of the twenty-odd UNAMA military advisers are Canadian officers.
[39] In the 28 October 2009 attack on a guest house in Kabul where many UN workers reside, it took a full hour for ISAF to reach the scene. Meanwhile, UN-hired security guards and an armed contractor held off the attackers from parts of the hotel. However, five UN foreign staff were killed in the attack.

more multilateral approach to solving the conflict, coupled with the increasing reticence of many NATO nations, a growing involvement of the United Nations can perhaps be expected.

The intent of the UNAMA mission is consistent with that of its parent organization, the United Nations, which seeks "to maintain international peace and security." While UNAMA advocates a peace and reconciliation process, the mission is careful not to be seen to be out of step with the two larger entities in Afghanistan, OEF and ISAF. Both the U.S. and NATO have opposed peace negotiations with Taliban leaders, while UNAMA remains ambivalent. The two larger missions also employ robust rules of engagement and significant firepower, unlike UNAMA.

As seen above, each of these missions has its own cause and intent. In principle, there is significant overlap between these justifications. When the missions are examined more critically later in this paper, however, major discrepancies will be pointed out and the justifications contrasted.

Who Authorizes Force?

For an intervention to be just, it must be approved by a legitimate authority.[40] Under current international law, only the UN Security Council can authorize the use of force.[41] The UN Charter (Article 51) also recognizes "the inherent right of individual or collective self-defence if an armed attack occurs against a Member of the United Nations, until the Security Council has taken measures necessary to maintain international peace and security."[42] But Article 51 does not give nations the unlimited right to act anywhere in the world with any amount of force in the name of

---

[40] The concept of "legitimate authority" in international law can be distinguished from the more traditional criterion of "proper authority," which means a ruler or government in the more traditional Just War literature. For examples of the later, see James Turner Johnson, *The War to Oust Saddam Hussein* (Lanham, Md.: Rowman & Littlefield, 2005), 38; Darrell Cole, *When God Says War Is Right* (Colorado Springs: Waterbrook Press, 2002), 78; Davis Brown, *The Sword, the Cross, and the Eagle* (Lanham, Md.: Rowman & Littlefield, 2008), chap. 4; and also Davis Brown, *Who Judges Wars?* in the same volume.

[41] The monopoly of the Security Council on the use of force is drawn from the provisions of the UN Charter. In article 2, para. 4, all Members are prohibited from "from the threat or use of force against the territorial integrity or political independence of any state." Regional arrangements or alliances are not forbidden but article 53 states that "no enforcement action shall be taken under regional arrangements or by regional agencies without the authorization of the Security Council." The UN Charter is available at http://www.un.org/en/documents/charter.

[42] This self-defence provision is given in Article 51 of the UN Charter.

self-defence. For sizeable interventions (including toppling governments), the Council remains the legitimate authority at the international level to endorse armed force, as reaffirmed in the "Responsibility to Protect" doctrine.[43]

Here there is a problem, for the Security Council authorized neither the U.S. invasion of Afghanistan nor the establishment of OEF, contrary to common belief. Many erroneously think that OEF gained approval from the Security Council through the Council's reaffirmation of the right to self-defence the day after the attacks of September 11, 2001.[44] On September 12, the Council did reaffirm "the inherent right of individual or collective self-defence in accordance with the Charter," but the resolution (1368) made no mention of Afghanistan or of U.S. military action. It certainly did not authorize an invasion of Afghanistan or the establishment of a U.S. military operation (OEF) to wage a Global War on Terror.[45] Over

---

[43] See: International Commission on Intervention and State Sovereignty, *The Responsibility to Protect* (Ottawa: International Development Research Centre), http://www.iciss.ca. The report does admit an exception if the Security Council is deadlocked and the humanitarian need is great. In such a case, the General Assembly or regional organizations can offer limited authorization.

[44] For example, Michael Pugh states: "Operation *Enduring Freedom* was authorized by the Council against the Taliban in Afghanistan." Pugh, Michael, "Peace Enforcement" in *The Oxford Handbook on the United Nations*, ed. Thomas G. Weiss and Sam Daws (Oxford: Oxford University Press, 2007), 370. The closest the Security Council comes is in Resolution 1368 of 12 September 2001, but it does not mention Afghanistan, the Taliban or the use of force. It simply calls on all states "to work together urgently to bring to justice the perpetrators, organizers and sponsors of the September 11 terrorist attacks and stresses that those responsible for aiding, supporting or harbouring the perpetrators, organizers and sponsors of these acts will be held accountable." Similarly, Amnesty International makes the same legal jump, stating: "Security Council Resolution 1368 adopted on 12 September 2001 granted international legal authority for OEF, condemning the 11 September attacks and affirming the right of states to individual and collective self-defence." See: Amnesty International, "Afghanistan Detainees Transferred to Torture: ISAF complicity?" ASA 11/011/2007, 13 November 2007, http://www.amnestyusa.org/document.php?id=ENGASA110112007&lang=e.

[45] Resolution 1368 (2001), the Security Council expressed sympathy and condolences to the victims of 9/11 and to Government of the United States of America. It called on states to bring to justice to the perpetrators and expressed "its readiness to take all necessary steps to respond to the terrorist attacks of 11 September 2001, and to combat all forms of terrorism, in accordance with its responsibilities under the Charter of the United Nations." In the Council's next resolution on terrorism, number 1373 of 28 September 2001, the Council created the Counter-Terrorism Committee. It makes no mention of Afghanistan or al-Qaeda.

the next few weeks, it became apparent that the Bush administration did not want to be limited by any international body, the Security Council included. The U.S. fought the Taliban both directly and indirectly by aiding indigenous anti-Taliban forces (the "Northern Alliance") without explicit Council approval. In fact, the Council did not pass a resolution on Afghanistan until 14 November, 2001, the day after the Taliban government fled Kabul under heavy U.S. bombardment. Resolution 1378 (2001) of that day merely expressed "support for the efforts of the Afghan people to establish a new and transitional administration" and encouraged "Member States to support efforts to ensure the safety and security of areas of Afghanistan no longer under Taliban control."[46] This was very different than authorizing force under the "Chapter VII" of the UN Charter. Chapter VII (enforcement) was not even mentioned in the resolution, nor were the prerequisite actions outlined in "Chapter VI" involving the "Pacific Settlement of Disputes."

While no international authorization was sought or received for OEF, national (U.S.) authorization was forthcoming. President Bush obtained Congressional approval on 18 September to use "all necessary and appropriate force" against those "he determines" responsible for the 9/11 attacks and those harbouring such organizations or persons.[47] Afghanistan was not mentioned explicitly. Essentially, Congress gave President Bush *carte blanche* on the use of force against these two types of targets. Shortly thereafter, Bush announced the likely military response, along with several demands he was making of the Taliban and al-Qaeda.[48] Military action under OEF began on 7 October, 2001 after a short Presidential radio address to the nation.[49]

---

[46] UN Security Council resolutions can be found at www.un.org/documents/scres.htm.

[47] The resolution affirmed the US was exercising "its rights to self-defense." 107th Congress, 1st Session, S. J. Res. 23, Joint Resolution "To authorize the use of United States Armed Forces against those responsible for the recent attacks launched against the United States," http://www.law.cornell.edu/background/warpower/sj23.pdf.

[48] Bush, "Address to a Joint Session of Congress and the American People," 20 September 2001.

[49] The White House: President George W. Bush, "Presidential Address to the Nation," 7 October 2001, http://www.georgewbush-whitehouse.archives.gov/news/releases/2001/10/20011007-8.html. Also on October 7, 2001, the US ambassador to the United Nations, John Negroponte, wrote to the President of the U.N. Security Council stating: "In accordance with Article 51 of the Charter of the United Nations, I wish, on behalf of my Government, to report that the United States of America, together

By contrast, ISAF was UN-authorized. It was created by the Security Council in resolution 1386 of December 2001. The resolution included the phrase of "acting under Chapter VII," though ISAF was not envisioned as an enforcement mission but as a security provider. The Council provided a mandate for ISAF and sanctioned its "taking all necessary measures to fulfil its mandate." The Council has reviewed and extended the mission every six months or annually since 2001.

The North Atlantic Council, NATO's highest decision-making body, agreed on 16 April 2003 that NATO would assume leadership for the operation of ISAF with UN agreement. The military alliance sought continuity for the UN-mandated mission as indicated by the title of the NATO announcement: "Same name, same banner, same mission as NATO enhances ISAF role."[50] The Security Council provided the mandate and the North Atlantic Council provided some political direction for the mission, while strategic command and control is exercised by NATO's main military headquarters, Supreme Headquarters Allied Powers Europe, located in Mons, Belgium. NATO Spokesman Yves Bordeur stated: "ISAF will continue to work within the UN mandate and will operate according to the current and future UN resolutions."[51] ISAF does, however, include at least a dozen non-NATO nations.

Thus ISAF is responsible to two higher bodies: the UN Security Council and NATO. NATO headquarters provides day-to-day supervision and direction. ISAF must also present quarterly reports to the Security Council. This reporting requirement is important if the Council is to influence the mission mandate and direction, and for mission accountability.

---

with other States, has initiated actions in the exercise of its inherent right of individual and collective self-defense following armed attacks that were carried out against the United States on September 11, 2001." Berlin Information Centre for Transatlantic Security, "Negroponte Letter to UN Security Council President," 7 October 2001, http://www.bits.de/public/documents/US_Terrorist_Attacks/negroponte.htm.

[50] NATO, "Same name, same banner, same mission as NATO enhances ISAF role," 16 April 2003, http://www.nato.int/docu/update/2003/04-april/e0416a.htm.

[51] NATO, "Announcement by NATO Spokesman Yves Brodeur on 16 April 2003 on NATO's intention to take over command of ISAF," 17 April 2003, NATO Online Library, http://www.nato.int/docu/speech/2003/s030416a.htm. On 2 Oct 2003, NATO offered to the UN its "Longer-term strategy for the North Atlantic Treaty Organization in its International Security Assistance Force role in Afghanistan." Enclosure in UN Doc. S/2003/970 of 8 October 2003, http://www.documents-dds-ny.un.org/doc/UNDOC/GEN/N03/547/44/pdf/N0354744.pdf.

ISAF reports sent to the United Nations, though sometimes late by four or five months,[52] provide a succinct overview of the diverse activities of ISAF and the challenges the mission faces. These provide a summary of activities such as judicial reform, training of an Afghan army and police force, and airport development, etc. Notably, any collateral damage caused by the Force's actions is rarely described. The task of keeping count of civilian casualties was taken up by UNAMA, which tracks fatalities caused by both pro-government forces (PGF) like ISAF, and Anti-Government Elements (AGEs) like the Taliban. It publishes these figures in the semi-annual *Bulletin on Protection of Civilians in Armed Conflict*.[53]

In contrast to ISAF, OEF has evidently assumed that it has no reporting requirements to the United Nations, though the Charter states that "measures taken by Members in the exercise of this right of self-defence shall be immediately reported to the Security Council."[54]

The only mention of OEF in Security Council resolutions is in relation to ISAF. The first reference came on 13 October, 2003, when the Council requested ISAF "to continue to work in close cooperation with" several entities, including OEF, in the implementation of the ISAF mandate.[55] Resolution 1659 (2006) called for closer operational synergy with OEF. Thus, it is fair to state that OEF was not "UN authorized" but it was eventually "UN recognized" as being in Afghanistan, some two years after its unilateral establishment.

In contrast to both OEF and ISAF, UNAMA is not only UN authorized but it is also UN run. The Security Council created the mission on 28 March, 2002, following the Bonn Agreement of 5 December, 2001.[56] Although UNAMA is classified as a "political mission," it is directed and supported by the UN's Department of Peacekeeping Operations. UNAMA coordinates the UN family of agencies operating in Afghanistan (UNDP,

---

[52] ISAF Report of 18 May 2006.
[53] United Nations Assistance Mission to Afghanistan, Human Rights Unit, "Afghanistan: Mid Year Bulletin on Protection of Civilians in Armed Conflict, 2009," July 2009, http://www.unama.unmissions.org/Portals/UNAMA/human%20rights/09july31-UNAMA-HUMAN-RIGHTS-CIVILIAN-CASUALTIES-Mid-Year-2009-Bulletin.pdf.
[54] UN Charter, Article 51.
[55] The Security Council: "2. Calls upon the International Security Assistance Force to continue to work in close consultation with the Afghan Transitional Authority and its successors and the Special Representative of the Secretary-General as well as with the Operation Enduring Freedom Coalition in the implementation of the force mandate…" United Nations Security Council, Resolution 1510, 13 October 2003, http://www.un.org/Docs/sc/unsc_resolutions03.html.
[56] UNAMA was created by Security Council Resolution 1401 (2002).

UNICEF, WFP, and so on), which are decentralized organizations and have their own governing boards at their international headquarters. Like all UN bodies (and OEF/ISAF), UNAMA operates with the consent of the host government.

Thus, the three missions each have different forms of authorization. The most controversial is that of OEF, which lacks explicit UN Security Council authority. As will be seen later, this can significantly reduce its legal and ethical legitimacy according to Just War theory, especially given that it engaged in regime change and employs the most permissive rules of engagement of the three missions.

When to Fight?

For armed force to be legitimate according to Just War theory it should be applied only as a "last resort," when all other means of conflict resolution have been exhausted. To what extent was OEF initiated as a last resort? When OEF employed force in the field, to what extent was it a last resort?

It was apparent to virtually everyone that the U.S. needed to take some form of action against the perpetrators of the September 11, 2001 attacks.[57] Within days of the attack, the U.S. fingered al-Qaeda as responsible. The organization's leader, Osama bin Laden, and his associates were known to be hiding in Afghanistan, where they had training camps. A week after 9/11, as the Central Intelligence Agency and the U.S. military were preparing to mobilize, President Bush made a series of demands, "not open to negotiation or discussion," to Taliban leaders.[58] The Presi-

---

[57] The direct perpetrators of the 9/11 attack were nineteen hijackers belonging to al-Qaeda who died when the planes crashed into the Twin Towers of the World Trade Center in New York City, the Pentagon in Washington and the a field in Pennsylvania. Most hijackers were from Saudi Arabia, but also United Arab Emirates, Egypt, Lebanon. Several trained in an al-Qaeda camp in Afghanistan. See: David Johnston, "Two years later: 9/11 Tactics; Official Says Qaeda Recruited Saudi Hijackers to Strain Ties," *New York Times*, September 9, 2003, http://query.nytimes.com/gst/fullpage.html?res=9803E4DD143BF93AA3575AC0 A9659C8B63.

[58] "And tonight, the United States of America makes the following demands on the Taliban: Deliver to United States authorities all the leaders of al Qaeda who hide in your land. Release all foreign nationals, including American citizens, you have unjustly imprisoned. Protect foreign journalists, diplomats and aid workers in your country. Close immediately and permanently every terrorist training camp.... These demands are not open to negotiation or discussion. The Taliban must act, and act immediately. They will hand over the terrorists, or they will share in their

dent's demands were to: "Close terrorist training camps; hand over leaders of the al Qaeda network; and return all foreign nationals, including American citizens, unjustly detained in your country." In his address of 7 October, on the eve of the first OEF strikes, Bush declared "none of these demands were met" and "the Taliban will pay a price."[59] Bush informed the nation and the world that he ordered "strikes against al Qaeda terrorist training camps and military installations of the Taliban regime in Afghanistan." Bush did not state that he was engineering a regime change. That was only implied but the goal became apparent a few weeks later.[60] The Taliban regime was overthrown in just 49 days.

There was no attempt to negotiate with the Taliban *de facto* government (even if it was not UN-recognized) for the hand-over of the al-Qaeda leadership. Prior to the aerial bombardment, the Taliban showed a willingness to send bin Laden for trial in an Islamic court or a third country.[61] However, the Bush Administration eschewed any bilateral dialogue, communicating its ultimatums instead through Pakistan, a neighbour decidedly unfriendly towards Afghanistan.[62] Other possible approaches were also pushed aside in favour of regime change. The U.S. did not limit itself to Special Force operations to locate, capture and try the al-Qaeda individuals deemed responsible for 9/11 attack, or to apply penalizing sanctions

---

fate." Bush, "Address to a Joint Session of Congress and the American People," 20 September 2001.

[59] Bush, "Presidential address to the Nation," 7 October 2001.

[60] "Our response involves far more than instant retaliation and isolated strikes. Americans should not expect one battle, but a lengthy campaign, unlike any other we have ever seen. It may include dramatic strikes, visible on TV, and covert operations, secret even in success. We will starve terrorists of funding, turn them one against another, drive them from place to place, until there is no refuge or no rest." Bush, "Address to a Joint Session of Congress and the American People," 20 September 2001.

[61] The Taliban proposed in early October to try bin Laden in an Islamic court in Afghanistan and also offered to hand bin Laden over to a third country for trial if they were given evidence of bin Laden's involvement in the events of September 11, 2001. The U.S. publically rejected these proposal and started its military operations. Douglas Frantz, "Taliban Say They Want to Negotiate With the U.S. Over bin Laden," *New York Times*, October 3, 2001, http://www.nytimes.com/2001/10/03/world/nation-challenged-afghans-taliban-say-they-want-negotiate-with-us-over-bin-laden.html.

[62] Darrel Moellendorf, "Is the War in Afghanistan Just?" *Imprints* 6, no.2 (2002), http://eis.bris.ac.uk/~plcdib/imprints/moellendorf.html. The border between Afghanistan and Pakistan has been a point of contention for the governments for decades, especially since 1993 when the Durand Line Agreement is alleged by Afghanistan to have expired, one hundred years after its signature.

against the Taliban for their support of al-Qaeda post 9/11, or even targeted assassinations against a number of al-Qaeda or Taliban leaders. "Last resort" was not a principle declared relevant by the Bush administration in 2001.

After the fall of the Taliban government, the Bush administration also did not follow the principle of last resort. When questioned during a 28 December 2001 press conference about when he believed that the war would be complete, Bush responded: "...Taliban gone, the country secure, the country stable, Al Qaeda cells rounded up, Taliban fighters brought to justice."[63] The Taliban and its allies were not invited or represented at the December Bonn conference. Bush stated what, in effect, were war aims for the Afghanistan campaign, including: "making sure the Taliban is out of existence."[64] In hindsight, years later with a resilient Taliban, it is apparent that these objectives were naïve and unachievable.

The last resort principle can also be applied at the tactical and individual level, as well as at the strategic (country leadership) level. Soldiers should not apply deadly force unless there are no other apparent ways to achieve their objectives. The use of armed force by OEF and ISAF personnel are governed by separate Rules of Engagement. It is much easier to use force in OEF than in ISAF. For instance, on aerial bombardment, Human Rights Watch reports:

> NATO and the US both require "hostile intent" for aerial munitions to be employed to defend their forces. [But] NATO defines "hostile intent" as "manifest and overwhelming force." The US Rules of Engagement defines hostile intent as "the threat of the imminent use of force," a much lower

---

[63] George W. Bush, "President, General Franks Discuss War Effort" 28 December 2001, The White House, Archives, http://georgewbush-whitehouse.archives.gov/news/releases/2001/12/20011228-1.html. President Bush also defined the war goals in the following succinct statement of 31 December 2001: "The definition of success is making sure the Taliban is out of existence, helping rebuild Afghanistan and disrupting this international terrorist network." The White House: President George W. Bush, "President Discusses Foreign Policy for Year Ahead" 31 December 2001, The White House, Archives, http://georgewbush-whitehouse.archives.gov/news/releases/2001/12/20011231.html.

[64] President Bush also defined the war goals in the following succinct statement of 31 December 2001: "The definition of success is making sure the Taliban is out of existence, helping rebuild Afghanistan and disrupting this international terrorist network." The White House: President George W. Bush, "President Discusses Foreign Policy for Year Ahead," 31 December 2001.

threshold than NATO for employing airstrikes, permitting anticipatory self-defense.[65]

After extensive research into casualties from airstrikes, Human Rights Watch's 2008 report found OEF to be responsible for more civilian deaths than ISAF due to OEF's heavier reliance on Special Forces (often lightly armed troops who call for air support when attacked) and its more permissive Rules of Engagement.[66] Due diligence was not taken by OEF especially in "unplanned situations":

> TICs (Troops in Contact) use far fewer checks to determine if there is a civilian presence. The tactical collateral damage assessment performed by the Joint Terminal Attack Controller (JTAC), a service member qualified in directing airstrikes on the ground is one of the only checks done, and, of necessity, such assessments often are made under the stress of hostile fire.[67]

In fact, both OEF and ISAF have relied heavily on air power, resulting in many fatalities, including of Afghan civilians and allied forces. An example of death by "friendly fire" is the first set of Canadian fatalities in Afghanistan, when four soldiers died in 2002 bombing after American pilots mistook Canadians in a designated firing range for hostile forces.[68] Routinely, the U.S. has kept bombers and fighter jets on patrol to provide close air support when called upon by ground troops.

From the beginning, OEF has relied much more than ISAF on Special Forces personnel to carry out search and destroy operations, including targeted assassinations. In Pakistan, OEF has made extensive use of CIA Reaper drones equipped with Hellfire missiles to assassinate Taliban and al-Qaeda leaders. In such attacks, many innocent civilian casualties have

---

[65] Human Rights Watch, "Troops in Contact: Airstrikes and Civilian Deaths in Afghanistan" September 2008, 31, http://www.reliefweb.int/rw/RWFiles2008.nsf/FilesByRWDocUnidFilename/SHIG-7JACE9-full_report.pdf/$File/full_report.pdf.
[66] Ibid., 4.
[67] Ibid., 6.
[68] The two F-16 pilots who dropped the 500-pound bomb onto the practice firing range, killing the four Canadian soldiers, were charged with involuntary manslaughter, aggravated assault and dereliction of duty for the April 2002 incident. But the charges were dropped by the Air Force in June 2003. David M. Halbfinger, "Charges Are Dropped in Bombing of Allies," *New York Times*, June 20, 2003, http://www.nytimes.com/2003/06/20/us/charges-are-dropped-in-bombing-of-allies.html?partner=rssnyt&emc=rss.

also been killed, often resulting in a strong backlash among local populations that, no doubt, have helped to swell the Taliban's ranks.[69]

OEF also established an extensive system to hold Afghan "detainees" both in Afghanistan and at special facilities abroad. Hundreds of captured fighters and other suspects were held as "unlawful combatants." This more closely resembles first resort than last resort since many were captured and held on mere suspicion, without charges and without due legal process. Allegedly the "worst of the worst" according to Secretary of Defence Donald Rumsfeld,[70] were flown to the U.S. base on Guantanamo Bay, Cuba. The U.S. refused to recognize the authority or applicability to detainees of the Geneva Conventions, which the U.S. had signed and ratified (though not the Additional Protocols).[71] The Bush administration purposefully sought to leave the Guantanamo detainees in legal limbo in a territory outside continental U.S.A., where they would, supposedly, be out of the reach of U.S. courts. But as several cases made it to the U.S. Supreme Court, several of the administration's military-justice practices were ruled unconstitutional. One of President Obama's first acts on assuming office was to order the closure of the Guantanamo detention centre within one year, following up a campaign promise—though the promise and the order remain to be fulfilled two years later.

The Afghan government is also ethically obliged to respect the last resort principle in its fight with the Taliban. It promotes "reconciliation," but rather than being a process of negotiation, such reconciliation to date has been mainly conceived in terms of the surrender of Taliban soldiers. Those seeking reconciliation are told they must first accept the Afghan Constitution, with the implication that the government of Hamid Karzai is the legitimate ruler and that the Taliban are illegal combatants. This position is

---

[69] Mazzetti, Mark, "The Downside of Letting Robots Do the Bombing" *New York Times,* March 21, 2009,
http://www.nytimes.com/2009/03/22/weekinreview/15MAZZETTI.html.
[70] Bob Herbert, "Madness and Shame," *New York Times*, July 22, 2008,
http://www.nytimes.com/2008/07/22/opinion/22herbert.html.
[71] The US signed the 1949 Geneva Conventions in 1949 and ratified them in 1955. However, it has not ratified either of the two "1977 Additional Protocols", designed to "strengthen the protection of victims of international (Protocol I) and non-international (Protocol II) armed conflicts and place limits on the way wars are fought." Protocol II was signed but not ratified, and Protocol I was neither signed nor ratified, though Human Rights Watch argues that Article I is accepted by enough countries that it has become Customary international law. See: Human Rights Watch, "Troops in Contact: Airstrikes and Civilian Deaths in Afghanistan" 34.

not acceptable, obviously, to the Taliban, who maintain that they were ousted illegally.

Unlike OEF, ISAF was not party to the overthrow of the Taliban regime in 2001. By the time ISAF was created in December of 2001, the United Nations had been presented with a *fait accompli*: the Taliban had been replaced by another regime, the leader of which, Hamid Karzai, had been hand-picked by the U.S. government. The UN-mandated ISAF mission was originally designed to have a light military footprint, in accordance with the views of the UN Special Representative in Afghanistan, Lakhdar Brahimi.[72] Thus ISAF operated in a defensive mode for the first few years, protecting only Kabul and its environs. In 2005, ISAF expanded to other provinces, seeking to extend governmental control over large swaths of territory still under Taliban control. At first the Taliban resisted, using conventional military tactics, and massing large numbers of its "soldiers" to hold territory. However, NATO gained substantial victories in such force-on-force encounters. For instance, after ISAF took responsibility for Regional Command South under Canadian leadership, it launched Operation Medusa to clear the Panjwai valley of Taliban fighters. Some 1,000 Taliban soldiers were killed, while Canada lost 16 and the U.S. lost two soldiers. The Taliban quickly learned to avoid such direct confrontations and increasingly resorted to attacks through improvised explosive devices.

Under President Obama, the U.S. approach to force has become more nuanced and sensitive. The principle of last resort, though not declared explicitly, now appears in ISAF counterinsurgency guidance. General Stanley McChrystal issued in 2009 directives to minimize force in order to reduce casualties and collateral damage. He further stated: "This directive does not prevent commanders from protecting the lives of their men and women as a matter of self-defence where it is determined *no other options* are available to effectively counter the threat."[73] The specific options were deleted from the publicly released document due to "operational security." But the last resort provision is clearly stated.

---

[72] United Nations Information Service, "Secretary-General, Special Representative Brahimi Tell Security Council Rapid Disbursement of Funds Pledged Essential for Afghan Recovery," 7 February 2002, United Nations, http://www.unis.unvienna.org/unis/pressrels/2002/sc7295.html.

[73] ISAF HQ (Commander ISAF, General Stanley McChrystal), "ISAF revises tactical directive", 6 July 2009, Press Release, http://www.nato.int/isaf/docu/pressreleases/2009/07/pr090706-tactical-directive.html, emphasis added. The directive itself is available (with some sections deleted for operational security) at http://www.nato.int/isaf/docu/official_texts/Tactical_Directive_090706.pdf.

Where to Fight?

In the Just War tradition, some locations are clearly out of bounds for targeting. For instance, bombs should not be dropped on medical facilities or civilian facilities and events, such as weddings. Furthermore, targets should be chosen so as to not inflict harm on innocent persons and civilian structures. This principle of *distinction* (sometimes called *discrimination*) between combatants and civilians is not only part of Just War theory but has become a key part of the law of armed conflict, including the Additional Protocols of the Geneva Conventions. In guerrilla warfare, however, distinction can pose a difficult challenge since insurgents often mix freely with the local civilian population.

The Taliban have often ignored the principle of distinction, which also has a basis in the Qur'an and in Islamic jurisprudence. In fact, some Taliban attacks deliberately target civilian population centres, frequently by suicide bombers, and Taliban spokesmen boast of the fact. Furthermore, the Taliban is also known to use "human shields," purposely mixing with civilians as a protective measure for themselves and perhaps to increase civilian casualties. However, violations by one side do not justify the weakening of the distinction principle by the other, especially for international forces seeking to abide by and to uphold international law.

The record of undesirable "collateral damage," especially from U.S. air strikes, is substantial and tragic. For instance, early in the war, the Red Cross compound in Kabul was hit by "stray bombs" on two occasions (16 and 26 October, 2001).[74] In 2007, an airstrike killed nine members of a family across four generations after a clash with militants in Jabar.[75] Some twenty-five civilians, including nine women and three young children, were killed in an air strike in Helmand province in 2007.[76] Further, in 2008, in the Shindand district aerial bombing killed more than ninety civil-

---

[74] Public Broadcasting Service (PBS), "U.S. Pummels Taliban Military Sites in Tenth Day of Strikes," *Online News Hour*, October 16, 2001, http://www.pbs.org/newshour/updates/october01/attack_10-16.html. "Red Cross warehouse hit again," *The Telegraph*, October 27, 2001, http://www.telegraph.co.uk/news/worldnews/asia/afghanistan/1360715/Red-Cross-warehouse-hit-again.html.

[75] "Official: NATO airstrike hits Afghan house, Family of 9 killed a day after Afghans allege U.S. Marines fired on civilians," *MSNBC*, March 5, 2007, http://www.msnbc.msn.com/id/17462080.

[76] AFX News Limited, "NATO Airstrike kills 25 Afghan civilians: police," *Thompson Financial*, 22 June 22, 2007, http://www.forbes.com/feeds/afx/2007/06/22/afx3847828.html.

ians, including sixty children, according to a UN report.[77] In July 2008, the bombing of a large wedding in Nangahar province caused the deaths of thirty-five children and nine women.[78] A few months later, a wedding in Kandahar City was bombed, allegedly killing over ninety people.[79] After a UN investigation exposed the high death rate in a bombing near Herat in May 2009, the U.S. revised its numbers from five to thirty-three civilian deaths.[80]

In 2008-09, President Karzai firmly and frequently insisted that foreign forces exercise greater discretion in aerial attacks and called for an end to civilian casualties. The Obama administration proved sympathetic to this call. On appointment in 2009, General McChrystal issued directives to minimize casualties. His Tactical Directive of 9 July stated that gaining the support of the population must be "our overriding operational imperative." McCrystal also noted that "excessive use of force resulting in an alienated population will produce far greater risks" than "carefully controlled and disciplined employment of force." He recognized the problem as not only as "a legal and a moral issue," but also as an "overarching operational issue." Therefore, he limited the use of force, especially close air support, against residential compounds and other locations where civilian casualties would be likely.

Even after the new policy of strictly minimizing civilian casualties came into effect in July of 2009, disaster struck as a U.S. plane bombed a gasoline tanker truck in Kunduz province, killing some seventy people. Ironically, this led the Taliban—who have regularly killed their countrymen in attacks—to call on the United Nations to investigate the bombing,

---

[77] United Nations, "The situation in Afghanistan and its implications for international peace and security: Report of the Secretary-General," UN Doc. A/63/372–S/2008/617, 23 September 2008.

[78] Human Rights Watch, "Troops in Contact: Summary"; UNAMA Human Rights Unit, "Afghanistan: Annual Report on Protection of Civilians in Armed Conflict, 2008," January 2009,
http://unama.unmissions.org/Portals/UNAMA/human%20rights/UNAMA_09february-Annual%20Report_PoC%202008_FINAL_11Feb09.pdf.

[79] Sameem, Ismail, "US Strike kills wedding party goes--Afghan officials," *Reuters,* November 5, 2008,
http://www.reuters.com/article/latestCrisis/idUSISL367820.

[80] *Agence France Presse*, "US-led strikes, clashes kill 100, mostly civilians," May 5, 2009, http://www.google.com/hostednews/afp/article/ALeqM5ipy2_iz7C9sv13zDZuViG0HcROUw.

saying, "if they respect human rights and the blood of human beings, they should determine the truth or falsity of this situation."[81]

In addition to air strikes, ground troops can also cause civilian fatalities, especially when firing on vehicles wrongly suspected of carrying improvised explosive devices. In this way many innocent lives have been lost, including those of women and children. For instance, in July of 2009, Canadian forces accidentally killed a young girl when their bullets ricocheted off of a motorcycle that failed to stop at a military checkpoint.[82] In another instance, U.S. Marines allegedly fired on cars and pedestrians as they fled a suicide attack, leaving up to ten Afghans dead.[83] Admittedly, the Taliban forces have a far worse record, compounded by the fact that they sometimes deliberately target civilians.

The Brooking Institution's "Afghanistan Index" shows the number of civilian casualties from both "anti-government" and "pro-government" forces (including the Afghan Government and all international forces). The casualty counts from both sides increased dramatically between 2006 and 2008, with pro-government force causing a jump from 230 to 828 casualties, and with 2009 looking even worse. An estimated 26% of all civilian casualties in 2008 were caused by airstrikes from pro-government forces.[84] The available UN statistics[85] are even more damning of pro-government forces, as shown in Table 1.

---

[81] *New York Times,* "Afghan Group Says NATO Strike Killed 70 Civilians," September 7, 2009, http://www.nytimes.com/aponline/2009/09/07/world/AP-AS-Afghan-Tanker-Attack.html.

[82] Dene Moore, "Soldier's warning shot kills Afghan girl" *The Toronto Star,* July 23, 2009, http://www.thestar.com/news/world/article/670480.

[83] *Associated Press,* "Official: NATO airstrike hits Afghan house. Family of 9 killed a day after Afghans allege U.S. Marines fired on civilians," March 5, 2007, http://www.msnbc.msn.com/id/17462080.

[84] Jason H. Campbell and Jeremy Shapiro, "Afghanistan Index", Brookings Institution 29 July 2009, http://www.brookings.edu/foreign-policy/~/media/Files/Programs/FP/afghanistan%20index/index20090729.pdf.

[85] "The situation in Afghanistan and its implications for international peace and security. Report of the Secretary-General," UN Doc. A/63/751-S/2009/135, para. 66, 10 March 2009.

Table 1: Civilian Fatalities in Afghanistan, 2007-08

Fatalities	2007	2008
by Anti-Government Elements	700 (46%)	1,160 (55%)
by Pro-Government Forces	629 (41%)	828 (40%)
by Others	194 (13%)	130 (5%)
Total civilian fatalities	1,523	2,118

ISAF troops routinely call for close air support when they find themselves under fire from insurgent forces. In some operations, indeed, they deliberately seek to *draw* fire from insurgents so that air strikes can eliminate the sources. Their rules of engagement, however, are stringent: they must abort the use of force (except in self-defence) when civilians in the vicinity might be injured. NATO affirms that ISAF forces have been given orders to consider "tactical withdrawal" rather than calling for air support in civilian-populated areas.[86] Nevertheless, "collateral damage" is frequent from airstrikes, as has been noted.

Because of the local backlash against NATO from its night raids into Afghan homes, ISAF has directed that entry into Afghan houses should be done by Afghan National Security Forces (ANSF) rather than ISAF soldiers. Since mosques have a special protected status for Muslims, according to the Qur'an,[87] the directive also stated that "no ISAF forces will enter or fire up on a mosque or any religious or historical site except in self-defence.[88]

---

[86] "We'll do anything we can to prevent unnecessary casualties, and we'll ensure that we'll have safe use of force. That includes not only airstrikes but ground operations.... If you can achieve the effect you're looking for without using a 2,000 pound bomb, if you can achieve the same effect you're looking for with a different kind of weapon then that's your responsibility as a commander on the ground... It's a question of requisite restraint." Brigadier General Richard Blanchette, Chief spokesman for NATO in Afghanistan, states in a press conference that NATO forces have been given orders to consider "tactical withdrawal" rather than calling in for air support in civilian-populated areas. Rondeaux, Candice, "NATO Modifies Airstrike Policy in Afghanistan," *Washington Post*, October 16, 2008, http://www.washingtonpost.com/wpdyn/content/article/2008/10/15/AR2008101503572_pf.html.

[87] See for instance, Surah 2:191 which stipulates: do not fight at a "Sacred Mosque, unless they (first) fight you there."

[88] ISAF HQ, "ISAF revises tactical directive."

What to Fight?

Shortly after September 11, 2001, the Bush administration chose to expand its war aims from destroying al-Qaeda to overthrowing the Taliban government in Afghanistan. An important underlying question for Just War theory is whether this expansion of the enemy was a proportionate response. While al-Qaeda was a legitimate target, did the U.S. have the moral right to force regime change in Afghanistan? The main supportive argument in favour of this view is that otherwise the Taliban would have continued to harbour terrorists, even in the face of U.S. surgical attacks. While such a statement is counter-factual and not verifiable, especially given the uneasy relationship that existed between the Taliban and their foreign terrorist visitors, it is true that the defeat of the Taliban dealt a heavy blow to al-Qaeda, forcing its fighters to move to the tribal belt of Pakistan. But an equally strong counterfactual argument also holds: a more precise series of attacks on al-Qaeda targets could have yielded better results, possibly even the capture of bin Laden. The search for a small network of individuals would have been much easier for U.S. intelligence agencies and Special Forces if the country had not been turned upside down through regime change. By whacking the whole "hornets' nest," so to speak, it became much harder to find the source of the trouble, as the early focus on al-Qaeda was dropped in favour of fighting the Taliban and, later, removing Saddam Hussein from Iraq. U.S. forces consequently could not find or capture the al-Qaeda leaders who had planned the 9/11 attacks.

No doubt part of the original incentive to overthrow the Taliban government (and later the Iraqi government) was the sheer ease with which it could be done. Dealing with the aftermath, however, proved much more difficult. This shows once again the time-honoured truth that removing a government is easier than removing an insurgency and winning the war is easier than winning the peace.

In addition, the costs and benefits of a wider war have to be taken into account. Has there been a *net benefit* to the overthrow of the Taliban government? The benefits of removing the government have to be weighed against the challenge of dealing with the Taliban insurgency in the long-term. Already, the costs have been high. In the first nine years of international intervention in Afghanistan, approximately 2,300 soldiers died, mostly from Taliban attacks, including by improvised explosive devices. This is about half the number of people killed in the original 9/11 attacks. The number of Afghan civilians who died far exceeds that of 9/11. What makes the statistics more alarming is that the annual number of fatalities is rising steadily for coalition forces, as shown in Table 2.[89]

Table 2: Annual Number of Coalition Fatalities (OEF and ISAF)

Year	US	UK	Canada	Other	Total
2001	12	0	0	0	12
2002	49	3	4	13	69
2003	48	0	2	7	57
2004	52	1	1	6	60
2005	99	1	1	30	131
2006	98	39	36	18	191
2007	117	42	30	43	232
2008	155	51	32	57	295
2009	317	108	32	64	521

Moreover, for many Afghans, the net benefit has been difficult to assess. The level of security is commonly said to be worse than during Taliban times, given that the influence of warlords and drug lords is greater, and that corruption in the Karzai government (especially its police force) is rampant. Though the Taliban meted out summary and brutal justice, they did control corruption and reduce drug production dramatically. The Taliban regime was even lauded by the U.S. government prior to the 9/11 attacks for its anti-drugs policy.[90] In 2009, democracy was under attack not only from the Taliban but from the candidates themselves. The Afghan-run election turned from being a source of national pride to being an embarrassment as the final results could not be announced for two months due to widespread fraud. Over a million ballots had to be discarded after a review by UN-supported agencies. Finally, the ongoing presence of international forces has caused great resentment to a proud people, who also suffered increasing numbers of civilian fatalities from coalition attacks (see Table 1 for 2007-08 fatality figures).

The international forces, which have been in Afghanistan longer than either World War (and almost as long as the two combined), are themselves experiencing fighting fatigue. Given that no victory is on the hori-

---

[89] Source: http://www.icasualties.org.
[90] Barbara Crossette, "Taliban's Ban on Poppy a Success, U.S. Aides Say", *New York Times*, May 20, 2001, http://www.nytimes.com/2001/05/20/world/taliban-s-ban-on-poppy-a-success-us-aides-say.html.

zon, several countries have sought a reduced role and others have pledged to withdraw. The Netherlands is due to leave Afghanistan in 2010 and Canada has pledged to remove its forces by 2011, in line with a parliamentary motion passed in March of 2008.[91]

Whatever the military proportionality of the U.S. response in 2001 and of international actions afterwards, there is a strong argument that the international community has a responsibility to rebuild Afghanistan. UNAMA currently embodies a vision of support for the Afghan people and government through non-kinetic (non-offensive) means. Elections are a key component of its work. For instance, UNAMA was put in charge of the elections of 2004, with ISAF playing a supporting role to provide security. On 9 October, 2004, UNAMA received an early victory when presidential elections were successfully held in Afghanistan, with minimal disruption. According to UN estimates, over 10 million people registered to vote, 42% of whom were female.[92] Hamid Karzai, leader of Afghanistan's transitional government, received 55.4% of the popular vote, running as an independent. The closest competitor out of the 17 other candidates, Yunus Qanuni of the Afghan National Party, received only 16% of the vote. Karzai, who had first been sworn in as President of Afghanistan on 9 December, 2001, was thus legitimized, at least until the 2009 elections. Those later elections were Afghan-run but the Electoral Complaints Commission, with a majority of UNAMA-appointed commissioners, found overwhelming evidence of fraud, enough to reverse the preliminary declared results of a Karzai victory with over 50% of the votes. The road to building a democratic Afghanistan is a long one involving both military and civilian efforts.

---

[91] The end date was specified in the following fashion: "the government of Canada notify NATO that Canada will end its presence in Kandahar as of July 2011, and, as of that date, the redeployment of Canadian Forces troops out of Kandahar and their replacement by Afghan forces start as soon as possible, so that it will have been completed by December 2011." See: "Afghanistan mission", House of Commons, 39th Parliament, 2nd Session, March 13, 2008, http://www2.parl.gc.ca/HouseChamberBusiness/ChamberVoteDetail.aspx?Language=E&Mode=1&Parl=39&Ses=2&FltrParl=39&FltrSes=2&Vote=76. Earlier motions had extended the mission: one passed on May 17, 2006 (two year extension to Feb 2009) and another passed on 13 March 2008 (two year extension to end 2011). See: Leader of the Government in the House of Commons and Minister for Democratic Reform, "Government Motion—Seeking to Continue the Mission in Afghanistan," Government of Canada, http://www.lgc.gc.ca/docs/media/press-presse-archives/pdf/20080208-2-eng.pdf.

[92] *CBC News Online*, "Afghanistan's presidential election" October 12, 2004, http://www.cbc.ca/news/background/afghanistan/afghanelection.html.

How to Fight?

Right conduct in Just War theory includes adherence to the international laws of armed conflict. In addition to the distinction principle mentioned above, there are many additional rules described in treaty law, especially the Geneva Conventions. However, the United States held that the Geneva Conventions were not binding in the Global War on Terror and hence they were not applied uniformly in OEF in Afghanistan and abroad. The Bush Administration claimed that terrorists were not lawful combatants so they did not deserve the rights and protections granted by the Geneva Conventions. The Global War on Terror not only bent the rules of armed conflict[93] but also distorted them to such an extent that even the U.S. Supreme Court ruled that certain U.S. practices were unlawful, especially in relation to detention.[94] Prominent in news coverage was the unlawful treatment of prisoners ("detainees") from Afghanistan and elsewhere held in the Guantanamo facility, which had been deliberately chosen since it was located outside the continental U.S.A. and hence presumed outside the reach of U.S. courts.

At Guantanamo, CIA interrogators employed a variety of coercive techniques to frighten suspects. In particular, water-boarding was used at least 266 times on two prisoners at the facility.[95] Top Obama administration officials later described the activity as illegal torture. Other atrocities disclosed included choking, mock executions and threatening a prisoner with a gun and power drill, and another with killing the detainee's children. Sleep deprivation was common. The growing list of atrocities led Obama's Attorney General Eric H. Holder Jr. to appoint a criminal prosecutor to investigate the interrogations of suspects.[96]

The U.S. was also accused of other crimes, some more indirect. It practiced "extraordinary rendition," whereby detainees were sent to countries that routinely practice torture, such as Syria and Egypt. As Amnesty Inter-

---

[93] George W. Bush, "President Discusses Creation of Military Commissions to Try Suspected Terrorists," 6 September 2006, The White House, Archives, http://georgewbushwhitehouse.archives.gov/news/releases/2006/09/20060906-3.html.

[94] In the US Supreme Court, three relevant cases (with references) were: Rasul v. Bush, 542 U.S. 466, 124 S.Ct. 2686 (2004); Hamdan v. Rumsfeld, 126 S.Ct. 2749 (2006); Boumediene v. Bush, 128 S.Ct. 2229 (2008).

[95] Shane Scott, "2 Suspects Waterboarded 266 Times" New York Times, April 20, 2009, http://www.nytimes.com/2009/04/21/world/21detain.html.

[96] Mark Mazzetti and Scott Shane, "C.I.A. Abuse Cases Detailed in Report on Detainees," *New York Times*, August 25, 2009,
http://www.nytimes.com/2009/08/26/us/politics/26intel.html.

national, for instance, has argued, such rendition is a violation of both U.S. and international law. Some 100-150 detainees have been "rendered" by the United States for detention and interrogation by governments in the Middle East. Human Rights Watch noted: "In an increasing number of cases, there is now credible evidence that rendered detainees have in fact been tortured."[97]

Similarly, the treatment of detainees in Afghanistan proper has also caused considerable controversy since coalition forces have not been able to guarantee that persons turned over to the Afghan government have not been tortured. This issue was particularly sensitive in Canada, which claims to treat detainees according to common article 3 of the Geneva Conventions. The country had in 1993 experienced the trauma of uncovering torture conducted by several of its soldiers in Somalia, leading to courts-martial of the soldiers directly involved and a multi-year governmental inquiry that led to the disbandment of the Canadian Airborne Regiment, to which the soldiers in question belonged. The tortuous path of Canada on the detainee issue is typical of a democratic nation struggling to fight a guerrilla war in a conscientious and law-abiding fashion.

The treatment of detainees by the Canadian Forces has been in question throughout Canada's Afghan mission. At the outset of Canada's military involvement in 2001-02, the Canadian Forces turned detainees over to U.S. forces to be held and questioned.[98] However, this stopped in 2002 as the treatment of detainees by U.S. officials came increasingly into question, particularly at Guantanamo Bay, souring the Canadian public domestically. As Canada took on the tough Kandahar mission in late 2005, it forged an agreement with the Afghan government to hand detainees over to Afghan forces. Under this deal, signed by Canadian Chief of Defence Staff Rick Hillier, Canadian forces notified the International Committee of the Red Cross of the transfers but did not check on the treatment of detainees thereafter.[99] Though the Red Cross monitored the conditions of transferred detainees, findings were only reported to the Afghan government. Canadian officials were therefore unaware of the detainees' status after

---

[97] Human Rights Watch, "Getting Away with Torture?" 23 April 2005, http://www.hrw.org/en/node/11765/section/2. For full report see: http://www.state.gov/g/drl/rls/hrrpt/2008/sca/119131.htm.
[98] *CBC News*, "The controversy over detainees: Are prisoners of war Canada's responsibility?" April 27, 2007,
http://www.cbc.ca/news/background/afghanistan/detainees.html.
[99] Paul Koring, "Amnesty Slams Canada over Afghan Detainees," *Globe and Mail*, March 31, 2009,
http://www.theglobeandmail.com/news/national/article743285.ece.

transfers took place.[100] Therefore it could be argued that Canada was complicit in torture, whether it was aware of it or not.

After an inquiry into the behaviour of Afghan officials found that torture and abuse was widespread, Amnesty International and the British Columbia Civil Liberties Association filed a complaint against the government of Canada and requested an injunction to terminate Canada's detainee transfer practice in 2007.[101] In the ensuing Federal Court case, it emerged that in fact the 2005 agreement for recorded detainee transfer could be circumvented by handing detainees directly to Afghan authorities within 96 hours, without formally taking them prisoner.[102] In such a case, the Red Cross would not be notified of the detainees' capture or transfer and the Canadian Forces could possibly be absolved of all responsibility for any breach of international law thereafter.[103]

In May of 2007, the Canadian government concluded a supplemental detainee transfer agreement with Afghanistan that included more stringent monitoring and preventative action against torture and abuse, as well as giving Canadian officials' "full and unrestricted access" to detainees in custody.[104] Still, after fresh evidence of widespread torture by Afghan officials was revealed, Canada halted detainee transfers altogether on 6 November 2007, using instead its own ad-hoc detainment facility at Kandahar Air Field. The transfers resumed two months later, after Canadian Officials cited sufficient reform, including increased record-keeping and a new Canadian-sponsored training program for prison officials.[105] However, in

---

[100] Then Defence Secretary Gordon O'Connor asserted several times that the Red Cross informed the Canadian Government of any mistreatment of the detainees. When it emerged that this had never been the case, O'Connor came under heavy criticism and was eventually transferred with Peter Mackay taking over the file in 2007. *CBC News*, "The controversy over detainees: Are prisoners of war Canada's responsibility?"

[101] Paul Koring, "Canada signs new Afghan detainee agreement," *Globe and Mail*, 31 March 2009, http://www.theglobeandmail.com/news/national/article756101.ece.

[102] Ibid..

[103] CBC News, "Canadian Forces Handle Some Detainees Differently, Documents Say," May 2, 2007, http://www.cbc.ca/canada/story/2007/05/02/detainees-afghan.html, and Koring, ibid.

[104] Koring, ibid.

[105] Graeme Smith, "Canada Resumes Afghan Detainee Transfers," *Globe and Mail*, February 29, 2008, http://www.theglobeandmail.com/news/world/article669955.ece.

May 2009 the Military Police Complaints Commission took up the detainee transfer issue and is to resume hearings in fall of 2009.[106]

The Military Police Complaints Commission also investigated the possible abuse of three Afghan detainees by Canadian Forces members held in 2006. The inquiry followed a civil complaint filed in 2007 by a University of Ottawa professor whose research uncovered suspiciously similar injuries amongst three detainees held by Canadian Forces in Kandahar in April 2006. The Canadian Military Police Complaints Commission took up the complaint in 2007 after the *Globe and Mail* brought the Professor's allegations to public attention.[107] In their final report in April 2009, the Commission cleared the Canadian Forces officials under question of any wrong-doing, stating that detainees had been handled, "professionally and humanely."[108] The report, however, found a "failure by the military police...to investigate the origins of the injuries of one of the detainees, when it was their duty to do so" and recommended increased educational programmes amongst other courses of action.[109] Overall, the issue of proper behaviour towards detainees continues to be a difficult one for Canada and its armed forces.

Detainee treatment after transfer to Afghan authorities has also been a challenge for the U.S., particularly after the U.S. State Department's 2008 annual report on the human rights situation around the world stated that women and children detainees face rape in Afghan prisons, whilst "security forces continued to use excessive force, including beating and torturing civilians," as well as "...pulling out fingernails and toenails, burning with hot oil, beatings, sexual humiliation, and sodomy."[110]

---

[106] Military Police Complaints Commission, "Commission Begins the Public Interest Hearing into the Allegations Regarding Afghan Detainees," 20 May 2009, Media Advisory, http://www.mpcc-cppm.gc.ca/alt_format/400/media/2009-05-20-eng.pdf.

[107] Paul Koring, "Military police failed to carry out obligations to detainees, probe finds," *Globe and Mail*, April 29, 2009, http://v1.theglobeandmail.com/servlet/story/RTGAM.20090426.wdetainees27/BNStory/undefined.

[108] Military Police Complaints Commission, "Final Report: Following a Public Interest Investigation Pursuant to Section 250.38 of the National Defence Act Of a Complaint Submitted by Dr. Amir Attaran Concerning the Conduct of the Task Force Afghanistan Military Police (Roto 1) at Kandahar Air Field in Kandahar, Afghanistan," 23 April 2009, http://www.mpcc-cppm.gc.ca/alt_format/300/3700/2007-003/2007-003-eng.pdf.

[109] Ibid.

[110] Paul Koring, "Torture, abuse still rife in Afghan prisons, U.S. human rights report says," *Globe and Mail*, February 26, 2009, http://v1.theglobeandmail.com/servlet/story/RTGAM.20090225.wafghan26/BNStory/International.

Improper conduct by U.S. forces in Afghanistan has in theory been investigated and punished via court-marshal under the Uniform Code of Military Justice. Unfortunately, many deadly incidents have gone unpunished, including cases of friendly-fire and civilian deaths. Furthermore, the U.S. has in fact insisted that its forces are immune from prosecution by the International Criminal Court.[111] The U.S. had signed the International Criminal Court Statute in the waning days of the Clinton administration, but that signature was declared null and void early in the Bush administration. In addition, the U.S. sought to sign immunity agreements with International Criminal Court signatories so that they would never turn over U.S. soldiers for prosecution. This undermining of the newly founded court was protested by many nations, particularly those who suffered punishment (e.g., through the withdrawal of U.S. aid) for not signing an immunity agreement with the U.S. However, the Obama administration is currently reviewing its policy towards the International Criminal Court.[112] To make matters more tense, the court prosecutor has initiated an investigation of atrocities committed by both sides of the war in Afghanistan. However, the International Criminal Court only takes cases in which national authorities are unwilling or unable to try offences committed by their soldiers. This puts U.S. actions in Afghanistan into a gray zone, while Taliban atrocities clearly violate international law.

Ethical Evaluation Using a "Just War Index"

To label the "war" in Afghanistan as either Just or Unjust without qualification would appear to be to oversimplify a complex problem, given that there are several operations involved and given that any such evaluation needs to consider all the criteria of Just War theory. A vague answer of "partially just" or "partially unjust" would also be unsatisfactory, since it would not offer sufficient moral clarity or specificity. Moreover, some Just War criteria may be well met while others are not at all met. In order to handle the level of complexity involved, therefore, this essay introduces the notion of a Just War Index.

In the Just War Index, each of the seven Just War criteria is evaluated. A range of 0 to 6 has been chosen to give adequate scope for the scoring of each of the criteria, and to allow some nuance in judgement. The following

---

[111] Jennifer Elsea, "U.S. Policy Regarding the International Criminal Court," 3 September 2002, Report for Congress, U.S. State Department, http://fpc.state.gov/documents/organization/13389.pdf.
[112] See: The American non-Governmental Organizations Coalition for the International Criminal Court, http://www.amicc.org/usinfo/administration.html.

broad meanings are associated with the scores available within the seven-point range: 0—completely unjust; 1—mostly unjust; 2—partially unjust; 3—neither just nor unjust; 4—partially just; 5—mostly just; and 6—fully just. The sum of the values for the seven criteria in view will thus give an overall score out of a potential score of 42. The overall score thus attempts to provide a measure of the justice of the war in its several dimensions.

The Just War Index is an analytical tool having heuristic utility, and is employed in order to explain and quantify an evaluation of the justice of the war. Obviously, each score must be explained. However, a comparison of the values for each criterion shows some missions to be more ethically justified than others in various ways. As with any ethical assessment, the results are perhaps subjective, being strongly influenced by the assessor's experience, world perspective and other factors. Nevertheless, evidence will be adduced to justify and support the values presented.

Usually Just War criteria are based on the information available at the time of the decision to go to war. This is appropriate, for instance, for making a judgement about a leader's actions at that time (*jus ad bellum*). In this paper's evaluation, however, the benefit of hindsight is applied to evaluate the military and associated operations, as they have turned out so far. Of course, the final outcome of the struggle in Afghanistan is not yet known (and may not be known for decades), so the assessment offered cannot be final. However, a view from the present time has its own merits, and might be of service in attempting to inform policy decisions that will impact upon that eventual outcome.

While the information provided above was designed to be descriptive and to present facts along with opinions, this assessment section allows for more stark moral judgement, presenting arguments in a manner that will be mainly short and to the point, but building on the considerations more extensively surveyed above. Such scoring necessitates the juxtaposition of the positive and negative sides of a nuanced argument. Extreme assessments (scores of 0 or 6) can rarely describe the real world, even for individual criteria. Though some of the seven criteria overlap significantly,[113] they are all of sufficient importance to merit independent assessment. Quantifying the criteria allows for clearer comparison of the missions and

---

[113] For instance, "proportionality of means" is often considered a component of right conduct (*jus in bello*). And "right intent" and "net benefit" are closely linked to the "just cause" criterion. Davis Brown argues that Right Intent is valid only in a narrow application of it. See Davis Brown, *The Sword, the Cross, and the Eagle: The American Christian Just War Tradition*, Lanham, Md.: Rowman & Littlefield Publishers, 2008.

the features of the missions, while the sum of the criterion scores can be used to evaluate each mission overall.

The American-led Operation Enduring Freedom (OEF) and the NATO-led International Security Assistance Force (ISAF) are each evaluated in what follows. The United Nations Assistance Mission in Afghanistan (UNAMA) is omitted because it does not use substantial armed force. However, an envisioned UNAMA II (robust peacekeeping) is assessed later.

1. Just Cause

The original cause of the U.S. invasion of Afghanistan under OEF was to defeat al-Qaeda and to capture its leaders. This was strongly justified after the attacks of 9/11. However, the U.S. government quickly moved as well to seek regime change in Afghanistan. This significantly broadened the definition of the enemy on the one side, and significantly diluted the justice of the cause on the other. President Bush's declaration that the United States would make no distinction between the terrorists and those who harbour them violated a basic provision of international law. It supposed a moral equivalency between the two that is not true to the original crime. It was also a recipe for an ever-widening war. The violence, for instance, quickly spread into Pakistan. Furthermore, the overthrow of the Taliban meant that much attention was diverted from the primary goal, and that complicating factors were introduced into the stability equation which have still not been resolved many years later. No doubt the Taliban government of Afghanistan in 2001 was deserving of some form of punishment, beyond the sanctions already applied by the United Nations, for its "delict" of harbouring the terrorist group al-Qaeda that had attacked the U.S. But waging war and overthrowing the government is the strongest form of punishment and one that diverted the U.S. from the primary goal, even if it did remove an odious rights-violating regime. Thus the justice of the cause for OEF cannot be negligible, but it cannot receive a high score either. For such reasons, the middle-range score of 3 out of 6 has been chosen.

ISAF was created after the Taliban's ouster, which the UN-mandated mission had to accept as a *fait accompli*. The mission was created by the international community as the interim government needed security assistance to function in Kabul and in other regions of the country. It engages in national capacity building. Although ISAF has not succeeded in its mandate of creating a secure and stable environment, its cause is deemed valuable and strongly justified. ISAF can easily be awarded 5 out of 6.

Just Cause: OEF: 3; ISAF: 5

2. Right Intent

Intent is one of the most difficult qualities to measure, but the Bush administration's approach in OEF makes judgement easier. The U.S. adopted a black and white view, dividing the world into those who are "with" them versus those who are "with" the terrorists. Initially, such a simple world view would seem to make the question of intent clearer. However, the nuanced reality of the world means the "with us or against us" distinction is artificial and inaccurate. Initially, the intent was articulated by a war-president who saw himself as the representative of good in the battle with evil. While the Obama administration has dropped this form of self-aggrandizement, along with the term "Global War on Terror," it is expanding the Afghan war with additional troops. It is also attempting to divest itself of some of the Bush administration's ideological goals of creating a democratic Afghanistan where individual liberties can thrive. Taking a more pragmatic approach rather than an ideological one, it has dropped much of the language that U.S. troops are there for humanitarian, nation-building and even school building purposes. The intent is now focused on a new goal: not to lose to the Taliban and al-Qaeda. A U.S. withdrawal from Afghanistan in the face of a resurgent Taliban would be seen as an unacceptable victory for the insurgents. Given the range of positive and negative factors, the intent behind OEF (2001 onwards) is quite mixed. Considering the many factors, a score of 3 seems merited.

The intent behind ISAF has been clearly articulated by the Canadian government, which has played a major role in the mission. Canada cited humanitarian grounds for the mission as it sent forces to ISAF in 2003, when ISAF forces were mostly confined to the Kabul region. Prime Minister Jean Chrétien stated: "We are committed to helping the Afghani people build a democratic, pluralistic society."[114] His successor, Prime Minister Paul Martin in 2004 cited the dual purposes of "reviving a failing state, for

---

[114] Prime Minister of Canada: Jean Chrétien, "Notes for an Address by Prime Minister Jean Chrétien at the Opening of the 58th Session of the United Nations General Assembly," 23 September 2003, Archives Canada, http://www.epe.lacbac.gc.ca/100/205/301/prime_minister-ef/jean_chretien/2003-12-08/stagingpm_3a8080/dfault.asp@language=e&page=newsroom&sub=speeches&doc=ungaspeech.20030923_e.htm.

humanitarian reasons and at the same time ensuring that it cannot be used as a base of operations for terrorists."[115]

A further look at Canada's motivation also reveals a sense of national pride. In 2006, Prime Minister Stephen Harper said the mission was to solidify Canada's leadership internationally: "...we are determined to demonstrate Canada's leadership on the world stage to regain the trust of our allies and to demonstrate that we will pull our weight in United Nations missions."[116] He also cited national security as a key objective: "because our national security and the safety of Canadians is at stake.... It [terrorism] must be confronted wherever we find it—at home or abroad."[117]

Similarly, NATO has sought in the Afghanistan context to prove that it could be a useful alliance at the forefront of international security and in the fight against terrorism. It has thus sought to build a stronger role for itself after the end of the Cold War. In Afghanistan, however, the alliance found a burden greater and of longer duration than many expected. Still, with the new people-centred ISAF approach, having the goal of winning hearts and minds, ISAF has recently shown itself to be a military alliance with adjusted priorities and with a *modus operandi* that goes far beyond simply killing Taliban enemies.

Right Intent: OEF: 3; ISAF: 5

3. Legitimate Authority

The OEF and ISAF missions have completely different authorizations. ISAF was authorized and mandated by the UN Security Council (resolution 1386 of 20 December, 2001). Its mandate, indeed, has subsequently been renewed on an annual or semi-annual basis. By contrast, the U.S.-led OEF has neither Security Council authorization nor mandate. It did gain U.S. domestic approval. Still, this falls short of the demands of the UN Charter and of the international rules governing the use of force, especially

---

[115] Prime Minister of Canada: Paul Martin, "Address by Prime Minister Paul Martin at CFB Gagetown, New Brunswick: Speech by the Prime Minister," 14 April 2004, Archives Canada, http://epe.lac-bac.gc.ca/100/205/301/prime_minister-ef/paul_martin/06-02-03/ and http://www.pm.gc.ca/eng/news.asp@id=172.

[116] Office of the Prime Minister: Stephen Harper, "Address by the Prime Minister on new Canadian government assistance for the reconstruction of Afghanistan," 15 June 2006, Government of Canada, http://www.pm.gc.ca/eng/media.asp?category=2&id=1204.

[117] Ibid.

for such large tasks as overthrowing an established government (even if it was one that was not widely recognized). From its creation after 9/11, OEF's use of the self-defence provision of the UN Charter has rung hollow, since no Security Council resolution authorized its use of force in Afghanistan. Many years after the U.S. invasion, the self-defence argument becomes even weaker, since Article 51 of the Charter limits self-defence to a period "until the Security Council has taken measures necessary to maintain international peace and security."[118] The Security Council has undertaken many measures, including the creation of ISAF. Furthermore, if OEF were operating under Article 51, it would be obliged to submit reports to the Security Council, which it does not do. By contrast, ISAF reports regularly, if not always punctually, to the Council. Thus, the scores for the two missions are judged to be even more dissimilar than the previous two for this criterion.

Legitimate Authority: OEF: 2; ISAF: 5

4. Last Resort

This provision of Just War theory states that all peaceful means should be exhausted before armed force is applied. Both OEF and ISAF are flawed from this point of view, since no attempt to negotiate with the opponent was made. This is particularly true of OEF before the overthrow of the Taliban government. The U.S. delivered ultimatums but made no effort at discussion, though several avenues remained to be explored, such as the Taliban offer to have bin Laden tried in a third country.[119] Furthermore, the U.S. has since remained adamant that no negotiations are possible with terrorists, ignoring that insurgent fighters include moderates and those simply defending their homeland against "foreign occupiers." While ISAF as a whole has not conducted negotiations, some nations in ISAF, includ-

---

[118] Article 51 of the UN Charter reads in full: "Nothing in the present Charter shall impair the inherent right of individual or collective self-defence if an armed attack occurs against a Member of the United Nations, until the Security Council has taken measures necessary to maintain international peace and security. Measures taken by Members in the exercise of this right of self-defence shall be immediately reported to the Security Council and shall not in any way affect the authority and responsibility of the Security Council under the present Charter to take at any time such action as it deems necessary in order to maintain or restore international peace and security."

[119] Bush, "Address to a Joint Session of Congress and the American People," 20 September 2001.

ing the United Kingdom and the Netherlands, have attempted limited local discussions and negotiations. For instance, in 2006, the commander of the British task force, Brigadier Ed Butler, negotiated a mutual withdrawal with the Taliban from Musa Qala, a town in Helmand province. Nevertheless, efforts to negotiate have not been sustained or supported by ISAF as a whole, and the battle with the Taliban has been waged without any consistent effort to explore peaceful means of dispute settlement, save a demand for Taliban surrender.

On a broader level, alternatives to force were hardly considered in 2001. As military historian Sir Michael Howard observed about the Global War on Terror, "the use of force is seen no longer as a last resort, to be avoided if humanly possible, but as the first, and the sooner it is used the better."[120] Furthermore, Howard proposed in October 2001 an entirely different approach to dealing with 9/11: "…many people would have preferred a police operation conducted under the auspices of the United Nations on behalf of the international community as a whole, against a criminal conspiracy whose members should be hunted down and brought before an international court, where they would receive a fair trial and, if found guilty, be awarded an appropriate sentence."[121]

Because OEF was involved at the outset of hostilities, when alternative (peaceful) means could have been tried, its score is considerably lower than that of ISAF, though they both ignored the "last resort" provision. OEF was a "first resort" to force, not a last one. Though an ultimatum was issued to the Taliban government after 9/11, no discussions or peaceful means of settlement were sought.

ISAF makes some mention of last resort in its Commander's 2009 Directive: "commanders [can] protect the lives of their men and women as a matter of self-defence where it is determined *no other options* are available to effectively counter the threat."[122] Negotiating with the Taliban leadership is certainly not one of the options currently used. Some local negotiations have occurred sporadically. In addition, ISAF has sometimes

---

[120] Michael Howard, "What's In A Name? How to Fight Terrorism (Lecture in London, October 30, 2001)," http://www.let.uu.nl/~Arend-Jan.Boekestijn/personal/historisch%20ambacht/Howard.htm.

[121] Quoted in Tania Branigan, "Al-Qaida is winning war, allies warned," *The Guardian*, October 31, 2001, http://www.guardian.co.uk/uk/2001/oct/31/afghanistan.highereducation.

[122] ISAF, "ISAF revises tactical directive". Emphasis added. The directive itself is available (with some sections deleted for operational security) at http://www.nato.int/isaf/docu/official_texts/Tactical_Directive_090706.pdf.

warned local residents in advance of planned attacks, asking fighters to set down their weapons and surrender before ISAF enters the area.

Last resort: OEF: 1; ISAF: 3

5. Net Benefit

The net benefit, after weighing the gains against the harm, has declined in recent years for both OEF and ISAF. As the missions prove unsuccessful in overcoming Taliban resistance and government progress is painstakingly slow, the mission outlook has become increasingly pessimistic and even the words "likely failure" have been used by commanders.[123]

On a positive note, there has not been a successful terrorist attack since 9/11 against civilian targets in Western countries from elements trained in Afghanistan. However, a few successful attacks and many attempts were made by indigenous terrorists who found international operations in Afghanistan so offensive that they vowed to retaliate against what they saw as an imperialistic West.

Thanks to the initial war waged by OEF, al-Qaeda no longer has safe haven in Afghanistan. It has now moved its base to the untamed and violent border areas of Pakistan. Overall, the Taliban is no longer in control of the central government in Afghanistan, though it now controls large swaths of Afghan land using guerrilla tactics and intimidation. Warlords, many of them once employed by OEF as a proxy force to overthrow the Taliban, are running many areas of Afghanistan. Since the Taliban times, the human rights situation has improved, especially for women, though the current government commits many human right violations and many Afghan regions are still under Taliban religious/cultural influence.

Since the final outcome of the intervention in Afghanistan is uncertain, it is impossible to judge the final net benefit. However, in recent years the insurgency in Afghanistan has shown signs of strengthening while both OEF and ISAF have lost ground. The conflict has been of far longer duration than expected and the resilience of the Taliban has exceeded predictions. For instance, on 1 May, 2003 during a visit to Kabul, Secretary of Defense Donald Rumsfeld actually declared an end to "major combat" in

---

[123] General Stanley McChrystal, the commander of OEF and ISAF forces, said he needed additional troops within the next year or else the conflict "will likely result in failure." See: Eric Schmitt and Thom Shanker, "General Calls for More U.S. Troops to Avoid Afghan Failure," *New York Times*, September 20, 2009.

Afghanistan![124] The same day, President George W. Bush declared "mission accomplished" aboard the aircraft carrier USS Abraham Lincoln, which was returning from Iraq. Both statements proved premature and naïve. At the time there were only 8,000 U.S. soldiers in Afghanistan. The necessity to continue fighting major combat operations brought the number of U.S. soldiers in 2010 to over 100,000, with NATO's number set to continue to decline.

A net benefit analysis measures progress, as well as setbacks in Afghanistan. The capacity of the Afghan National Army has grown considerably. It has in fact surpassed its original recruitment goals, having some 135,000 soldiers by end of 2010, and is expected to reach 172,000 by 2012.[125] The economy has grown substantially, though the contribution of the illegal drug trade is still strong. New markets have opened with neighbouring countries for Afghan farmers. Some 500,000 hectares of land have been rehabilitated since 2004, often using new irrigation systems. Cereal production almost doubled between 2001 and 2007, and agricultural cooperatives have grown exponentially, increasing the number of employed from 7,400 in 2002 to 142,600 in 2007. Electricity production tripled between 2002 and 2008. Some 20,000 kilometres of rural access roads have been constructed or repaired, and Afghanistan's main national transport artery, the 3,000 km "ring road," is almost entirely re-paved and re-furbished (at huge international expense).[126]

On the education front, between 2001 and 2008, 3,500 schools were built, while 19 universities are now providing higher learning. Seven million children are enrolled in school, 2 million of whom are female.[127] Health-wise, 85% of Afghans have access to a basic package of health services.

While some specific figures are encouraging, the overall quality of life picture is more discouraging. Life expectancy at birth is still only 43.6 years.[128] The UN Human Development Index 2009 ranks Afghanistan sec-

---

[124] *Cable News Network (CNN)*, "Rumsfeld: Major combat over in Afghanistan," May 1, 2003, http://www.cnn.com/2003/WORLD/asiapcf/central/05/01/afghan.

[125] The Afghan National Army had some 82,000 troops in 2007. See: NATO, "Afghanistan Report 2009," July 2009, 12, http://www.nato.int/nato_static/assets/pdf/pdf_2009_03/20090331_090331_afghanistan_report_2009.pdf.

[126] Ibid., 37-38.

[127] Ibid., 32.

[128] United Nations Development Programme, *Human Development Report 2009*, Afghanistan, http://www.hdrstats.undp.org/en/countries/country_fact_sheets/cty_fs_AFG.html.

ond last (only surpassing Niger) in its list of 182 nations.[129] This abysmal rank stands despite almost a decade of international aid and reconstruction efforts, and the immense help provided by NATO countries. Afghanistan received over $36 billion of aid for development and reconstruction from 2001-2009, according to the Afghan government, although this number is likely an underestimate.[130]

The costs of the military campaign are enormous. The U.S. spent $223 billion for OEF from fiscal years 2001-2009. The bill in the fiscal year 2008 was $34 billion. Combined with Operations Iraqi Freedom and Noble Eagle (homeland security), the Congressional Research Services has predicted that by the fiscal year 2010, "war funding since the 9/11 attacks would total over $1 trillion."[131] These are "incremental" costs, which are in addition to normal peacetime military costs, the baseline funding for which pays for salaries and normal equipment purchases.

The cost in national treasure is exceeded by the cost in national blood. The number of lives lost can be precisely counted: as of December, 2010: 1,414 Americans, 345 British and 153 Canadians had died. Overall, the NATO-led coalition had lost over 2,200 lives.[132] A negative consequence of the military fatalities has been a growing split in the NATO alliance. With many contributors imposing limitations on the use of their forces ("national caveats") and some nations such as Germany unwilling to send forces into high-intensity combat areas, there is a growing distinction between those carrying the "heavy burden" of combat and those limiting themselves to less lethal projects. Furthermore, the declared withdrawals, of the Netherlands forces in 2010 and Canada's combat forces in 2011, threaten to further strain relations between ISAF partners, and particularly with the United States, which is assuming a larger burden.

Within Afghanistan, the corruption of the Karzai government, the spectre of increased warlordism, widening banditry, and higher opium produc-

---

[129] *Rawa News*, "In Brief: Afghanistan slipping down UN human development index," http://www.rawa.org/temp/runews/2009/10/05/in-brief-afghanistan-slipping-down-un-human-development-index.html.

[130] Elisabeth Bumiller and Mark Landler, "Civilian Goals Largely Unmet in Afghanistan," *New York Times*, October 12, 2009, http://www.nytimes.com/2009/10/12/world/asia/12civil.html?_r=1.

[131] Amy Belasco, "The Cost of Iraq, Afghanistan, and Other Global War on Terror Operations Since 9/11," Congressional Research Service, Report RL33110, 15 May 2009, 46, www.fas.org/sgp/crs/natsec/RL33110.pdf. The average cost per deployed troop (in war operations) in the financial year 2006 was $325,000.

[132] These are the three nations with the greatest number of fatalities, based on figures available on 3 November 2009, http://www.icasualties.org/OEF/index.aspx.

tion remains alarming. Human rights abuses by government forces as well as insurgents persist, especially in the South. The Afghan National Police remains notoriously corrupt.

The negative effects of the Afghanistan war are not confined to that country but have spilled over into neighbouring Pakistan. The anti-American movement coalesced with the December 2007 creation of *Tehrik-i-Taliban Pakistan* (literally, "Students' Movement of Pakistan"). The Pakistani movement not only destabilizes Afghanistan by providing fighters and refuge, but threatens the stability of Pakistan itself. A series of bloody bombings have rocked the country and resulted in savage fighting between government forces and insurgent/Taliban fighters in the tribal areas on the Afghan border. This conflict is spreading from northern areas of Pakistan to its major cities, including its capital.

Thus, the net effects of the overthrow of the Taliban (OEF) have not been overall positive, giving OEF a score of at most 3. ISAF does slightly better since it engages in many more humanitarian and reconstruction projects with modest success, giving it a score of 4. Both missions have disappointingly little to show for their immense efforts after almost a decade.

Net Benefit: OEF: 3; ISAF: 4

6. Proportionality of Means

Both OEF and ISAF employ far more sophisticated and lethal weaponry than do the insurgents.[133] OEF has conducted air strikes from B-1 Lancer strategic bombers, B-2 Spirit stealth bombers and B-52 Stratofortress bombers. F-14 Tomcat and F/A-18 Hornet fighter jets have flown combat missions from aircraft carriers. Tomahawk cruise missiles were launched from both U.S. and British ships and submarines. Unmanned Aerial Vehicles, like the Predator drone armed with Hellfire missiles, have been a weapons system of choice due to their long "loiter" capabilities and remote piloting with no possibility of loss of American life. On land, OEF and ISAF forces use Leopard main battle tanks, Bradley fighting vehicles, M777 155mm Howitzer artillery, and heavy machine guns, among other weapons. The insurgent forces are limited to small arms: rocket-propelled

---

[133] For more on the weapons systems (including photos with extensive captions), see: U.S. Air Forces Central, "Media Gallery," U.S. Air Force, http://www.centaf.af.mil/photos/mediagallery.asp?galleryID=1063; Tony Holmes, "F-14 Tomcat Units of Operation," (Oxford: Osprey Publishing, 2008); BBC News, "Timeline Afghanistan: Air Strikes" October 7, 2009, http://news.bbc.co.uk/2/hi/americas/1584660.stm.

grenades, assault rifles, mines, booby traps and improvised explosive devices.

This asymmetry in forces does not necessarily imply that coalition means were disproportionate. Sophisticated weaponry may be necessary for the protection of coalition forces, particularly when the enemy is indistinguishable from the civilian population. It is often necessary to use high technology and precision weapons to detect and destroy insurgents at night and prevent harm to civilian populations. However, the amount of firepower used has been immense, and air strikes in particular have been heavily criticized because of the large numbers of civilian casualties. Typically, between five hundred and a thousand civilians a year have died from coalition attacks. In particular, the five hundred pound bomb has caused widespread destruction. Though not particularly lethal, night raids are considered extremely offensive and disproportionate by Afghan citizens because coalition forces enter homes without permission while the occupants are sleeping. After kicking down doors, their presence traumatises occupants, including the carefully protected women and children.

OEF has relied heavily on Special Forces to conduct search and destroy missions as well as targeted assassinations. ISAF and UN project managers have sometimes complained that their development efforts, with the goal of winning the "hearts and minds" of locals, have been rendered ineffective, if not sabotaged, by OEF's uncoordinated attacks.

Some comparisons of figures also give a sense of the (dis)proportionality. The number of Taliban forces is typically estimated at only 10,000 to 20,000 strong. Other insurgent groups may have the same number in total. The OEF and ISAF together made up some 140,000 in 2010. However, this abundance of forces does not ensure victory. At its height, the Soviet Union had deployed some 118,000 troops and it was not able to create stability in the country.[134]

In comparison to the Soviet occupation, however, the current intervention has been much less bloody (more proportionate). Over a period of ten years (1979-1988), the Soviets suffered some 13,300 fatalities and caused an estimated 1.1 million Afghan fatalities. Coalition forces between 2001 and 2010 suffered approximately 2,200 fatalities and caused an estimated 10,000 Afghan fatalities (rough extrapolation from Table 1).

The coalition hopes to build the Afghan Security Forces to a level that can defeat or at least contain the Taliban without foreign forces. Nevertheless, the Soviet experience shows that even by developing large numbers

---

[134] Richard F. Nyrop, Donald M. Seekins, *Afghanistan: A Country Study*, (Washington, DC: United States Government Printing Office, 1986), XVIII–XXV, http://www.gl.iit.edu/govdocs/afghanistan/Afghanistan-Chapter1.pdf.

of government forces, such a victory is not certain. Overall, by 1988 the government had over 450,000 security forces available, though their loyalty then was questionable, as it is today.[135] The pro-government Afghan forces by end of 2010 are much smaller in number: 130,000 active army troops and 110,000 police. Still, this number is much larger than the estimated number of insurgent (mostly Taliban) forces.

In summary, given that OEF deploys greater firepower, more offensive capability, more targeted assassinations, and is less transparent than ISAF, its proportionality factor is deemed less (3) than ISAF's (4), but not by much. Both types of coalition forces, desperate to defeat the Taliban, have sought military dominance using overwhelming force. The failure of such a strategy to achieve victory has shown that what matters is not only the level of force but the strategy and conduct of the forces involved.

Proportionality of Means: OEF: 3; ISAF: 4

7. Right Conduct

The loss of civilian lives in coalition attacks, particularly from the air, has been both considerable and very tragic. Both OEF and ISAF forces have engaged in questionable and sometimes objectionable practices. In cases where insurgents have used civilians as "human shields," blending into the population to defend themselves, the resulting civilian casualties have been explicable, if not defensible. However, on too many occasions the use of force has been excessive and the choice of targets inappropriate, as evidenced by frequent Afghan and international newspaper headlines. This is particularly true for OEF, which commands most of the air strike assets. Although civilian fatalities are not deliberate for the most part, due

---

[135] The Soviets built up the Afghan security forces to over 300,000 in 1988 from 87,000 at the time of the Soviet invasion in 1979. In 1988, the year of the Soviet withdrawal, the regular military forces reached 90,000 troops. Border guards—considered a separate force—had a strength of around 42,000. The gendarmerie (Tsarandoy) and the secret police (KhaD), heavily armed and organized alongside military lines, reached 92,000 and 68,000, respectively. Special Guards, the elite units that guarded the regime in Kabul, numbered about 11,500. This makes 303,000 government forces. In addition, the Soviets also paid for 150,000 militia to serve on the side of government (Tribal 62,000, GDR 35,000, self-defence 53,000). See: Anton Minkov & Dr. Gregory Smolynec, "3-D Soviet Style: Lessons Learned from the Soviet Experience in Afghanistan," Defence Research and Development Canada, DRDC CORA TM 2007-36, 26 Oct 2007, http://www.cradpdf.drdc.gc.ca/PDFS/unc66/p528465.pdf.

caution appears not to have been exercised either by OEF or by ISAF forces.

The issue of improper conduct by international forces extends from excessive fatalities to the treatment of detainees. As outlined above, OEF has employed detention facilities and methods illegal under international law. To a lesser extent, ISAF forces have been complicit in this potential war crime by handing over detainees to the U.S. and to the Afghan government. The Afghan government's domestic intelligence agency, the National Directorate of Security, is known to commit frequent human rights abuses such as torture. Furthermore, though most ISAF countries, including Canada, have from the beginning affirmed that behaviour will "fully accord with the Laws of Armed Conflict"[136] OEF forces are not beholden to such a commitment.

Right Conduct: OEF: 3; ISAF: 4

Final Just War Index Scores

Each mission (OEF and ISAF) has been evaluated under the seven specified criteria of the Just War. The simple addition of scores results in the following totals: OEF: 17 out of 42 (40%); and ISAF: 29 out of 42 (69%). Clearly, the numbers should not be taken as an objective result having scientific validity. They are in many ways, rather, a quantitative reflection of the wider views expressed in this paper, which, as such, help to crystallise the degree of justification for the Afghanistan conflict in the author's mind. While acknowledging the perspectival nature of the judgements made, however, what this analysis suggests is that ISAF can legitimately be seen to have substantially greater moral justification than OEF. Readers will naturally have their own views, and can also arrive at their own scores if they so desire.

The difference in scores does not mean that the two missions are competitive. The two are, in certain ways, to be considered as complementary. In many ways they carry the same flaws. What this seems to imply from a moral, if not also a practical point of view, is that a third type of force is well worth considering.

---

[136] Department of National Defence Art Eggleton, "MND Statement in the House of Commons—Ottawa, Ontario," 19 November 2001, Minister's Speeches Archive, National Defence and the Canadian Forces, Government of Canada, http://www.forces.gc.ca/site/news-nouvelles/view-news-afficher-nouvelles-eng.asp?id=517.

Evaluating a Future Peacekeeping Force

Although the creation of a "robust peacekeeping" force is not currently under active discussion, one can readily envision a future mission based on current UN missions working in similarly challenging environments, particularly the current UNAMA mission in Afghanistan and the UN Mission in the D.R. Congo.[137] Just War theory allows one to assess the ethical value not only of past and present operations but also of envisioned plans. Indeed, the criteria in view in Just War theory were designed specifically to help leaders and thinkers assess the legitimacy of *future* actions.

A new mission would maintain the cause of nation-building and promoting a peace process, like UNAMA. But any "UNAMA II" in the Afghanistan context would require a sizeable military and police component, numbering in the tens of thousands, ideally drawn predominantly from Muslim nations to make it more acceptable to the population and the insurgents. It would be deployed with the consent of the belligerent parties, including the Afghan government, NATO, the U.S. and the main insurgent groups. It would be the result of negotiations, well beyond the current halting efforts of the Saudi authorities. Whether or not all the parties would accept this deployment cannot be taken for granted, but it cannot be dismissed out of hand, either. As the current stalemate of the Afghan war wearies all sides, the prospect for a UN peacekeeping force increases. Even if the U.S. and NATO gain the upper hand and greater stability is established, it is likely that a peacekeeping force will be introduced to facilitate a U.S./NATO drawdown if not withdrawal. In the opposite scenario, if the war becomes worse for NATO and the U.S., they might well seek to reduce the number of their troops deployed, handing over the difficult situation to the UN.

Peacekeeping forces have frequently served as a key stabilization tool. For the Taliban and other insurgents, the UN force would be far more impartial than the existing ones (OEF and ISAF). The UN force would also be less threatening because its mandate would be to support a peace process and because it would not act in an aggressive manner. It would avoid adopting the "enemy-centred" mentality that is characteristic of both OEF and ISAF. It would assume a defensive posture, as is the case for almost

---

[137] The proposal for a UN peacekeeping force in Afghanistan was made by the author in his testimony to the Canadian House of Commons Standing Committee on Foreign Affairs and International Trade (SCFAIT) on March 22, 2007, http://www2.parl.gc.ca/HousePublications/Publication.aspx?DocId=2785497&Language=E&Mode=1&Parl=39&Ses=1.

all modern peacekeeping operations, though it would probably need to be more robust than any current mission.

Because its approach and military activities would be more defensive and peacebuilding in character, the Just War Index scores would naturally be higher. With a purpose similar to UNAMA, the just cause score would be high (such as 5). The intent of the mission would be clear: to foster and maintain peace, as the term "peacekeeping" implies. Though the UN Security Council might be bowing to U.S. pressure in any deployment of such a force, the intent would still be benevolent, resulting in a high score (5).

Given that all UN peacekeeping forces are created and mandated by the UN Security Council and funded through the General Assembly, the international legitimacy of the mission would also be high. UNAMA II would need to obtain the consent of the Afghan government and of the main parties to the conflict, which is something that might take time to achieve. But given this prerequisite, a high "Legitimate Authority" score is likely (5). This, however, is not a perfect score, since the legitimacy of the government and the insurgents may be in question, especially given the fraud committed in the 2009 elections.

Like most peacekeeping forces, UNAMA II would be expected to use force only as a last resort. The Rules of Engagement for modern UN missions contain such a provision explicitly. Peacekeepers are not offensive fighting forces, though they are combat-capable. Their mandate is multi-dimensional, and the goal is clearly peace, so a peacekeeping mission must strive to be an example of using last resort. Unless there are overly aggressive force commanders, the last resort provision would likely be fully met (score: 6).

When OEF and ISAF were first established in 2001, most expected that stability would be achieved in a matter of months. Such exaggerated expectations could not be held for any UNAMA II, given the experience of the other two Afghan missions and of difficult peacekeeping operations in other parts of the world. However, the net benefit of UNAMA II should be positive, given the constructive role that is currently played by UNAMA with its small cadre of uniformed personnel. Furthermore, there remains hope that a peace process supported by a peacekeeping force could eventually lead to stability. Peacekeeping forces have greater staying power than most combat forces. Some peacekeeping operations have been in existence to verify and oversee agreements for more than 50 years. Thus, the net benefit of such a mission could reasonably be expected to be very positive (score: 5).

A model for UNAMA II might be the United Nations Transitional Authority in Cambodia (1992-93). The main insurgent group in Cambodia, the Khmer Rouge, was an ideological and military entity more devastating and tyrannical even than the Taliban. While in power (1975-79), the Khmer Rouge sponsored a genocide that resulted in several million deaths. Afterwards, it fought a brutal insurgency. In 1990, however, the Khmer Rouge was finally brought to the negotiating table. It joined the Paris peace process, and even sought to run candidates in an envisioned election. But the rebel group became confused about whether to participate in the election or to undermine it. This division within its ranks was one of the factors that led to its slow breakup and marginalization. Eventually, several of its remaining leaders were brought before a hybrid UN-Cambodian court to meet justice.

Whether Taliban leaders will face their day in court is uncertain, though the International Criminal Court is now investigating atrocities in Afghanistan. In any case, through a peace process the insurgents can be represented and their concerns voiced. Possibly the groups will gradually become marginalized as they lose popular support, like the Khmer Rouge. The United Nations Transitional Authority in Cambodia provided a great net benefit to the Cambodian peace process, even though after it withdrew in 1993, internal politics allowed one party (the Cambodian People's Party, under Hun Sen) to seize and maintain power. More importantly for this exercise, however, the Khmer Rouge subsequently ceased to be a force in Cambodian politics or to threaten the people or the state.

The resources needed for a future UN peace operation in Afghanistan would be much more modest than those provided for ISAF and OEF, though considerably larger than in Cambodia, where 17,000 military personnel and 3,500 police were involved. A future UNAMA II in Afghanistan might have over 30,000 uniformed personnel. Unlike OEF and ISAF, it would not drop bombs in air strikes, though at first ISAF or OEF forces might provide such protection in urgent cases. UNAMA II might deploy attack helicopters (as the UN does presently in its Congo operations) but these would use missiles only when local negotiations have failed and the United Nations must stop an attack that is under way—and then after giving warnings. Thus the means used could be expected to be less forceful than in the case of OEF or ISAF currently. The problem is more likely to be an under-resourced and overly-defensive combat capability than an overuse of force. Thus, the proportionality of force component of the Just War Index could be expected to be satisfactory (no "overkill"), resulting perhaps in a score of 5 out of 6.

The main critique of a potential UNAMA II is that it would not be able to handle Taliban attacks. However, if it were not perceived as an enemy or occupying force, as a result of negotiations, it might not be subject to insurgent attacks in quite the same way or to the same extent that American and ISAF forces have been. A UN force would also likely gain greater acceptance in the local population. The current mission, UNAMA, is popular among locals in Afghanistan, beating out the Afghan and international security forces for approval in opinion polls.[138] Though it has suffered occasional and sometimes horrendous attacks, UNAMA has not withdrawn from Afghanistan, and is increasing safety measures for its staff.

A UNAMA II mission would no doubt have to face the challenge of determining the right level of force and the right means to deal with potential belligerents, as, for example, in the case of any "spoilers" of the peace process. Peacekeeping operations, however, are obligated to apply the rules of the Geneva Conventions and the laws of armed conflict, and the United Nations is developing a detainee policy. Though UN forces might have a tendency to avoid offensive operations, they can do so as a last resort. A few violations of international rules on the use of force could undoubtedly be anticipated, given the weak command and control capability in peacekeeping operations, the mixture of many national forces, and the high threat level. But overall, the score for right conduct could be expected to be high (another 5).

This completes the Just War Index criteria evaluation of an envisioned UNAMA II. A comparison of the Just War Index totals for OEF, ISAF and UNAMA II is now be presented in Table 3. As can be seen, UNAMA II obtains on such reckoning the highest score by far, over double the OEF score, with ISAF in between. While there is an arbitrary element to the numbers, they do help get a sense of relative merit in the eyes of the assessor. They also help contrast the separate character of the three missions, using standard criteria, which will hopefully make the writer's conclusions clearer.

---

[138] Daisaku Higashi, "Challenges of Constructing Legitimacy in Peacebuilding: Case of Afghanistan," 1 September 2008, UN Peacekeeping Best Practices Unit, United Nations, http://www.peacekeepingbestpractices.unlb.org/PBPS/Pages/PUBLIC/ViewDocument.aspx?docid=901&cat=34&scat=0&menukey=_4_3.

Table 3: Summary of Scores for OEF, ISAF and a Hypothetical UNAMA II

Criteria	OEF	ISAF	UNAMA II
Just cause	3	5	5
Right Intent	3	5	5
Legitimate Authority	2	5	5
Last Resort	1	3	6
Net Benefit	3	4	5
Proportionality of Means	3	4	5
Right Conduct	2	3	5
Total (out of 42)	17	29	36
Total (as percentage)	40%	69%	86%

Conclusion: a Third Force?

No approach to armed force can be ethically perfect and indeed, many ostensibly unjust strategies may even have some merit. In comparing ISAF with OEF, however, the ethical evaluation above seeks to show that OEF has serious ethical deficiencies. At its start in 2001, the aim of OEF was greatly expanded from punishing al-Qaeda to Afghan regime change, without anticipating the long-term consequences of that policy. It was based on a simplistic dichotomization of "good versus evil," "either with us or against us," that immediately failed to make a distinction between terrorists and those harbouring them. As the military arm of the Global War on Terror, OEF did not take into account either the diversity of world views involved, or the morally nuanced and uncontrollable nature of conflict. Neither was OEF legitimated under international law through Security Council authorization. It was definitely not a last resort mission in Afghanistan, as no efforts were made at peaceful settlement or at meaningful discussions with the Taliban government. The net benefit has proven rather slender, given the ongoing fighting and terrorist activity in Afghanistan and Pakistan. Finally, OEF's conduct has been highly questionable at times, particularly in the treatment of detainees in Afghanistan and at the Guantanamo facility. All these characteristics justify the low overall score. If the passing mark were arbitrarily set at 50%, the OEF mission at 40% would not pass the ethical test. One might well conclude that it would be better, therefore, if the OEF mission in Afghanistan were to be rolled into that of ISAF, rather than to continue as at present.

ISAF, for its part, is not so heavily burdened, but it has ethical deficiencies as well. While it supports the just cause of providing security for reconstruction, and while it is UN-authorized, it has been implicated in many civilian fatalities, and it has not adopted means for peaceful settlement (negotiations) with its enemies. Also, the net benefit has been far from the desired level, especially with the continuing insecurity in the country. Still, the mission has considerable ethical traction and merits the reasonable (and above passing) score of almost 70%.

UNAMA II is, of course, merely an imagined mission that might well not live up to the high scores suggested (86% overall), but there are genuine grounds for the high ethical evaluation. It would have the just cause of bringing peace to the war-torn country of Afghanistan. Admittedly, this would necessarily involve making compromise with some unsavoury Taliban leaders, which itself poses difficult ethical questions. Such a pragmatic strategy is, however, not without precedent. The mission, furthermore, would certainly be UN-authorized and UN-run. It ought ideally to involve a large number of forces from Muslim nations to help establish legitimacy and to avoid the problematic prospect of the arrival of yet more Western "occupying" forces. It would, finally, have the advantage of being seen as more impartial and as distinct from the current U.S. and NATO missions in the country. The force would adopt a defensive posture, using its limited combat power and only when necessary, as a last resort. It ought accordingly to be implicated in far fewer civilian fatalities. In this way, it could help win the "hearts and minds" of the local population.

If peacekeeping would be more ethical, then the question remains: Could it do the job, and stand up to Taliban attack? Certainly it could not do so alone. For the immediate future, in fact, there will need to be a robust coalition of forces that act in tandem to stop the Taliban from overrunning large areas of Afghanistan. Over time, however, as the peace process strengthens and more Taliban units and fighters sue for peace, the role of UNAMA II could increase. While it is unlikely that a peacekeeping force would be accepted by senior Taliban leaders at the negotiating table in the near future, as they become increasingly war-weary in their fight with U.S.-led forces, separate, UN-led negotiations and forces will likely become more appealing to them. As the peace process gained strength, warfighting and counterinsurgency efforts could be expected to decrease while the peacekeeping mission increased in size and strength. This, indeed, could be part of the exit strategy for coalition forces after a decade or more of fighting. Thus the missions are not to be seen as mutually exclusive.

In fact, what is proposed here is that any UNAMA II mandate would be complementary to ISAF, for though the two could never be identical, as counterinsurgency and peacekeeping employ different strategies, the two are inherently related. Counterinsurgency has the principal goal of defeating an insurgency, and uses the building up of effective government as a means to that end. In peace operations, by contrast, both objectives exist but the order of priorities is reversed. The purpose is to build a representative government that serves the population through an inclusive peace process. One of the means to this end (and one of its consequences also) is to end the insurgency. In peacekeeping, in short, the strategy is less offensive, the method is less aggressive, and the approach is more inclusive.

Most civil wars of the past century have ended in some form of negotiated settlement. The United Nations has gained tremendous experience helping settle internal conflicts through negotiation and peacekeeping. Its track record after the end of the Cold War of successful missions to help end civil wars is impressive, including as it does conflicts in El Salvador, Nicaragua, Guatemala, Namibia, Mozambique, Angola, Sierra Leone, Liberia, Cote D'Ivoire, D.R. Congo, Nepal, and East Timor. It does have some blemished and even clearly failed missions on its record (notably Somalia and Rwanda), but the United Nations has learned from these difficult experiences. The United Nations has greatly increased its capacity in the twenty-first century. This is one more reason to give the United Nations and peace a chance in Afghanistan.

THE NATO CLUB AND AFGHANISTAN: NORTHERN, RICH, AND WHITE NATIONS DEFEND THE IMPERIAL PALACE[1]

ERIKA SIMPSON

NATO and the Imperial Palace

Since its inception in 1949, the North Atlantic Treaty Organization (NATO) has grown from an American-led alliance of twelve countries, to sixteen, to nineteen allies, and most recently to twenty-eight Western and formerly Eastern European states. The entire process of NATO expansion can be likened to enlarging a club to take in more and more purportedly liberal-democratic nations that see themselves as allied with the club's leader. While the NATO club ostensibly operates according to consensus decision-making, in practice important decisions are always made by the alliance leader, in a way which has more in common with autocracy than democracy. For instance, during the first round of expansion after the end of the Cold War, the United States unilaterally decided to expand the alliance from sixteen to nineteen nations, including within it the Czech Republic, Hungary, and Poland. Then the U.S. delineated the territorial guidelines of the second round of expansion that accepted Baltic nations of Estonia, Latvia, and Lithuania, along with Slovenia, Slovakia, Bulgaria and Romania, but not Albania, Ukraine or Belarus. Albania joined as late as 2009, along with Croatia. While members of the expanding NATO alliance tend to view the NATO club benignly, in Russia, every political leader and political party has consistently opposed NATO expansion as a threat to peace.[2] Yet, despite Russian objections, NATO and its near allies see it functioning as a kind of peacekeeping alliance.

---

[1] The author would like to thank Dr. Darren Marks and Dr. Walter Dorn for their commentary.
[2] Erika Simpson, "New Threats to the Alliance's Security and Strategies to Reform NATO," *The Transatlantic Quarterly* (Winter/Spring 2005): 47-51.

In many parts of the world such as Afghanistan, Iraq, Kosovo, North Korea, and Serbia, however, American forces in particular are seen as foreign invaders, and NATO forces are not readily distinguished from American forces. For defenders of NATO's wars in Kosovo and Afghanistan, furthermore, there seems to have been a tendency to dismiss reports of "collateral damage" in these conflicts as inconsequential, even though it includes the aerial bombing of villagers, the slaughter of uneducated peasant farmers, the house-to-house brutalization of women, and even the illegal imprisonment and torture of combatants, including in some cases child soldiers. But while those inside the NATO fold may regard such excesses as the norm, outside the fold, NATO actions have proven to be highly objectionable. Undeniably, the human tendency is to find our own reasons for undertaking war and to interpret such war as "just" in those terms, seeing our own cause as rightful. The American satirist Mark Twain wrote of this tendency in the "The War Prayer" over a century ago:

> O Lord our Father, our young patriots, idols of our hearts, go forth to battle—be Thou near them! With them—in spirit—we also go forth from the sweet peace of our beloved firesides to smite the foe. O Lord our God, help us to tear their soldiers to bloody shreds with our shells; help us to cover their smiling fields with the pale forms of their patriot dead; help us to drown the thunder of the guns with the shrieks of their wounded, writhing in pain; help us to lay waste their humble homes with a hurricane of fire; help us to wring the hearts of their unoffending widows with unavailing grief; help us to turn them out roofless with little children to wander unfriended the wastes of their desolated land in rags and hunger and thirst....[3]

In a similar attempt to frame offensive actions in our own time as justified in the sight of the Almighty, former U.S. Defence Secretary Donald Rumsfeld is said to have regularly illustrated his top-secret intelligence briefings for President George W. Bush with prayers from the Bible. For example, a picture of a F-18 fighter jet taking off from an aircraft carrier was accompanied by a prayer, "If I rise on the wings of the dawn, if I settle on the far side of the sea, even there your hand will guide me, your right hand will hold me fast, O LORD—Psalm 139:9-10."[4]

---

[3] "The War Prayer" is available online at http://www.midwinter.com/lurk/making/warprayer.html and was found after Twain's death among his papers. It was first published in Albert Bigelow Paine's anthology, Mark Twain, *Europe and Elsewhere* (New York: Harper & Brothers, 1923).

[4] "Donald Rumsfeld's holy war: How President Bush's Iraq briefings came with quotes from the Bible," *Daily Mail*, 20 May, 2009, http://www.dailymail.co.uk/news/worldnews/article-1184546.

Yet, as the satirist Twain saw, it is surely necessary to ask whether our time-bound and culturally-specific conceptions of justice and of the rightness of our cause (including those so confidently expressed in our prayers to God) can prevent us from seeing things more deeply and honestly. Postmodernism, for instance, might teach us that there are no universal truths or Platonic Ideals; our understanding is, rather, constructed, relative, and contextual—which means that perhaps we ought not to claim too much for the justice of what we may at times say and do. Even in classical sapiential thought, there have been legions of great thinkers over the centuries who have realized that "truth…is stronger than all things."[5] St. Thomas Aquinas' monumental treatise, *Summa Theologiae*, was composed over the years 1267-73 and still helps to form the bedrock of the Just War tradition. Yet as Sophy Burnham points out in *The Ecstatic Journey,* near the end of his life, Thomas experienced a moment of "infused contemplation," after which he said that everything he had written, thought, argued, and defined during his brilliant theological life "was no better than straw or chaff."[6] In keeping with such claims, if we approach with due scepticism all the rhetoric about NATO needing to be in Afghanistan as part of "the war on terrorism," and as part of a "just war" to defend Afghan civilians, or even as part of a justifiable strategy to root out al-Qaeda in Wajikistan, Afghanistan, and Pakistan, then we need to ask why there are over a hundred thousand U.S.-led NATO forces in Afghanistan. Could it be that there is some sense in which NATO is merely part of the structure of a kind of Imperial Palace in which the privileged reside, and thus that it is bent on protecting the existing privileges of those people—northern, rich, and predominantly white people? If that were indeed the case, then responsible NATO members would need to inquire more closely as to who the "enemy" is, exactly, and precisely why the conflict has occurred.

In the present re-examination of our *Weltanschauung*, the "Imperial Palace," as I have called it, is not of course a building, nor is it only or altogether a geo-political territory, as might be expected from the reference made hitherto to NATO, but it is also a state of mind and condition of life. The Imperial Palace can perhaps be best understood as that privileged condition that is desired by those who live in the rest of the world, or the "Global Village," as I shall call it. The Imperial Palace, as such, houses about one-third of the world's population, which lives on what is, by global standards, an extraordinarily rich income. Conversely, the Global

---

[5] 1 Esdras 4:38, NRSV. In a similar vein, Joseph Campbell often quoted the Vedas, "Truth is one, the sages speak of it by many names," cited in Phil Cousineau, ed., *The Hero's Journey* (San Francisco: Harper, 1990), xi.
[6] Sophy Burnham, *The Ecstatic Journey* (New York: Ballantine Books, 1997), 4.

Village, which lives outside the Palace wall, contains two-thirds of the world's population, is often shockingly poor, without adequate education, and commonly suffers from ill health and violence. In the Global Village, in fact, most people suffer in some way from hunger and malnutrition, and over half live in squalid housing or are homeless. One principal reason for this is that the Imperial Palace garners over two-thirds of the world's entire income, while the rest subsists on the other one-third. While many citizens of the Imperial Palace implicitly recognize that such injustice cannot go on forever, they are at the same time driven by fear to arm themselves, in part against the Global Village, and to spend more and more money on military defence because they cannot fathom how to live in peace with their neighbours. The leader of the Imperial Palace, unsurprisingly, is far and away the global leader in military spending: the United States of America. U.S. military spending accounted for an astonishing 41.5% of the world total in 2008, followed by China with 5.8%, and the NATO allies, France and the United Kingdom with 4.5% each.[7]

In addition to addressing some of the huge inequalities, the gaps in living standards, and the terrible injustices of the world that can lead people to become terrorists, those living in the Imperial Palace need to redefine their security at the individual, state and systemic levels. The word "security" itself is often taken to imply an absolute condition: something is either secure or insecure. But real security, this paper assumes, symbolizes something deeper which remains indefinable, and yet that is attainable at far lower levels of military spending and defence preparation. By questioning our traditional assumptions about how to achieve security from many different levels of analysis, in short, we can develop more creative strategies which actually enhance security.[8] This essay takes a systemic level approach and suggests that NATO cannot defend the Imperial Palace in its present campaign in Afghanistan, that the Alliance should instead withdraw, and that other forms of engagement are needed.

The Emperor Has No Clothes

It is a cliché (and yet a true one) to point out that old ideas about defending the Imperial Palace no longer apply. As Robert Kaplan has put it, employing the metaphor of "a stretch limousine in the potholed streets of New York City," the old ways of thinking about security no longer seem

---

[7] Stockholm International Peace Research Institute, "Recent Trends in Military Expenditure," http://www.sipri.org/research/armaments/milex/resultoutput/trends.

[8] Erika Simpson, 'Redefining Security,' in Alex Morrison, ed., *The McNaughton Papers* vol. 1 (Toronto: Canadian Institute for Strategic Studies, 1991), 57-75.

convincing: "Inside the limo are the air-conditioned post-industrial regions of North America, Europe, the emerging Pacific Rim, and a few other isolated places, with their trade summitry and computer-information highways. Outside is the rest of mankind, going in a completely different direction."[9] So for instance, traditional concepts about how to defend NATO's geographical territory by means of the nuclear deterrent have been made redundant by the massive geo-political changes of recent years. In a world of sub-state terrorists, in short, relying entirely on classical geo-spatial concepts such as "counter-strikes" and "pre-emptive doctrine" does not work because these concepts no longer have credibility. There have long been debates associated with the applicability of deterrence doctrine but even long-time defenders of traditional realist concepts must doubt the possibility of pre-empting terrorist attacks using weapons of mass destruction.[10]

During the Cold War, it is true, strategists assumed that by threatening massive retaliation, nuclear weapons could credibly prevent an enemy from attacking. Then the attacks of 11 September, 2001 demonstrated that the "guarantees" provided by the threats of pre-emption or retaliation cannot in fact any longer succeed in preventing attack—it being impossible to retaliate against sub-state opponents like suicide bombers. At the same time, and adding to the problem of signalling credible deterrence in this new situation, all the traditional arguments against classical deterrence still hold true. There are many ways in which deterrence and/or pre-emption could fail, including misunderstanding, miscalculation, poor communication, irrational leadership, and accident. These types of problems are only exacerbated in a multi-polar, rather than a bi-polar world.[11]

Further questions abound about how to defend the Imperial Palace in our changed situation, because the former paradigmatic differences among realists and liberals, hawks and doves, and neo-realists and liberal institutionalists no longer hold true. During the Cold War, the belief systems of both defenders and critics of the deterrence strategy were fairly stable and

---

[9] Robert Kaplan, *The Coming Anarchy* (New York: Vintage Books, 2000), 24.
[10] Erika Simpson, "New Opportunities to Question US Reliance Upon Nuclear Weapons," *INESAP Information Bulletin*, 28 (April, 2008): 14-19, http://www.inesap.org/node/72.
[11] Erika Simpson, "The new U.S. doctrine of pre-emptive warfare and its implications for nuclear deterrence and disarmament," in David Krieger, ed., *The Challenge of Abolishing Nuclear Weapons* (Piscataway, NJ.: Transaction Publishers, 2009), 141-154.

coherent, even if they were opposed to each other.[12] But now they are undergoing such rapid revision and change that it has become difficult to know whom to label as a hawk or dove. When classical realists such as Zbigniew Brezinski argue for intervention in Kosovo on humanitarian grounds, and when hawks like Henry Kissinger sign op-eds in favour of nuclear abolition, or when doves like former Canadian Foreign Minister Lloyd Axworthy favour NATO's bombing of Serbia, traditional belief systems have clearly been undermined. Adding to the perplexity are the contrasting arguments of "liberal-internationalists" like President Obama, who long seemed undecided about whether greater or lesser troop contributions are needed for fighting the war in Afghanistan.[13] In short, in the new world in which we live, many of our inherited, and most basic assumptions about how to defend the Imperial Palace no longer work.

The only adages that may still hold true for realists and idealists everywhere are "the security dilemma" and "common security." The first English School concept dictates that whatever offensive measures one side takes to increase its security necessarily decreases its would-be opponent's security, resulting in endless arms races and more "(in)security dilemmas" on all sides.[14] Accordingly, one way to emerge out of the security dilemma or structural "prisoner's dilemma" unscathed is to undertake only defensive measures, which are difficult to execute because the enemy tends to perceive defensive measures as offensive due to miscommunication and

---

[12] Erika Simpson, *NATO and the Bomb* (Kingston & Montreal: McGill-Queen's University Press, 2001).

[13] It is difficult to define liberal-internationalist principles as they are nowhere written down but for some analysis of the basic precepts, see Erika Simpson, "The Principles of Liberal Internationalism according to Lester Pearson," *Journal of Canadian Studies* 34, no. 1 (Spring 1999): 64-77. Primary evidence of President Obama's liberal-internationalist beliefs can be found in many of his foreign policy speeches and election speeches but perhaps the most iconic and telling was his speech to the UN General Assembly, September 23, 2009, http://www.reuters.com/article/topNews/idUSTRE58M3MV20090923. On President Obama's indecision, see for example, "Obama Rules Out Large Reduction in Afghan Force," *New York Times*, 7 October, 2009.

[14] The concepts of the security dilemma and of common security have deep intellectual roots. See, for example, Ken Booth on the non-traditional agenda of security in Booth, *Theory of World Security* (Cambridge: Cambridge University Press, 2007) and Peter Stirk on Herz's concept of the security dilemma in Stirk, "John H. Herz: realism and the fragility of the international order', *Review of International Studies* 31 (2005): 285–306. Notably Secretary of State Hilary Clinton recently reviewed deliberative efforts by the Obama administration to enhance our "common security" in her remarks at the CTBT Article XIV Conference in New York, September 24, 2009, http://www.armscontrol.org/ClintonCTBTStatement.

misunderstanding.[15] More tantalizingly, another effective way to change outcomes that has been historically-proven, though perhaps not as yet really understood within the Imperial Palace, is to change perceptions so that they more adequately reflect the underlying need for "common security." Arguably Mikhail Gorbachev understood the need for common security thinking, initiating changes which led to nothing less than the end of the Cold War. Were we sufficiently attentive to this precedent in the present situation, it might suggest to us that the citizens of the Imperial Palace and of the Global Village could also change their thinking and band together for the sake of the common security of all on planet earth.

Is this merely idealistic? Is yet another cliché in view? Or does perhaps a deeper truth beckon?

(In)Security Dilemmas and Imperial Overstretch

One of the major problems faced today is that the (in)security dilemmas experienced by the citizens of the Imperial Palace and the Global Village have been exacerbated by an imperial overstretch. Afghanistan is actually called "out-of-area" by NATO, since the allies committed six decades ago to defend each other's physical territory. What was never agreed is that they should defend countries outside of NATO's area. Indeed, not only Afghanistan, but also Bosnia and Kosovo, have all been "out-of-area" wars in which NATO was not formally obliged under Article V of its 1949 Charter to intervene. Article V declares in Three Musketeers fashion that "an attack against one of us is an attack against us all." But in fact, Article V has only been invoked once, in the wake of 11 September, 2001 when NATO allies pledged to come to the defence of the United States after the World Trade Center and Pentagon bombings. Yet the war that it is currently fighting in Afghanistan can scarcely be seen any longer as a defence of the United States. The problem here, I wish to suggest, is one of imperial overstretch—and of an overstretch that began well before 9/11, as NATO had already overreached its territorial limits by attacking Serbian President Slobodan Milosovic over ethnic cleansing in Kosovo.[16] It was this policy that it has renewed once more by choosing to fight al-Qaeda and the Taliban in Afghanistan.

---

[15] For more analysis of such strategies, see Erika Simpson, "Games, Strategies, and Human Security," in M.V. Naidu, ed., *Perspectives on Human Security* (Brandon, Manitoba: Canadian Peace Research and Education Association, 2001), 139-49.

[16] For a critique of NATO's out-of-area war on Serbia, see Erika Simpson, "New Threats to the Alliance's Security and Strategies to Reform NATO."

Until recently, NATO defenders have argued that NATO cannot lose in Afghanistan, not merely because of the security needs of Afghanistan, but because losing in Afghanistan would inevitably undermine NATO's credibility. The assumption was that a loss in Afghanistan—avoidance of which has become one of NATO's chief priorities from an organizational and resource standpoint—would spell the end of NATO's credibility on the world stage as the true defender of international security. Thus the prospect of defeat must not be countenanced because it would effectively mean the end of NATO itself.[17] Only in the last two years have NATO leaders and military commanders publicly entertained the idea that a gradual pullout from Afghanistan might be inevitable. While previously the notion of somehow forsaking Afghanistan induced warnings about whole-scale abandonment and fear of NATO's concomitant loss of credibility, steady rises in the casualty rate, slow progress in the war, and the Obama administration's changed stance in particular have fuelled more public hesitancy among elite decision-makers.[18]

Until the 2008 American election, most of the elite within the Imperial Palace accepted old-fashioned realist concepts such as balance of power politics, containment and deterrence. NATO was seen in this context as an instrument of collective defence, and its members were united to defend against a threat from outside the pact. In the case of Afghanistan, the threat came from without, and was such that "peace enforcement" (i.e., warfighting) seemed to make sense. The option of first- and second-generation peacekeeping and peacemaking encountered internal resistance within the Alliance, the idea that "preparing for peace can prevent war" being comprehensively trumped by the idea that "preparing for war can ensure peace." It mattered neither that Afghanistan was not part of NATO's *Partnership for Peace* (formerly the North Atlantic Cooperation Council), nor that Afghanistan could scarcely be considered for possible NATO membership.

---

[17] Confidential and off-record interviews by the author of high-level NATO policymakers at NATO headquarters in Brussels in January of 2007 and various policymakers, Members of Parliament, and Cabinet Ministers, including Canada's Minister of Defence, conducted in Ottawa and Nova Scotia in February of 2006, February of 2007 and July of 2008.

[18] Space constraints prevent a full analysis of the growing divides within elite American opinion, but for a cogent overview of the different emerging perspectives see the analysis by Richard N. Haass, President of the Council on Foreign Relations, "In the Afghan War, Aim for the Middle," *Washington Post,* 11 October, 2009.

Notably, some long-time and prominent NATO defenders have advocated the idea that the alliance should consider expanding to include wealthy industrialized and industrializing countries outside North America and Europe, such as Japan, Australia, and possibly even Mexico. The underlying assumption seems to be that a "Global NATO" might be established, so as to include wealthy countries that have a history of close defence cooperation with the United States.[19] Thus the fact of Mexico's non-membership in the North American defence perimeter is becoming an increasingly relevant question.[20]

What emerges from such observations is perhaps that the boundaries of NATO's territory are largely in our minds, being associated with various preconceptions about the "us" versus "them" question. Such preconceptions, however, can rapidly change. The recent twentieth anniversary of the fall of the Berlin Wall is a reminder that it took only a few years, and not decades or generations, for NATO to welcome with open arms former Warsaw Pact members into its membership. Apparently the advantages for the NATO allies of drastically expanding its regional collective defence organization—possibly even at the expense of efforts to reform and extend the universal collective security afforded by the UN—outweighed the disadvantages of extending Article V protection to former Warsaw Pact countries. On 1 May, 2004, NATO enlarged to include most of the European Union, including Bulgaria, Romania, Slovenia, Slovakia, Estonia, Latvia, and Lithuania.

These newer NATO allies had already invested heavily to upgrade their aged defence systems so as to abide by official (and unofficial) guidelines in order to be invited into the NATO club. Thus massive military expenditure was involved in the shift. As one RAND Corporation study indicated early on, combined spending by the newer and would-be allies was expected to rise to $130 billion over ten years. How could former Warsaw Pact countries afford to spend these billions on defence, when their own economies were lagging? As the RAND study accurately predicted, those countries that lacked funds were provided with massive loans and grants by the "friendly" NATO governments. Thus it was that,

---

[19] General (ret.) Klaus Naumann, General (ret.) John Shalikashvili, Field Marshal The Lord Tinge, Admiral (ret.) Jacques Lanxade and General (ret.) Henk van den Breemen, *Towards a Grand Strategy for an Uncertain World* (Noaber Foundation: 2007), http://www.csis.org/files/media/csis/events/080110_grand_strategy.pdf.

[20] For more on such "impossible thoughts," see David Haglund, "Pensando lo Imposible: Mexico and the Issue of NATO Membership," paper presented to the International Studies Association, New York City, February 15, 2009.

within less than a decade, NATO expanded at great expense to include most of the former Warsaw Pact countries.[21]

It is impossible either to prove or disprove the claim that American leaders were drawn to the idea of NATO expansion because of the lure of hefty defence procurement contracts and increased influence. But clearly, there were economic as well as political advantages in the strategy taken. Several resulting contradictions in NATO policy have proved difficult to reconcile without referring to the lure of defence contracts to be gained amid this new expansion of the American empire. For example, while NATO pursued greater cooperation with new Eastern European allies, NATO expansion risked a major new security dilemma, in increasing tensions with Russia (which the end of the Cold War had seemingly resolved in the case of the old Soviet Union). There were distinct risks run that the expansion—both in its first and second rounds—could lead Russia to move its conventional and nuclear arsenal into new defensive positions along a newly-defined border, effectively a new Central Front. Expanding NATO, in short, risked inciting old hatreds, new insecurities and even more paranoid leaderships.[22] Nevertheless, the U.S. under both Presidents Bill Clinton and George Bush insisted on the policy of the rapid enlargement of NATO.

Arguably, however, it was NATO expansion that in turn incited Russia to extend its own sphere of influence into the "near abroad" of Kalingrad, Belarus, Georgia and Ukraine. The rearmament of Hungary and threat to place radar installations in the Czech Republic and Poland contributed to new tensions in Central Europe. NATO enlargement seemed merely to create a new dividing line in Europe similar to the old one that wound its way through Germany and East Berlin. Certainly it is true that the decisions taken to enlarge the American sphere of influence have increased the new Eastern European allies' sense of security. But it has not happened without price. It has led to the distressing situation in which a new generation of young defence ministers in NATO nations such as Poland are becoming some of the strongest defenders of classical nuclear deterrence doctrine internationally, and in particular of the necessity for the United States to extend its nuclear deterrence, as a security guarantee over against

---

[21] Erika Simpson, "NATO expansion," *International Journal* 54, no. 2 (Spring 1999): 324-339.
[22] Erika Simpson, "The greater threat from Russia," *Metro Europe*, 10 August, 1999.

Russia.[23] The Imperial Palace has thus became mired yet again in a security dilemma, one already made acute on the international scene after 9/11 and the decision to attack al-Qaeda and the Taliban, and amid the lingering conflicts in Afghanistan, Pakistan, and Wajikistan, not to mention Iraq.

The citizens of the Imperial Palace may like to delude themselves that NATO expansion will not have grave implications for future conflict prevention, management, and resolution. They may like to assume that NATO's nuclear weapons are essential, according to NATO's strategic concept, and that it is only the possession of nuclear weapons by "rogue states" such as Iran and North Korea that is problematic. They may, however, also therefore continue to think in ways that ensure entrapment in arms spirals and never-ending (in)security dilemmas. But as NATO members, should we not rather seek to strip away the old Cold Warrior's style of thinking, realizing the opportunity presented for forging new global partnerships, and find ways to become more constructively engaged?

Constructive Engagement and Withdrawal from Afghanistan

Constructive engagement—as President Obama has evoked for us so well in speeches that exude liberal internationalist values—necessarily means the pursuit of more multilateralist measures.[24] To follow this course, however, the United States and its NATO allies need to learn to look beyond themselves, and in particular to work more closely with the UN, with partner organizations such as the Middle Powers Initiative, and with new coalitions of states, such as the New Agenda Coalition.[25] One long-overdue debate that needs to take place with a view to engineering more useful forms of constructive engagement would be to consider whether or not the U.S. and NATO's defence spending might be a greater threat to world security than the menace of small-scale tyrants. Unquestionably, despicable behaviour by Taliban tribal leaders, by dictators of the world such as Saddam Hussein, or by anti-imperialists such as Kim Jong-Il of North Korea, deserve to be condemned and roundly opposed in rele-

---

[23] Off-record comments to the author by a high-level U.S. State Department official, in light of papers on tailored deterrence that were presented to the International Studies Association, New York City, February 16, 2009.

[24] For example, on the need for more multilateralist strategies, see his aforementioned speech to the UN General Assembly, September 23, 2009, http://www.reuters.com/article/topNews/idUSTRE58M3MV20090923.

[25] For more information on new coalitions, like the Middle Powers Initiative, see the website of the Global Security Institute at http://www.gsinstitutei@org.

vant international fora. But perhaps the greater threat to global security is the astounding fact that the 2009 U.S. budget allocated $542 billion to the Pentagon and $196 billion to Iraq for a total of $738 billion, or more than *half* the entire U.S. discretionary budget.[26] Ought we to be content with the absurd notion that nearly a trillion dollars on an annual basis be devoted to protecting the Imperial Palace—especially as the strategy is in many ways so ineffective? Where will astoundingly-high U.S. military spending, dangerously mounting debt, and constrained choices lead?

The cost of such policy is more than financial. If the United States as the alliance's leader involves its NATO allies in more and more out-of-area operations—similar to Kosovo, Afghanistan, and Iraq—then the rest of the world may come to perceive NATO troops merely as defenders of the American empire, and so very negatively. Arguably, NATO members really ought to increase their overseas commitments to peacekeeping and peacemaking—but NATO itself ought not to in the business of peace enforcement. There needs, in short, to be a return to the UN as the chief guarantor of international security.

The most recent NATO Summit Declaration, issued by the Heads of State in April 2009, makes many worthy declarations:

> Our security is closely tied to Afghanistan's security and stability. As such, our UN-mandated International Security Assistance Force mission (ISAF) in Afghanistan, comprising 42 nations, is our key priority. We are working with the Government and people of Afghanistan, and with the international community under the leadership of the United Nations Assistance Mission in Afghanistan. Together, in a comprehensive approach combining military and civilian resources, we are helping the Government of Afghanistan build a secure, stable and democratic country, respectful of human rights. We stress the importance of the protection of women's rights. The international community aims to ensure that Al-Qaeda and other violent extremists cannot use Afghanistan. Today we have issued a Summit Declaration in which we reiterate our strategic vision and set out actions that demonstrate our resolve to support Afghanistan's long-term security and stability.[27]

These are all noble sentiments on behalf of the UN and NATO. All NATO members would no doubt prefer that Afghanistan and Pakistan became safe for all citizens, not safe havens from which to launch terrorist

---

[26] For the budget figures, see http://www.notmypriorities.org, which also notes that the budget figures are unsustainable because they do not include funds for the bailout or the economic stimulus package.

[27] NATO Strasbourg/Kehl Summit Declaration, April 2008, http://www.nato.int/cps/en/natolive/news_52837.htm.

attacks. Nobody would dispute that Afghan ownership of their own institutions, such as their military and police forces, remain crucial for sustained progress. Strong constructive engagement by countries in the region will also be critical and, to this end, any pledges to reinforce NATO's cooperation with all Afghanistan's neighbours, especially Pakistan, should always be welcome.

On the other hand, for NATO's own sake, and for the sake of its own long-term survival and credibility, any more strong pledges by NATO to fight against the Taliban and al-Qaeda in Afghanistan should be questioned. The reason, quite simply, is that NATO's war as presently waged in Afghanistan is destined to fail. Why will NATO fail? The reason often given is that the continuing low-level war against Taliban and al-Qaeda forces in Afghanistan and Pakistan is being waged by too few forces—though, in the near future, about 150,000 U.S. troops and coalition allies will be present on Afghan soil. But were even more troops than these committed, the project would still fail, because sheer military firepower and personnel will never be the key to victory in the Afghanistan context. Nor does it fundamentally matter whether strong troop contributors, such as Canada and the Netherlands, eventually reduce their troop contributions in 2010-2011 in favour of other NATO allies taking up the burden. Indeed, the issue of whether Afghan troops can be trained to take over police and military functions is another red herring that continues to preoccupy us.[28] In the final analysis, I wish to suggest, NATO will fail because its present strategy can provide no solution to the problem of opium production in Afghanistan—without tackling which, all our efforts are futile.

The deeper structural problems surrounding the opium trade in Afghanistan get short shrift in the media and in scholarly treatments because for decades, our assessment of the threats to international security have been overly influenced by traditional American military threat analyses. We thus continue to assume that committing more troops, training more military and police, and even building more schools in the non-Taliban influenced areas of Afghanistan are viable solutions to its intractable problems. But these solutions are no solutions, or are at best very partial and

---

[28] This preoccupation is evident in my own work. For examples, see Erika Simpson, "Afghanistan panel recommends re-orienting Canada's mission but staying the course," *Embassy Magazine: Canada's Foreign Policy Weekly*, January 23, 2008; and Cris de Clercy and Erika Simpson, "Is Afghanistan panel just a crass bid to deflect critics?" *London Free Press*, October 17, 2007. I might also cite an excellent thesis written under my supervision by an officer in the Canadian Forces, Keith Cameron, "Risk, Cost and Control in NATO Burdensharing: Apportioning Atlas' Load'," MA thesis, University of Western Ontario, 2008.

inadequate ones. Instead, we need to unite with like-minded nations, and in conjunction with UN monitoring agencies and other international bodies, to make a more timely and accurate threat assessment that takes seriously the menace of the international drugs trade, and of the ways in which it is destroying the prospect of peace in Afghanistan. To do this, however, requires more than a campaign in a far country. In particular, the great need is to reduce the drugs trade with and within the Imperial Palace. For as things stand, we are destined to fail in Afghanistan because of the continuing global demand for opium.

One of the things that needs to be recognized in this context is that current programs aiming at opium poppy eradication in Afghanistan never work well because other types of crops need fertile land, whereas opium crops can survive on infertile land that does not need irrigation. An opium poppy crop has many advantages for peasant farmers struggling to survive, especially because it is not perishable. The opium poppy can grow almost anywhere. The product is relatively easy to transport and smuggle, and millions of willing customers exist for it in the Imperial Palace. Efforts to eradicate opium production will fail in Afghanistan so long as licit crops cannot be sold for as much money as illicit poppy seeds, and so long as the choice of impoverished farmers must be to grow the more lucrative crop merely to survive.[29] NATO simply does not have the resources to stamp out the annual Afghan opium industry—even if it is one that largely finances the Taliban.[30] Although Afghanistan's opium cultivation fell in 2009 by 22% from 2008 levels, a second annual decline, Afghanistan still

---

[29] I am indebted to a former student for writing a paper that illuminated the depth and breadth of the opium trade problem in Afghanistan, Eli Lipetz, "Opium and Afghanistan: New Solutions to an Old Problem," presented at the International Pugwash Conference in Cairo, Egypt in 2006, and available on the Pugwash Canada website at http://www.pugwashgroup.ca/events/documents/2006/2006.11-Lipetz_essay.pdf. For further studies developing the same line of argument, see: Frank Kenefick & Larry Morgan, *Report submitted U.S. Agency for International Development in Afghanistan: People and Poppies, the Good Evil* (Kabul, Afghanistan: 2004); David Mansfield, "The Role of Opium as a Source of Informal Credit in Rural Afghanistan," World Bank, http://siteresources.worldbank.org/ INTAFGH ANISTAN/Resources/AFRFW_4_Role_of_Opium_as_Source_of_Credit.htm; and Rachel Morarjee, "Taliban Goes for Cash Over Ideology," *The Financial Times,* 26 July, 2006. It is interesting to note that the Taliban pays its soldiers well, which may explain its successes in recruiting. Taliban fighters receive twice as much pay as Afghan soldiers, and four times as much as Afghan police. See Anna Badkhan, "Afghan government failure reopens door to the Taliban," *The San-Francisco Chronicle,* 17 September, 2006.

[30] "Salvaging Afghanistan," *New York Times* editorial, February 20, 2009, A30.

grows far more opium than the current global demand, which is steady at about 5,000 tons a year. Some of that excess crop is being hoarded, the UN Office on Drugs and Crime reports, so that "stockpiles of illicit opium now probably exceed 10,000 tons—enough to satisfy two years of world [heroin] addiction."[31]

The bitter truth of the matter is that opium will continue to be produced in Afghanistan so long as the citizens of the Imperial Palace desire heroin—or until a cheap, synthetic, and legal alternative to heroin is made available to them. It may be a difficult thing psychologically for leaders of the Imperial Palace to take responsibility for their own nations' complicity in the tragedy of Afghanistan due to the failure of their domestic anti-drugs strategies. It is always easier to blame the "other." Thus we have seen various extraneous arguments about why NATO could fail in Afghanistan, rather than a sustained focus on the deeper causes for that likely failure, stemming from the worldwide drugs trade (and, indeed, the illegal trafficking in small arms and light weapons that goes with it).

The argument that NATO could fail in Afghanistan because the Soviet Union failed in Afghanistan between 1979-89 is also heard, the point being that unless the U.S. and its recalcitrant NATO allies contribute far more resources than did the Soviets, they too will fail.[32] But this too is a distraction, not least because this argument is based on a poor historical analogy. The Soviet Union deployed some 104,000 troops, but suffered far higher casualties in a rather different war; it withdrew in 1989 after almost 20,000 of its soldiers had been killed and 50,000 had been wounded. Moreover, such a high number of casualties would be unacceptable within NATO, even among its most committed allies such as Canada (which has already suffered a casualty rate widely considered to be unsustainable).[33] The argument in favour of increasing the number of forces is also irrelevant to combating the fundamental problem besetting NATO's involvement in Afghanistan, namely the drugs trade.

It is also a common distraction to argue that NATO will fail because of al-Qaeda and the Taliban's effective use of guerrilla tactics. It is to be expected that the Taliban will continue to attack rural and urban populations

---

[31] Matthew Rosenberg, "UN Reports a Decline in Afghanistan's Opium Trade." *Wall Street Journal,* 2 September, 2009, A9.

[32] For a recent example of this type of argument, see Sebastian L. v. Gorka, "How to Win in Afghanistan." 24 September, 2009, available on the Hudson Institute website, http://www.hudsonny.org/2009/09/how-to-win-in-afghanistan.php.

[33] On the operation's unsustainability, see for example the wide array of critics in Lucia Kowaluk and Steve Staples, eds., *Afghanistan and Canada* (Toronto: Black Rose Books, 2009).

using suicide bombers, there will be more scorched earth campaigns, and various warring tribal factions also will continue to destroy Afghanistan's infrastructure. In reply, NATO defenders will likely continue to warn, as NATO has done in the past, that NATO must commit to providing more peace enforcement (i.e. engage in more warfighting) in order to provide scope for more peacebuilding (e.g. road and school construction).[34] Both sides blame each other for contradictory behaviour and for adopting nefarious tactics, while the war escalates in terms of violence and the numbers of killed each month.

Meanwhile, al-Qaeda cells will continue to justify their violent campaigns as a jihad against the United States and the Christian West. More widely within Islam, debate will continue concerning the claim of Salafists generally that it is the duty of Muslims to engage in violent jihad to protect their religion when an outside force encroaches on Islamic land. Competition among belief systems will continue to be further intensified by interpretations of American support for Israel as an aggression against Islamic faith, and this reading of the meaning of current history will be pitted against Israeli perceptions of an anti-Zionist conspiracy to eradicate Israel as a Jewish state. Belief systems, however, though important intervening variables that help explain the severity of outcomes, do not adequately account for the fundamental structural causes of conflict.

Among those who advocate violent jihad, there is the phenomenon whereby extremist recruiters from the military cells of al-Qaeda, the Hamas, the Islamic Resistance Movement, and so forth nurture young men (and women) for the "holy war." These recruiters circulate in schools and mosques, and have notably adopted the internet to serve their cause, dropping the idea of dying for God into the conversation, and then zoom in on those who take the idea seriously, much like recruiters for cults prey on other depressed or disenchanted university students. Then their training system focuses on all the verses in the Koran that refer to the glory of dying for God. Scriptures are used in this way, and underground sermons idealize the afterlife as a carefree garden with golden palaces, good food, and even-tempered women. Potential suicide bombers get the idea they are about to sit next to God; the whole process is described as the martyr's wedding and so presented as a joyous occasion. In addition, they are reassured that their families will be given money, scholarships, and other subsidies.

---

[34] On the implicit contradictions in NATO's stance, see Astri Suhrke, "A Contradictory Mission? NATO from Stabilization to Combat in Afghanistan," *International Peacekeeping* 15, no. 2 (April 2009): 214-236.

Attempting to ban such recruitment methods and to quell extremist indoctrination are partial solutions to these fundamental problems. Moderate Muslims themselves, above all, need to combat the idea that the Garden of God awaits the so-called "martyrs" that al-Qaeda and the like cultivate. Over the long run, we can only hope, more humane sources arising from the depths of the Islamic tradition itself, along with the forces of education and globalization, will help to combat the idea that this perversion of the idea of martyrdom is preferable to life—just as similar forces have moderated traditional Christian belief systems concerning ideas such as Heaven and Hell. Yet one of our problems is that studies show that suicide bombers are not necessarily unified by any ideology, belief system or underlying commonalities; they seem at times to appear out of nowhere, like randomly-caused cancers. Extremists who take up arms in the hope of martyrdom, or who take the short route to that goal by becoming suicide bombers, may be young or old, rich or poor, highly educated or unschooled, male or female, and either victims of violence or very ordinary people raised in normal homes, and we do not yet know why they choose to become suicide bombers.[35] Until we understand the common causes of their behaviour, it may be premature to counsel combating the Taliban and al-Qaeda as if they were cult victims or the last vestiges of antiquated ways of religious thinking in a secular world. And among the best ways of finding out the underlying reasons for their behaviour is something that our leaders, the media and the establishment of the West generally are, for the most part, unprepared to countenance: the kind of face-to-face dialogue that alone would make it possible to hear what they have to say.

In this context, a relatively unknown factor may also be of importance. When the Taliban temporarily held power in Afghanistan, it actually opposed drug use, and established a better record than has NATO in terms of opium poppy eradication. The Taliban's drug eradication program, implemented in 2000-2001, led to a 94% decline in opium cultivation. In 2001, according to UN figures, opium production fell to 185 tons.[36] It might be that a NATO withdrawal from Afghanistan would actually slow the production of opium in Taliban-run pockets of the country. At present, admittedly, the Taliban is using hundreds of millions of dollars of profits from the drug trade to fight against foreign invaders, but previously it forbade poppy production and condemned drug use. One possible advantage of negotiation with the Taliban in Afghanistan, therefore, and perhaps of an

---

[35] Stuart Sim, *Fundamentalist World* (London : Icon Books, 2004), 26-27, 222.
[36] Michel Chossudovsky, "Who benefits from the Afghan Opium Trade?" http://www.globalresearch.ca/index.php?context=va&aid=3294.

eventual power-sharing agreement, might be a significant reduction in the amount of opium that is produced by Afghan farmers.[37]

It is likely also that the departure of perceived foreign invaders might lead to a significant decline of support for the Taliban in many areas. The rise of support for the Taliban can be traced back to 1979, when the Soviet Union invaded Afghanistan, marking a turning point for the development of radical Islam. A number of Islamic religious leaders called for a defensive jihad, aided by the Reagan administration in the United States no less, to combat the Soviet "infidels." For example, Osama bin Laden's right-hand man Aynan al-Zawahiri was an influential Egyptian writer and physician who persuaded many Muslims to fight in Afghanistan against the Soviets. It was during that war that al-Zawahiri met Osama bin Laden in Pakistan, and then that the two realized that their skills could complement each other's. In 1988, they consolidated their groups, creating what is today known as al-Qaeda. Today, however, al-Qaeda operatives and Taliban leaders rail not against the Soviets, but against the West—and Christianity—as represented by the U.S. and NATO, the latest foreign invaders in an area that has been fought over for centuries.

As we are now the foreign invaders, we need to find a way to leave Afghanistan, taking our weapons of warfare, and our cultural domination with us. There is new prospect that the Afghan people, in an inclusive movement involving at least the more moderate supporters of the Taliban (who seem increasingly reluctant to cooperate with al-Qaeda operatives), may be able to set up their own governing councils, organize an Afghan-oriented infrastructure, and train future generations for something other than civil war or violent jihad. It might turn out that an Afghan government that had a place within it for the Taliban would be better able to provide Afghans with social services, medical attention, and schools than we imagine. In large pockets of the region, government would no doubt be very traditional in terms of its values, and even oppressive by our standards, but values can change, given time. No doubt medieval attitudes toward women in Afghanistan, concerning schooling for girls, for instance, would be slow to change—but change is inevitable when people and cultures open up to the forces of education and globalization.[38]

---

[37] Rosenberg, "UN reports a Decline in Afghanistan's Opium Trade."

[38] On the other hand, there are powerful arguments that the Taliban would endlessly resist the forces of globalization. Human Rights Watch has recently reported on how the Taliban uses violence and the threat of violence to shut down schools at http://www.hrw.org, and there is no question that human rights were violated during the Taliban's period in power, including rights to freedom of expression, association, and assembly, the right to work, education, freedom of movement, and

Much of the change needed in Afghanistan in any case cannot be imposed by outside force, but can only be grown as something indigenous—sometimes painfully, no doubt, and in a process extending over generations. What is imperative is that a space in which this can happen be provided. What is clearly unacceptable is the status quo. The results of the 2009 elections in Afghanistan demonstrate that corruption still abounds at the highest levels. Meanwhile, drugs money continues to fund warlord and Taliban activity. In the vacuum generated by such destructive forces, there can be no legitimate power structures, including those provided by the corrupt and intransigent Karzai government. Responsible military withdrawal from Afghanistan is therefore needed, so that Afghanistan's own leaders, including those presently sympathetic to the Taliban, will have to face their real problems: the difficulties of state building, development, education and reform. Rather than fight NATO forces, they will need to devote their energy to strengthening their own police and military forces. Rather than blame the West for imposing corrupting educational practices, they will need to find ways to provide public education for themselves, having broad support among the people. Many more tasks, including reform of the political system, poppy eradication, and drugs and small arms interdiction will necessarily preoccupy them. They may well develop abhorrent policies in the short-term—such as we saw in the Karzai government's own draft legislation allowing rape within marriage—but domestic pressures and the response of the international community (including the international Islamic community) should stamp out such policies in the long-run.

Eventually, pre-pubescent girls in Afghanistan will not be married to old men, and girls will go to school, just as happens elsewhere in the Muslim world, even in countries with highly oppressive regimes. The truth is that the change needed in Afghanistan will likely take three generations or more to come about, which is as tragic as it is inescapable—and that it cannot happen as long as we stand in the way.[39] Thus, trusting and abet-

---

health care. Some disturbing examples of current Taliban attitudes vis-à-vis human rights are evident in letters posted around rural villages. For example, one letter read: "Respected Afghans: Leave the culture and traditions of the Christians and Jews. Do not send your girls to school." See, for example, A. Widney Brown and Farhat Bokhari, "Humanity Denied—Systematic Violations of Women's Rights in Afghanistan," *Report Prepared for Human Rights Watch,* Section V, and available at the Human Rights Watch website cited.

[39]For the argument that real change takes three generations to develop, see David Helde (with Daniele Archibugi), *Cosmopolitan Democracy* (Cambridge: Polity Press, 1995).

ting the forces of global change and of human progress are better options than supporting NATO's current strategy—which is merely creating enemies faster than we can kill them.

MUSLIM OPPOSITION TO THE WAR IN AFGHANISTAN: THE CASE(S) OF BANGLADESH AND TURKEY

RASHED CHOWDHURY[1]

Public Opinion and the Pain of Afghanistan

In 2008, an Ipsos Reid survey showed that 37% of Canadians wanted to see a withdrawal of Canadian troops from Afghanistan.[2] In comparison, as many as 72% of Turks were in favour of a NATO withdrawal from Afghanistan the same year, according to a Pew survey. A 2007 Pew poll (the last year for which data is available) shows that an even higher proportion of Bangladeshis, 89%, were in favour of NATO withdrawing its troops from Afghanistan.[3] Canada and Turkey are both NATO members, and both have been involved in NATO's Afghanistan mission since its inception. Yet Turkish public opinion on Afghanistan seems more akin to that of Bangladesh, with which Turkey shares not the ties of a military alliance, but rather the bonds of a common faith.

Can differences in religion explain the differences between the way a majority of Turks and Bangladeshis, on the one hand, see the war in Afghanistan, and the way the majority of Canadians see it, on the other? It certainly can, if one subscribes to the notion of a "clash of civilizations," as propounded by Bernard Lewis and popularised by Samuel Huntington. For Huntington, "a civilization is...the highest cultural grouping of people

---

[1] I would like to acknowledge funding provided to me by McGill University (2008-2009) and the *Fonds québécois de recherche sur la société et la culture* (2009-2010), which made this paper possible.
[2] Canwest News Service, "Support for withdrawal from Afghanistan declines, but divisions remain," *Ottawa Citizen*, 26 January 2008.
[3] Pew Research Center, "Support for War in Afghanistan: Should the U.S. and NATO keep troops in Afghanistan or remove them?" Pew Global Attitudes Project Key Indicators Database, http://pewglobal.org/database/?indicator=9&group=10&response=Remove%20their%20troops.

and the broadest level of cultural identity people have...."[4] Although ostensibly dealing with the interactions of seven different "civilizations," Huntington's theory largely focuses on perceived conflict between "Islam" and "the West.."[5] Thus, it would come as no surprise to him that religion may be a better predictor of public opinion on a particular issue than membership in a culturally diverse organisation such as NATO.

The convenience of a theory such as Huntington's is that, in many ways, it eliminates the need for analysis. As Huntington puts it, "The underlying problem for the West is not Islamic fundamentalism. It is Islam....The problem for Islam is not the CIA or the U.S. Department of Defense. It is the West...." In his view, "the basic ingredients that fuel conflict between Islam and the West" are the sense on the part of Muslims and Westerners that their culture is superior to the other.[6] Thus, Huntington presents us with a ready-made explanation for any past, present or future confrontation between Westerners and Muslims, seemingly obviating the need to look at causes or context.

Applying Huntington's theory to Turkish and Bangladeshi public opinion on the war in Afghanistan would give us the idea that the Turks and Bangladeshis, being majority-Muslim peoples, are bound to oppose any deployment of Western force anywhere in the world simply because it is Western. The actual actions of the United States and its allies, and the methods employed by them, would be rendered irrelevant. Similarly, in the Huntingtonian model, Muslims would support those fighting against the West, whatever their methods, simply because they are fighting against the West. As Hungtinton puts it, "Protests against anti-Western violence have been totally absent in Muslim countries.... In civilizational conflicts...kin stand by their kin."[7]

The reality is, however, that neither "the West" nor "Islam" is a static and monolithic entity. Neither Westerners nor Muslims are automatons endlessly replaying a set scenario. As Richard Bonney puts it, "Instead of fixed traditions...cultures need to be seen as dynamic rather than static; as relative, not absolute; as complex and varying from person to person, from group to group, and over time; cultural identities need to be seen as multi-layered."[8] Thus, what I aim to demonstrate here is that Muslim public

---

[4] Samuel P. Huntington, *The Clash of Civilizations and the Remaking of World Order* (New York: Touchstone, 1996), 43.
[5] Ibid., 209-218.
[6] Ibid., 217-218.
[7] Ibid., 217.
[8] Richard Bonney, *False Prophets: The 'Clash of Civilizations' and the Global War on Terror* (Oxford: Peter Lang, 2008), 230.

opinion is not the static product of timeless "culture," but, rather, a dynamic response to unfolding events. It is not dogmatically opposed to "the West," with which it shares many traits and concerns.

To some extent, Turks and Bangladeshis do perceive events in Afghanistan through the prism of Islamic solidarity. However, they do not see themselves as being at war with the West as a result of events in faraway Afghanistan. They simply want the United States and its allies to modify its policies toward Afghanistan to reflect shared values, such as freedom, democracy, and the sanctity of human life. Ironically, NATO claims to be fighting in Afghanistan precisely to uphold these same values. Thus, what we have is not a clash of civilisations, but rather a disagreement (albeit on a large scale) over how best to achieve goals that most Westerners and Muslims hold in common. As will be shown, both Turks and Bangladeshis perceive the current NATO approach as being overly focused on warfighting, with insufficient attention paid to the human cost involved.

There are several reasons why I selected Turkey and Bangladesh in particular for this paper. First and foremost, they are both Muslim-majority countries with significant populations. In fact, Bangladesh has the fourth-largest number of Muslims in the world, while Turkey has the fifth-largest.[9] Together, their Muslim population accounts for over 10% of the world's Muslims. Turkey and Bangladesh are both imperfectly democratic countries, with freely elected governments presiding over political systems that suffer from corruption and a history of military interference in politics.[10] The politics of the two countries are quasi-secular, although Islam plays an important mobilising role in both. Anomalously, religious institu-

---

[9] Bangladesh has 156 million inhabitants, 83% of whom are Muslims, giving us a figure of 129 million Muslims. Turkey, meanwhile, has a population of 77 million, of whom 99.8% are Muslim, which gives us approximately 77 million Muslims. See CIA, *The World Factbook*, 2009, https://www.cia.gov/library/publications/the-world-factbook/.

[10] On the Bangladeshi political system and its swings between civilian and military rule, see Willem van Schendel, *A History of Bangladesh* (Cambridge: Cambridge University Press, 2009), 200-201. On similar developments in Turkey, see Aylin Güney, "The Military, Politics and Post-Cold War Dilemmas in Turkey," in *Political Armies: The Military and Nation Building in the Age of Democracy*, ed. Kees Koonings and Dirk Krait (London: Zed Books, 2002), 164-166. According to the 2008 Corruption Perceptions Index, compiled by Transparency International, Turkey has the 58th-best corruption record in the world, while Bangladesh has the 147th-best (out of a total of 180 countries studied). By comparison, Canada is ranked 9th, while Afghanistan is 176th. The index is available at http://www.transparency.org/news_room/in_focus/2008/cpi2008/cpi_2008_table.

tions enjoy greater autonomy in Bangladesh, where Islam is, on paper, the "state religion." The Turkish state, though ostensibly fully secular, pays the salaries of mosque imams, and even goes to the extent of supplying them with Friday sermons. While the state funds some Islamic seminaries in Bangladesh, all Islamic seminaries in Turkey are state-funded.[11]

Turkey and Bangladesh both have long-standing and proud traditions of participation in international peacekeeping. Bangladesh currently contributes to 12 different UN peacekeeping missions, while Turkey is a participant of ten. Bangladesh is, at present, the second-largest contributor of troops and the largest contributor of policemen to the UN. In recent years, both Turkish and Bangladeshi troops have served in peacekeeping operations in the Middle East, Africa and the Balkans. In general, both Bangladeshis and Turks tend to support the foreign peacekeeping roles played by their armed forces.[12] Thus, the opposition in the two countries to a continuation of the war in Afghanistan does not stem from distaste towards all foreign military deployment. In fact, both countries are currently engaged in Afghanistan, although, out of the two, only Turkey is playing a military role. As of 14 December 2009, there were 720 Turkish troops deployed in Afghanistan (compared to 2,830 Canadian soldiers).[13] Bangladesh, on the other hand, is involved largely through non-governmental organisations (NGOs), such as the Bangladesh Rural Advancement Committee (BRAC), which has become the biggest source of micro-credit in Afghanistan.[14] The level at which the two countries are currently involved in Afghan affairs has not come under strong domestic criticism. Thus, it is not all involvement in Afghanistan that a majority of Turks and Bangladeshis oppose; instead, it is the war in its current form that they are against.

---

[11] Gareth Jenkins, "Symbols and Shadow Play: Military-JDP relations, 2002-2004," in *The Emergence of a New Turkey: Islam, Democracy, and the AK Parti*, ed. M. Hakan Yavuz (Salt Lake City: University of Utah Press, 2006), 187; Angel Rabasa and F. Stephen Larrabee, *The Rise of Political Islam in Turkey* (Santa Monica, Calif.: RAND Corporation, 2008), 11-12; Syed Serajul Islam, "The Politics of Islam in Bangladesh," in *Religious Fundamentalism in Developing Countries*, ed. Santosh C. Saha and Thomas K. Carr (Westport, Conn.: Greenwood Press, 2001), 177, 181.

[12] UNB, "Dhaka pledges more peacekeepers for UN; Obama lauds Bangladesh's contribution," *Daily Star*, 25 September 2009; Akif Kireççi, "Turkey in the United Nations Security Council," *Today's Zaman*, 21 January 2009; Mahmud Ayub, "Sixty years of peacekeeping," United Nations Turkey, http://www.un.org.tr/index.php?LNG=2&ID=201.

[13] NATO, "Troop Contributing Nations," n.d., http://www.isaf.nato.int/en/troopcontributing-nations/index.php.

[14] Arun Devnath, "The invisible hand of microfinance," *Daily Star*, 8 April 2009.

In a democratic society, newspapers, and the media as a whole, both foster the creation of public opinion, and are themselves a product of public opinion. As Irving Crespi points out, it was newspapers, deploying modern means of communication to the business of news gathering and dissemination, which "fostered the emergence of collective opinion on a national scale" in the first place.[15] At the same time, the loyalty of the newspaper reader is, to some extent, a product of whether he or she finds his or her opinions reflected in the positions taken by the newspaper.[16] In imperfectly democratic societies such as Bangladesh and Turkey, this dialectical relationship between newspapers and the reading public is somewhat modified by the fact that the media have to censor themselves to some extent when it comes to topics which the government or a powerful institution (such as the army) finds sensitive.[17] Nevertheless, both Turkey and Bangladesh possess a media scene that is vibrant and largely free. Thus, I believe that the evidence for the argument that follows, drawn from two Bangladeshi newspapers and two Turkish ones, is broadly reflective of public opinion in the two countries.

In my selection of newspapers, I have aimed for both linguistic and ideological diversity in order to capture as wide a range of opinions as possible within the scope of the study. Thus, among Bangladeshi newspapers, I have selected the *Daily Star*, which is the leading English-language, secularist daily in Bangladesh, and the *Daily Ittefaq*, the main Bengali-language daily, which has a background in Islamic socialism. The Turkish newspapers I selected are the secularist, Turkish-language daily *Hürriyet*, and the pro-Islamist English-language daily *Today's Zaman*.[18]

Using Google Advanced Search, I conducted searches of the four newspapers' online archives in order to find articles on the war in Afghanistan published between May 2008 and May 2009. Of the articles that turned up in each newspaper archive, I used the top 50 results. The ranking

---

[15] Irving Crespi, *The Public Opinion Process: How the People Speak* (Mahwah, N.J.: Lawrence Erlbaum Associates, 1997), 80.
[16] Walter Lippmann, *Public Opinion* (Mineola, N.Y.: Dover Publications, 2004), 178.
[17] "Country Profile: Turkey," BBC News, 5 August 2009, http://news.bbc.co.uk/2/hi/europe/country_profiles/1022222.stm#media ; "Country Profile: Bangladesh," BBC News, 28 July 2009, http://news.bbc.co.uk/2/hi/south_asia/country_profiles/1160598.stm#media.
[18] On the newspapers' history and orientation, see World-newspapers.com, http://www.world-newspapers.com/ ; Manu Islam, "Ittefaq, The," *Banglapedia*, http://www.banglapedia.org/httpdocs/HT/I_0125.HTM; "Pakistan: Prophet of Violence," *Time*, 18 April 1969. Incidentally, the word *ittefaq* means "agreement"; *hürriyet* means "freedom," while *zaman* means "time."

of search results in Google is a function of links to the pages referred in them. Thus, all other things being equal, a page matching the search criteria will be placed above a similar page if it receives more incoming links, and also if it is linked to by more popular pages.[19] As a result, taking the first 50 search results per newspaper website enabled me to focus in on the most widely read and quoted articles published in these four newspapers on the war in Afghanistan over the course of the year.

Several common themes emerge from the four newspapers, pointing to the similarities between the concerns that have arisen in Bangladesh and Turkey over the continued prosecution of war in Afghanistan by NATO and its allies. At the same time, some of the themes central to reporting on the war in Afghanistan are more-or-less unique to Bangladesh and Turkey, pointing to the distinct geographic and political realities of the two countries.

Bangladesh: Worried about the Conflict Spreading

The *Daily Star* is, in general, strongly opposed to both the Taliban and to the U.S. presence in Afghanistan. The most frequent complaint of the *Daily Star*'s columnists regarding the war is that it represents an instance of U.S. aggression. Far from being giving credence, the notion that the U.S. is merely acting in self-defence is not even mentioned. The *Daily Star* is also insistent in its criticism of the United States regarding what it sees as avoidable civilian deaths in Afghanistan. Instead of seeing NATO forces as being in Afghanistan at the invitation of the Afghan government, as is often portrayed in the Canadian media, the columnists of the *Daily Star* see the NATO presence as illegal and imposed by force from outside. Moreover, a prime concern at the *Daily Star* is the gradual spread of the war into Pakistan, which has much closer historical ties to Bangladesh than does Afghanistan.

Thus, in a *Daily Star* article on airstrikes carried out by U.S. unmanned aerial vehicles (UAVs or drones), Liaquat Ali Khan, a Professor of Law at Washburn University in Topeka, Kansas, writes that "the majority of the victims [of the U.S. airstrikes] are poor. They have little to do with the militants who are fighting the NATO occupation forces in Afghanistan." Khan thus takes a morally neutral position between NATO and the Taliban, regarding the former as occupiers and the latter as "militants." The

---

[19] "Corporate Information: Technology Overview," http://www.google.com/corporate/tech.html.

people he sides with are the civilians (in this case Pakistani) who are caught in the middle.

Indeed, Khan believes that U.S. armed forces have not "serve[d] the cause of liberation" anywhere since World War II. He uses Pakistan as a case in point. The country has, in his words, "been a submissive American ally for more than sixty years," yet has not been spared American aggression. Khan sees the reason for such behaviour on the part of the United States in the "unexamined self-righteousness" which drives U.S. foreign policy. In this fashion, the United States "continue[s] to impose deadly military solutions over complex geopolitical problems." Khan sees Barack Obama as merely continuing the policies of George W. Bush in a new part of the world and predicts that "killing indigenous people in Pakistan under the Obama flag will be as unsuccessful as has been killing Iraqi people under the Bush flag." According to Khan, the U.S. drone attacks in Pakistan are illegal under international law, even with Pakistani approval, "when the collateral damage is fully assessed and aggregated."

Finally, as far as the military value of the drone strikes is concerned, Khan sees them as being counter-productive. In his view, "they invite retaliation from militants and sow resentment in the Muslim world." The only solution, in Khan's view, is for the United States to conduct its war on terror "under the rule of law," which would include a halt to air strikes in Pakistan. Khan does not mention similar and much more frequent U.S. air strikes on Afghan territory. His concern lies mostly with Pakistan, and he points out that the United States is not making itself any friends in the Muslim world with what he sees as its high-handed policies.[20]

In an article on the wars, military and economic, being fought by the Obama administration, the freelance writer Mumtaz Iqbal raises the stated reason for the NATO presence in Afghanistan, before quickly brushing it aside. Iqbal acknowledges that the U.S. claims to be militarily engaged in Afghanistan and Pakistan in order to destroy al-Qaeda. However, in Iqbal's view, success in Pakistan would not mean an improvement for U.S. security; after all, "a terrorist attack doesn't have to be executed by Al-Qaeda personnel in Pakistan; 9/11 wasn't." Furthermore, Iqbal argues that "Al-Qaeda's destruction may not end the Afghan insurgency." According to Iqbal, the Taliban are actually Pashtun nationalists, whose insurgency is "fuelled by deprivation from power in Kabul that Pakhtuns consider their birthright." While accusing the Taliban of being in thrall to a "medieval obscurantism," Iqbal still argues that the prime reason for the Taliban insurgency against NATO is that the Pashtuns "regard NATO as an occupa-

---

[20] Liaquat Ali Khan, "Sending in the drones," *Daily Star*, 22 April 2009.

tion force." Moreover, NATO air strikes "cause civilian casualties and alienate the population."[21]

Nader Rahman writes in the *Star Weekend Magazine* (distributed with the *Daily Star*) that the gradual U.S. withdrawal from Iraq and simultaneous ramping up of its military presence in Afghanistan is nothing but "a diversion of resources from one half-failed conflict to another." Rahman recognises that the Iraq war is one Barack Obama "never wanted." Nevertheless, unlike Obama, Rahman sees no essential difference between the two wars. In Rahman's view, the war in Afghanistan is as much a war of choice as the Iraq war. Obama is increasing the U.S. military presence in Afghanistan and spilling it over into South Asia simply because "he feels it must be done, much like Bush felt [the United States] 'must' go into Iraq." Thus, Rahman dismisses Obama's claims of a "new direction" in foreign policy, and sees Obama as someone "mired in the Bush way of waging wars."[22]

Harun ur Rashid, the former Bangladeshi permanent representative to the UN Office in Geneva, disagrees with Nader Rahman's view on the war in Afghanistan, calling it "necessary" and upbraiding George W. Bush for having "abandoned" it. Rashid rejects the Taliban's claims to speak on behalf of Muslims. In his view, "their goal is totally misplaced and contrary to the true teaching of Islam." Nevertheless, according to Rashid, the U.S. presence in Afghanistan has so far only strengthened the hand of both the Taliban and al-Qaeda. The United States, he argues, has done nothing to counter "unemployment, deprivation, desperation and lack of social justice" in either Afghanistan or Pakistan. Under these circumstances, many young men are radicalised, and "want a reason to fight for God" (in the words of a Taliban commander), and many others join up with the Taliban because it simply makes economic sense. As Rashid points out, the Taliban pay their fighters $8 a day, while the Afghan National Army can only manage $4 a day. To complicate things further for the United States, it has, according to Rashid, hopelessly lost the public relations war in Afghanistan, with the result that "most Afghans now believe that...the Bush administration's real goal [was] to set up permanent bases in Afghanistan and occupy the country forever." Rashid's conclusion is that "America cannot defeat the extremists if Afghans and Pakistanis don't see their lives improve."[23]

---

[21] Mumtaz Iqbal, "Obama's 3 ½ wars," *Daily Star*, 4 April 2009.

[22] Nader Rahman, "Exit Strategy," *Star Weekend Magazine* 8, no. 60 (6 March 2009).

[23] Harun ur Rashid, "The new US Afghanistan-Pakistan plan," *Daily Star*, 18 April 2009.

An Associated Press story that appeared in the *Daily Star* further seems to indicate a disconnect between the aims and methods of the U.S.-led alliance in Afghanistan. Although the article takes the form of a news story rather than an editorial, it offers an overtly negative assessment of President Hamid Karzai's choice of the "powerful warlord" Mohammad Qasim Fahim as one of his running mates in the 2009 presidential election. The AP cites a report by Human Rights Watch, issued in 2005, which alleges "widespread and systematic human rights abuses and violations of international humanitarian law" by Fahim's troops. According to Brad Adams, the Asia director of Human Rights Watch, Fahim "is widely believed by many Afghans to be...giving cover to criminal gangs and drug traffickers." This statement stands in sharp contrast to one issued by the U.S. embassy in Kabul, according to which "the election is an opportunity for Afghanistan to move forward with leaders who will strengthen national unity."[24] Although not in so many words, the AP article accuses the United States of hypocritically backing an alleged war criminal in the interest of its military goals in Afghanistan. I would suggest that the choice on the part of the *Daily Star* to publish this particular article, out of all the AP dispatches coming out of Afghanistan, is significant.

It is important to stress, however, that the *Daily Star* evinces little sympathy for the Taliban as a movement. The freelance journalist Syed Maqsud Jamil describes the Taliban as "Mullah Omar's turbaned terror." Nevertheless, according to Jamil, some Afghans are drawn to the Taliban as a response to collateral damage in NATO bomb raids. In his words, "wayward bombing and loss of innocent civilian lives will only harden the Afghan mind."[25]

Similarly, the Pakistani novelist Uzma Aslam Khan, writing in *Star Weekend Magazine*, calls the Pakistani Taliban then occupying the Swat Valley "a band of criminals," adding that what they implemented in Swat was "their grotesque version of Islamic law." Nevertheless, Khan is strongly opposed to the U.S. policy of attacking Taliban bases on Pakistani territory. Comparing today's Pakistan to Vietnam-war-era Cambodia, Khan argues that U.S. bombings only lead to "an escalation in the number of those joining the Taliban," in addition to "whipping up anti-government and anti-U.S./NATO sentiment among common Pakistanis."[26]

---

[24] AP, "Karzai chooses warlord as running mate," *Daily Star*, 5 May 2009.
[25] Syed Maqsud Jamil, "Ruhollah Nikpai's Afghanistan," *Daily Star*, 26 August 2008.
[26] Uzma Aslam Khan, "Transforming a Wonderland into a Gangland," *Star Weekend Magazine*, 27 February 2009.

Thus, the message of the *Daily Star* is unequivocal. In its view, the Taliban, both in Afghanistan and Pakistan, is an unsavoury group that wants to impose an extreme and unpopular interpretation of Islamic law on the territory it holds. Nevertheless, in their current guise, NATO military operations against the Taliban only serve to enhance the popularity of the insurgents, largely because of the high death toll among civilian Afghans and Pakistanis who happen to be in the proximity of Taliban activity. Elections in Afghanistan are dominated by warlords. Thus, current U.S.-led NATO policy in Afghanistan is doing nothing to promote the long-term stability of the country.

Whereas the *Daily Star* is, to some extent, willing to give the United States and its allies in Afghanistan the benefit of the doubt when it comes to their intentions (while decrying their methods), the Bengali-language *Daily Ittefaq* sees the NATO presence in Afghanistan as simply a case of imperialism. Thus, according to an article by Shahadat Hossain Khan, "following the terrorist attacks on the United States, the country launched its aggression against Afghanistan." Thus, Khan acknowledges the NATO claim that the alliance is in Afghanistan in order to defeat al-Qaeda, but refuses to grant this claim legitimacy. Khan argues, moreover, that the United States will not succeed in Afghanistan as long as there is no credible Afghan government in place (thus denying the legitimacy of the Karzai administration).[27]

Just as with the *Daily Star*, however, this does not mean that the *Daily Ittefaq* has any particular sympathies towards the Taliban. In an unsigned article, the *Ittefaq* correspondent in London writes that, in his view:

> It is because of the Anglo-American imperialist [*shamrajjobadi*] laying of hands on Pakistan and Afghanistan that the Taliban are becoming popular in the two countries. The ordinary people are supporting the Taliban in an attempt to resist imperialism. If the imperialist troops are withdrawn from these two countries and their peoples are given the opportunity to decide their own fate, they would choose democracy. The Taliban would find no support.

According to the London correspondent, the reason that the Taliban was able to gain power in Afghanistan in the first place was U.S. "economic and military" support. Once again, he calls for the need to "immediately stop British and American aggression" in Afghanistan. Furthermore, he calls for a comprehensive peace conference, with Taliban partici-

---

[27] Shahadat Hossain Khan, "Afgan loraiye kibhabe jitbe markinira" [How the Americans are going to win in the Afghan struggle], *Daily Ittefaq*, 18 April 2009. Here and below, the translations from Bengali are mine.

pation, as a means of ending the war in Afghanistan. As he points out, "this is how the Irish terrorist problem was peacefully resolved. It was not done through war." Thus, the correspondent compares the Taliban to the IRA and is not loath to use the word "terrorist" to describe them. Nevertheless, he repeatedly uses the words "imperialist" and "imperialism" to describe what he sees as Anglo-American "aggression" in Afghanistan and Pakistan. Thus, the two sides, to him, are morally equivalent. The way out, in his view, is in democracy, but only a democracy free from NATO occupation.[28]

The *Daily Ittefaq* printed an Agene France-Presse (AFP) story about an interview given to CNN by the Pakistani president, Asif Ali Zardari. In the interview, Zardari asked the United States to stop allowing its troops to cross into Pakistani territory in order to strike at militants. Zardari claimed that Pakistan was more capable of pursuing militants on its own territory than anyone else. His comments followed an incident in which Pakistani troops opened fire on two U.S. helicopters that had entered Pakistani airspace.[29] This article helps us contextualize the consistent claim by *Ittefaq* columnists that any U.S. military activity in Pakistan represents American aggression. After all, even the pro-American Zardari administration is openly opposed to it. An AFP article printed in the *Daily Ittefaq* regarding a trilateral summit between Barack Obama, Hamid Karzai and Asif Ali Zardari mentions U.S. Secretary of State Hillary Clinton expressing her "pain" over civilian deaths caused by U.S. bomb raids. Notably, there is no mention made by Obama of civilian deaths caused by the United States in Pakistan.[30]

Reporting by the *Daily Ittefaq* gives an impression of overwhelming callousness on the part of NATO forces in Afghanistan towards Afghan civilians. For instance, an article on civilian deaths reports on Hamid Karzai's announcement that over 30 Afghans had been killed in a NATO airstrike. The report cites statements by villagers who witnessed the attacks, according to whom the number of civilians killed was not 30, but rather somewhere between 70 and 150. Karzai thus appears to be either unaware of the situation, or to be intentionally minimising it. The eye-witnesses to

---

[28] "Pakistaner biponno ostitto o okhondota gota upomohadesher sharthei keno rokkha kora proyojon?" [Why the integrity of Pakistan must be preserved for the sake of the entire Subcontinent], *Daily Ittefaq*, 3 May 2009.
[29] AFP, "Shimanto elakay jongi domon amader kaj, Juktorashtrer noy CNNke president Zardari" [The task of suppressing militants in the border area is ours, not that of the United States: Zardari to CNN]. *Daily Ittefaq*, 30 September 2008.
[30] "Jongi birodhi loraiye noya Pak-Afgan front gothon" [The formation of a new Pak-Afghan front in combating militants], *Daily Ittefaq*, 8 May 2009.

the incident claimed that most of those killed were women, children and elderly people who had taken refuge in a village that was later targeted by NATO planes. The report closes with testimony from a young girl named Shafika, who had lost seven of her relatives in the air strike, and was herself wounded.[31] This report was published a fortnight after an illustration of Pentagon-authorised torture methods appeared in the *Ittefaq* under the heading "Interrogation methods."[32] Reports such as these certainly contribute to the impression that the U.S. military and its NATO and Afghan allies are morally bankrupt.

Nevertheless, the *Daily Ittefaq* is also firmly opposed to the support given to the Taliban by some sections of the Bangladeshi religious right. Reporting on a meeting organised in Chittagong by Bangladeshi veterans of Afghan wars, the *Ittefaq* takes an overtly negative stance against them. The meeting was held in order to launch the new Islamic Democratic Party (IDP). According to *Ittefaq* reporter Komol De, however, the IDP is simply "the current form of the banned ultra-fundamentalist organisation Harakatul Jihad." Abdul Ghafur, an IDP functionary, told the *Ittefaq* that, "Our older leaders took part in the war in Afghanistan in order to help Muslims. But they never hurled bombs inside our country, and were never arrested in possession of bombs. Throwing bombs is not in keeping with Islam. We want to institute Islamic government in the country." Another party official, Ariful Islam, admitted that certain members and even leaders of the party were involved in militant activity in Bangladesh, and had been expelled from the party as a result. In Ariful Islam's words, "We hate militancy." It does not seem, though, that De was convinced.[33]

In contrast, the *Daily Ittefaq* gave positive coverage to a round table entitled "Islam and Militancy," organised by the Bangladesh Islami Front [sic], an Islamist political party. At the round table, Syed Najibul Bashar Maijbhandari, the chairman of the Bangladesh Tarikat Federation (another Islamist party), claimed that, "Militancy will soon become the main problem of our country if we cannot suppress it right now. The reason is that of those Bangladeshi militants who went to fight in Afghanistan, the majority are now inside the country." A professor of the University of Dhaka pointed out that "there is no refuge for murderers" in Islam. A *madrasa*

---

[31] "Dershotadhik lok nihoto howar ashonka" [Fears of over a hundred and fifty people having been killed], *Daily Ittefaq*, 7 May 2009.
[32] "Bondi nirjatoner chhobi prokash korbe Pentagon" [The Pentagon will publish pictures of prisoner torture], *Daily Ittefaq*, 26 April 2009.
[33] Komol De, "Chottograme prokashshe kormi shommelon korlo Hujir shohojogira" [Harakatul Jihad collaborators openly hold an assembly in Chittagong], *Daily Ittefaq*, 11 April 2009.

teacher who participated in the round table also called for the government to "suppress" those "who are pursuing militant activity using Islam."[34]

Thus, the *Daily Ittefaq* is by no means an anti-Islamic or even anti-Islamist newspaper. Nevertheless, as we have seen in our discussion of some of its articles, it is very much against Islamist militancy either in Bangladesh or, for that matter, in Afghanistan. From the *Ittefaq*'s perspective, the way to put an end to this militancy, when it comes to Afghanistan, is to withdraw NATO forces and allow the establishment of a genuine, popular democracy there.

Turkey: Feeling Ignored

The primary difference between Bangladesh and Turkey in relation to the ongoing war in Afghanistan is that Turkey is a NATO member with troops deployed in Afghanistan, whereas Bangladesh is not. Reading the Turkish press, however, you would hardly know that Turkey is present in Afghanistan as a U.S. ally. Instead, the opposition to the war in its current shape is, if possible, even more vociferous in the Turkish press than it is in the Bangladeshi press.

There is a sense in reading the Turkish press that Turkey feels slighted and overlooked in the way the war has been conducted by its NATO partners. Thus, when asked whether the United States would be requesting Turkey to beef up its presence in Afghanistan, the Turkish defence minister, Vecdi Gönül, replied, "I do not know what America is going to do. I do not know what they are going to talk about, either. No information on that whatsoever has reached us."[35] Thus, Ankara seems to be smarting at having been relegated to a second tier within NATO. The Turkish military also does not seem to see the Afghan war as one worth pursuing further in its current form. Dismissing the possibility of Turkey's sending additional troops to Afghanistan, the former chief of staff of the Turkish armed forces, M. Yaşar Büyükanıt, said, "If we were to send troops there, what is it going to be like when the remains of [Turkish] martyrs start arriving from there? How will we explain that to the Turkish nation? That is not possible." Büyükanıt added that Turkey has its own "struggle against terrorism" to conduct on its territory, and thus cannot spare any troops to

---

[34] "'Islamer shathe jongibader kono shomporko nei'" ["There is no connection between Islam and militancy"], *Daily Ittefaq*, 6 May 2009.
[35] "Gönül 'Planladığımız bazı şeyler var'" [Gönül: "We have planned some things"], *Hürriyet*, 12 March 2009. Here and below, the translations from Turkish are mine.

fight terrorism in Afghanistan. According to Büyükanıt, the Turkish armed forces are not a "depot" to dip into at will.[36]

Thus, the Turkish government and army are, in a sense, washing their hands of the war in Afghanistan (while not withdrawing existing Turkish troops from there), and increasingly viewing it as a war of choice, rather than a war of necessity. *Hürriyet* itself takes a similar position, branding the war, in one headline, "Obama's war."[37] In fact, there is some suspicion in Turkey that, had the United States really wanted to defeat the Taliban, it would have done so by now. Thus, *Hürriyet* carried a piece describing allegations by the *Anis* newspaper of Afghanistan, according to which the United States has intentionally kept Afghanistan in a state of instability in order to have control over the "oil and gas" resources of Central Asia.[38] In another article, *Hürriyet* reports Hamid Karzai's mounting frustration with NATO's inability to defeat the Taliban, and its carelessness when it comes to civilian casualties. In Karzai's words, "This war has been going on for seven years. We cannot understand how a small force like the Taliban has been able to continue to exist." Karzai also remarked that NATO seems to be engaged in bombing villages and killing civilians instead of fighting against terrorism.[39]

In contrast to the allegedly dubious role being played in Afghanistan, Turkey's role there is portrayed very positively by *Hürriyet*. According to one article, Turkey provided "education, clothing and stationery allowances to 15,000 Afghan families" and medical aid to "750,000 Afghan citizens." Presumably as a result of the difference Turkey is making, the Turkish forces are made to feel welcome in Afghanistan. According to the report, "Afghan citizens have been displaying warmth towards the Turkish police [in Kabul]." The article makes no mention of any aid given to Afghanistan by Turkey's NATO allies, or other countries, for that matter.[40]

That is not to say that *Hürriyet* is hostile to ordinary soldiers from other NATO countries serving in Afghanistan. For instance, in a moving article on Corporal Sarah Bryant, the first female British soldier killed in Afghanistan, the newspaper reports that "Two years ago, on a summer

---

[36] "Büyükanıt: Ya Afganistan'dan şehitler gelirse" [Büyükanıt: What if martyrs come from Afghanistan], *Hürriyet*, 16 April 2009.
[37] "Obama'nın savaşı" [Obama's war], *Hürriyet*, 28 March 2009.
[38] "ABD hakkında şoke eden iddia" [A shocking claim about the U.S.A.], *Hürriyet*, 28 August 2008.
[39] "Karzai, ABD ve NATO'dan şikayetçi" [Karzai complains against the U.S.A. and NATO], *Hürriyet*, 27 November 2008.
[40] "Türkiye'den 15 bin Afgan aileye yardım" [Help from Turkey for 15 thousand Afghan families], *Hürriyet*, 11 December 2008.

day, she became a bride. Yesterday, in Afghanistan, she gave her life...."
It also reports that Cpl. Bryant's father said, "She will never come home again. I cannot believe it. I will go on waiting for her."[41]

On the other hand, when it comes to higher-ranking officers in the armed forces of a fellow NATO member, *Hürriyet* is much less sympathetic. In a rather long article, *Hürriyet* reporter Kasım Cindemir reports from Washington, D.C. that Admiral John Stufflebeem, a military adviser to George H.W. Bush, is being investigated for allegedly carrying on an eight-month affair with a junior officer inside the White House 18 years ago. According to Cindemir, repeated attempts at investigating the affair had been quashed in the past.[42] The picture painted in the article of the state of discipline in the higher echelons of the U.S. armed forces, and, indeed, the White House, is not a kind one.

This does not mean, however, that *Hürriyet* has any sympathy for the Taliban. The columnist Yavuz Çekirge accuses the Taliban of hypocrisy, saying that "the Taliban, which is fighting... to establish a utopian 'Shariah,' is in the process of taking control of the world drug trade."[43] In another article, *Hürriyet* reports that some Afghan children are "applying special make up" and bandaging their eyes in order to "present themselves as war victims." An accompanying photograph shows a little girl with a seemingly mutilated face. The implication may be that not all the alleged civilian victims of the NATO campaign in Afghanistan are genuine. On the other hand, it is also an indictment of the present state of affairs in Afghanistan, where a child has to take on the gruesome image of someone with a half-burned face in order to get a bite to eat.[44]

Of the four newspapers examined here, the English-language daily *Today's Zaman* devotes the most space to the war in Afghanistan. It is also perhaps the most vociferous in its criticism of the failings of the U.S.-led coalition in Afghanistan. One of the features of the war most commented on by *Today's Zaman* is the high rate of civilian casualties that have resulted from NATO bombing. For instance, in an article tellingly entitled, "Will the civilian massacres stop?" the columnist Ali Bulac comments on a U.S. air strike that killed 37 civilians, most of whom were women and children: "The world community, which holds the US responsible for oc-

---

[41] "Afganistan'da öldü" [She died in Afghanistan], *Hürriyet*, 20 June 2008.
[42] Kasım Cindemir, "Amiral, Beyaz Saray'da kimse seks yaptı" [An admiral had sex with someone in the White House], *Hürriyet*, 12 May 2008.
[43] Yavuz Çekirge, "Taliban rejimi..." [The Taliban regime...], *Hürriyet*, 25 April 2009.
[44] "Korkmayın acımayın" [Do not be afraid, do not have pity], *Hürriyet*, 2 October 2008.

cupations in Palestine, Iraq and Afghanistan, has difficulty understanding civilian massacres. Especially in Afghanistan, US warplanes carry out air strikes against civilians on a regular basis, killing people indiscriminately." Thus, Bulac presents the air strike not as an isolated incident, but rather as part of an almost deliberate U.S. policy. Going beyond the charge of U.S. "imperialism" raised in the *Daily Ittefaq*, Bulac blends the U.S. military presence in Iraq and Afghanistan with the Israeli occupation of Palestinian territories. According to Bulac, "the primary reason for growing anti-American sentiments in the world is the ongoing tragedy in Palestine and…the baseless American occupation of Afghanistan." Bulac does not bring up the fact of Turkey's participation in that "occupation."[45]

In another article, Bulac ridicules the notion, brought up by U.S. vice-presidential candidate Sarah Palin, that U.S. soldiers ought to be going into the field "on a task that is from God," and as part of "God's plan." In Bulac's view, Palin's hope of a divinely inspired U.S. military mission, in the face of "what happened and is happening in Afghanistan and Iraq," is an insult to God. After all, "in the US operation in Afghanistan, hundreds of children have been killed in [U.S.] bomb attacks."[46]

Eventually, Bulac comes to the extraordinary conclusion that NATO has been deliberately targeting civilians in Afghanistan in order to keep the war going. In Bulac's words, "There is strong evidence that the strategy that NATO has been pursuing recently in Afghanistan largely relies on forcing Taliban forces to stop resisting by aiming for innocent targets." Bulac compares this "strategy" to Israel's bombardment of civilian targets in the Gaza Strip. Bulac backs up his assertions by citing figures published by the *Guardian*, according to which "829 [civilians] were killed by U.S., NATO and Afghan forces" in 2008. Bulac does acknowledge, however, that the Taliban had killed 1,160 civilians in the same year. He expresses disquiet over alleged British plans (his source once again being the *Guardian*) to start viewing anyone with Islamist sympathies in Britain as an "extremist." The list would include people who support the implementation of the Shariah, or armed resistance to occupation. It would even extend to people "who refuse to condemn the killing of British soldiers in Afghanistan or Iraq." According to Bulac, "the overwhelming majority of Muslims in the UK" will thus be branded extremists. As a result, they will be "prevented from accessing public funds and state aid." According to Bulac, the connection between civilian deaths in Afghanistan and the British gov-

---

[45] Ali Bulac, "Will the civilian massacres stop?," *Today's Zaman*, 7 November 2008.

[46] Ali Bulac, "Will Bush be remembered for shoes?" *Today's Zaman*, 19 December 2008.

ernment's new definition of extremism is that anyone protesting against "NATO forces' killing of innocent people in Afghanistan" in the U.K. risks being declared an extremist. In Bulac's view, it is policies such as these that lead to the radicalization of Muslims.[47]

Writing yet again about civilian deaths in Afghanistan, Bulac complains about the double standards of Reuters and, by extension, of the West, whereby the murder of 44 wedding guests in the Turkish city of Mardin is seen as shocking, whereas a U.S. air strike in which 100 people were killed is seen as normal. He also blames the United States for Taliban suicide bombings, saying that they are the direct outcome of the "US-led NATO occupation."[48] İbrahim Kalın cites a RAND Corporation report, entitled "Defeating Terrorist Groups," according to which, in Kalın's words, "the...presence of US troops in Muslim countries has created a better recruiting ground for al-Qaeda and the like."[49]

Today's Zaman presents a completely different view of the role of Turkish troops in Afghanistan, however. Whereas the Turks' NATO allies (in particular the United States) are presented as illegitimate occupiers of Afghan soil, the Turkish presence in Afghanistan is depicted in the newspaper as not simply benign, but rather selfless and charitable. In an interview with the newspaper, the Afghan consul general, Azim Naseer Zia, observes that "when the Turkish soldiers are going out [sic] in the streets in Afghanistan with their emblems, the people are more friendly with them than with any other forces." The reason is, according to Zia, that the Afghans "identify with the Turks." Furthermore, "the Turks are not considered foreigners in Afghanistan." Zia cites a long history of past Afghan-Turkish cooperation, reminding the *Zaman* reporter that many Afghans volunteered to fight for the Ottoman Empire in World War I.[50]

A *Today's Zaman* report on reconstruction in Afghanistan, while acknowledging the contributions of U.S. Provincial Reconstruction Teams (PRTs), mainly focuses on the work done by the one Turkish PRT, based in Wardak Province. The reporter, Namık Kemal Parlak, points out that it is the only "civilian-run PRT in the country." He praises its "many accomplishments," including the construction of "seven schools, one medical center, two deep freezer facilities, two water reservoirs, a fruit drying facility, 10 wells, a police training center, a police station, a gymnasium and

---

[47] Ali Bulac, "Exclusion from the system," *Today's Zaman*, 20 February 2009.
[48] Ali Bulac, "Model method for massacres," *Today's Zaman*, 8 May 2009.
[49] İbrahim Kalın, "Fate of the war on terror: some modest advice for the Obama administration," *Today's Zaman*, 28 November 2008.
[50] Kerim Balcı, "'If the Afghan boat sinks, the West will also sink'," *Today's Zaman*, 19 April 2009.

a mosque." By contrast, Parlak gives this sort of detailed description of only one single project undertaken by the 12 American PRTs operating in Afghanistan. Parlak adds that the Turkish PRT is highly esteemed by U.S. forces.[51]

An article by Çağlar Avcı reports on a group of 37 volunteer Turkish doctors providing medical assistance to 3,000 Afghans in four days. Avcı cites Orhan Coşkuner, who heads a Turkish medical NGO involved in the project, as saying that, through health care and education, Turkey is "trying to answer the call for help made by the Afghan people, who have suffered a great deal due to years of war." Avcı also mentions a 16-year-old Afghan patient who said that the arrival of the Turkish doctors made him feel "like I was no longer abandoned to my fate." According to Avcı, the doctors were "welcomed by a crowd carrying Afghan and Turkish flags." Thus, according to the article, the Turks are in Afghanistan to respond to the dire need of a people who have suffered from "years of war" and have no hope of help from elsewhere.[52] Similarly, Haşim Söylemez describes how the Afghans have "had to deal with" Soviet occupation, "Taliban rule," "civil war" and "American military intervention."[53] What these narratives conveniently leave out is Turkey's own participation in NATO, Turkey's presence in Afghanistan as an "occupier" alongside its allies, and its participation in the "years of war" that have afflicted Afghanistan.

In fact, another *Zaman* columnist, Beril Dedeoğlu, tackles this point by arguing that "in Afghanistan, Turkey is the sole [NATO] country that is not seen as an occupier by the Muslim people." The implication here is that Turkey is something other than an occupier in Afghanistan simply by virtue of its being a Muslim country. Indeed, according to Dedeoğlu, Turkey is in a position of greater respect in Afghanistan than Afghanistan's own president, Hamid Karzai. In her view, Karzai is nothing more than "the political representative of the 'West' in the internal supervision of Afghanistan." Karzai's standing in Afghanistan is, according to Dedeoğlu, "extremely dubious."[54] Ömer Taşpınar describes Karzai's government as "very weak, dysfunctional and utterly corrupt." According to Taşpınar, "many of the most corrupt elements in Kabul are allies of the West and

---

[51] Namık Kemal Parlak, "Taliban not the only problem in Afghanistan," *Today's Zaman*, 27 February 2009.

[52] Çağlar Avcı, "Turkish doctors examine 3,000 Afghans in four days," *Today's Zaman*, 29 April 2009.

[53] Haşim Söylemez, "The dark road of Afghan drug trafficking reaches to Turkey," *Today's Zaman*, 24 December 2008.

[54] Beril Dedeoğlu, "The Afghanistan-Pakistan dilemma," *Today's Zaman*, 4 April 2009.

have thus gained a kind of immunity."[55] Thus, in the view of *Today's Zaman* columnists, not only is the West (primarily personified by the United States) failing to bring real democracy to Afghanistan, but it is also sheltering individuals whose activities are inimical to the interests of the Afghan people. Yet even Karzai, who presides over this "dysfunctional" set up, regularly says that civilian deaths caused by NATO activities are "unacceptable."[56] Thus, in the view of *Today's Zaman*, U.S. policy in Afghanistan is completely divorced from reality and counterproductive.

The preceding discussion may have created the impression that *Today's Zaman* would not mind a Taliban victory in the war in Afghanistan. That, however, is far from the truth. In fact, the *Zaman* columnist Fikret Ertan writes that "the Taliban is more sophisticated and bolder now...and it needs more attention and resources with which to tackle it."[57] Thus, in *Zaman*'s view, the Taliban remains a threat to be "tackled." It is the current approach to the problem that the newspaper is strongly against.

As a solution, Ömer Taşpınar suggests that "Turkey should have a large role in...the Afghanistan mission." In his view, NATO "desperately needs a greater Muslim presence." Taşpınar laments the fact that, at a time when NATO "needs much better public relations in the Islamic world," it decided to select the former Danish prime minister Anders Fogh Rasmussen for the position of secretary-general. Rasmussen is unpopular in the Muslim world for refusing to apologise for the cartoons of the Prophet Muhammad until forced to do so by riots in the Muslim world and the boycott of Danish consumer goods by many Muslims. Taşpınar reminds his readers that 12 Afghans were killed in one such riot in Afghanistan, making Rasmussen a far from ideal figure to head NATO. Taşpınar thus describes Rasmussen's selection as "quite unfortunate."[58]

Columnist Şahin Alpay is "astonished, if not shocked" at Rasmussen's selection as NATO secretary-general. According to Alpay, Rasmussen's impending appointment contradicts Barack Obama's ostensible attempts to mend fences with the Muslim world. Moreover, Rasmussen is unacceptable to Turkey not only because of the cartoon controversy, but also because of issues of more particular concern to Ankara. For one, while in office as Danish prime minister, Rasmussen was "opposed to the accession

---

[55] Ömer Taşpınar, "Afghanistan is not Iraq," *Today's Zaman*, 23 February 2009.
[56] "Red Cross: Many Afghans killed after US bombings," *Today's Zaman*, 7 May 2009.
[57] Fikret Ertan, "Taliban bolder and more sophisticated," *Today's Zaman*, 20 July 2009.
[58] Ömer Taşpınar, "NATO, Afghanistan and Turkey's role," *Today's Zaman*, 13 April 2009.

of Turkey...to the European Union." Secondly, he allowed "a television station affiliated with the Kurdistan Workers' Party (PKK), regarded by both the US and the EU as a terrorist organization, to broadcast from Denmark." Thus, on several counts, "Rasmussen heading NATO is a very bad idea."[59]

The columnist Bülent Keneş sees Rasmussen's appointment to the position of secretary-general as part of a pattern of anti-Muslim behaviour on the part of NATO. He points out that, as early as 1994, Willy Claes, the secretary-general at the time, said that "NATO's new target and mission is to deal with radical Islam." According to Keneş, Claes's words are "alive in the memories of Muslims." Keneş points out that, "except for new member Albania, Turkey is NATO's only Muslim member," and is thus better informed than other member-states about the way in which NATO policies play in the Muslim world. However, instead of taking Turkey's advice on Rasmussen, its fellow NATO members decided to "[exert] pressure, even threats" to get Turkey to back down. Keneş describes Rasmussen as someone "hated by hundreds of millions of Muslims" because of the cartoon issue. Therefore, in his view, Rasmussen's appointment is "either... an intentional provocation or... serious strategic blindness." Keneş predicts that "the Taliban, al-Qaeda and radicals in other areas" will "easily recruit new members" using pervasive anti-Rasmussen sentiments in the Muslim world.[60] Sure enough, *Today's Zaman* later published a Reuters report, according to which the Taliban had called Rasmussen "the major enemy of Islam's Prophet" and had promised an "intensification of [the] war" against NATO.[61]

Following Anders Rasmussen's victory, columnist İbrahim Kalın observes that "the situation in Afghanistan cannot be won or improved with a military mission." He points out that "sending 150,000 US troops to Iraq was a mistake," and predicts that "sending them to Afghanistan would be a disaster." According to Kalın, any intensification of the US military presence in Afghanistan will "only strengthen the hand of al-Qaeda and the extreme elements within the Taliban." The result would be a new "Vietnam" for Obama. *Today's Zaman* does not want to see the Taliban, or its one-time ally al-Qaida, to emerge victorious in the war in Afghanistan. On the other hand, the unanimous position of its columnists seems to be that the present course, as pursued by NATO (with only incidental and positive

---

[59] Şahin Alpay, "Rasmussen for NATO: A very bad idea," *Today's Zaman*, 30 March 2009.
[60] Bülent Keneş, "Rasmussen un-welcomed," *Today's Zaman*, 6 April 2009.
[61] Reuters, "New NATO chief is Islam's 'major foe,' Taliban says," *Today's Zaman*, 17 April 2009.

involvement by Turkey) is nothing short of disastrous, both for Afghanistan and for the world at large.

An Opportunity for Engagement

As Richard Bonney points out, the "clash of civilizations" theory has been extraordinarily popular in the United States in recent years. Indeed, perhaps "no thesis has had a comparable influence on Western, especially American, strategic thinking since the end of the Cold War."[62] If that is the case, it unfortunately follows that segments of American and other Western policymakers abandoned the analysis of developments in Muslim societies for a facile, one-size-fits-all notion of "Islamic" opposition to anything Western. As we have seen in the analysis presented above, the notion that Turks and Bangladeshis oppose the war in Afghanistan simply because it is Western-led is false. In the four newspapers I have examined, it is very hard to find a single positive mention of the Taliban. Rather, the Taliban are seen as a fanatical, even terrorist movement, that ought to be defeated, but not at the price of countless Afghan civilian lives. Furthermore, from a purely practical point of view, all four newspapers point out that the high level of civilian casualties in Afghanistan continually pushes more Afghans into the arms of the Taliban. The solution most often proposed in the four newspapers is an American (and NATO) withdrawal, combined with the establishment of real democracy. The current Afghan political system, with warlords wielding disproportionate political power, is seen in both Bangladesh and Turkey as a sham.

These are all points that the United States and its allies can discuss with the Muslim world. If Barack Obama's initiative of greater engagement with the Muslim world is to bear fruit, the issue of Afghanistan needs to be addressed by the United States not just in Pakistan, but also in other parts of the Muslim world, such as Bangladesh and Turkey. Turkey in particular, as a Muslim power of rising international importance and simultaneously a staunch ally of the West, should not be allowed to continue feeling left out of NATO decision-making. I agree with Juan Cole that "the pressing conflicts between the North Atlantic nations and the Muslim-majority ones can in most instances be resolved more successfully by engagement than by dirty wars and covert operations."[63]

As for Canada, the good and bad news is that not one of the articles I examined in the four newspapers mentioned the country by name. Thus, it

---

[62] Bonney, *op. cit.*, 35.
[63] Juan Cole, *Engaging the Muslim World* (New York: Palgrave Macmillan, 2009), 5.

is safe to say that Canada's contribution to peace in Afghanistan, valiant though it is, is being almost completely ignored by the public in the Muslim world. While this may be unfair, the advantage to Canada from such a situation is that it has very little damage to repair in its relations with the Muslim world. Following the planned withdrawal of most Canadian troops from Afghanistan in 2011, Canada can, if it wishes, seek to deepen relations with the Muslim world without the negative associations of the war in Afghanistan to encumber the efforts. On the other hand, the United States certainly has its work cut out for it.

AFGHANISTAN'S VILLAGES AND DISTRICTS: NOTES ON A FORGOTTEN PRIORITY

REMMELT C. HUMMELEN

A Primer on Afghanistan

Afghanistan, a mountainous country of approximately 652,000 square kilometres, shares borders with China, Iran, Pakistan, Tajikistan, Turkmenistan, Uzbekistan and a sector of the disputed territory of Jammu and Kashmir that is controlled by Pakistan. About half of its territory is more than 2,000 metres above sea level. To give a sense of scale, Afghanistan is larger than France, which is the largest country in western Europe with about 545,000 square kilometres, but has a lower population than France, numbering an estimated 28 million, as opposed to France's 62 million. There is, however, another notable difference in demographics. In France, only 22% of the population lives in rural areas; in Afghanistan, by contrast, about 75% of the population is rural.[1]

Afghanistan is divided into provinces, which are subdivided into districts. Districts and villages form an immensely important social network for ordinary families and serve key functions in the national economy. In June 2005, the Afghan Ministry of the Interior recognized 398 districts, divided between the 34 provinces. Each district generally has a commercial centre that serves as the capital. The District centre serves as a place where villagers can do their selling and buying of agricultural produce and obtain other items such as household goods. Standard items not available in a district market can generally be obtained from a market located in the provincial capital. The district centre will typically have a police post, medical services, etc. More sophisticated services such as a hospital would, in most instances, be located in the provincial capital. Depending on the area, veterinary services might also be available. As is well known, there are instances when a district or province will have their own lan-

---

[1] World Resources Institutes, http://www.wri.org/, citing United Nations figures for 2010.

guage in addition to the national languages of Dari and Pashto: Uzbeki, Turkmani, Baluchi, Pashai, Nuristani, Pamiri (alsana), and other languages spoken in the country.

There are over 33,000 villages in Afghanistan, housing, as has been noted, the majority of the population. Because of their isolation, many have become self-reliant and the intervention of foreign powers has, in many cases, only reinforced their desire to remain self-sufficient. But that resolve has had side effects including poverty, drug abuse, poor sanitation and low crop yields. In some areas, farmers are forced to cultivate poppy in order to earn a subsistence income. This brief paper argues that the international community needs to engage much more creatively and constructively with the reality of life in Afghanistan's villages and regions if the causes of discontent among the great majority of Afghanistan's people are to be addressed.

The author has had the privilege of working in Afghanistan on three occasions, first in 1994 (pre-Taliban) to 1995 (with Taliban) with the United Nations International Drug Control Program (UNDCP, now the United Nations Office on Drugs and Crime, or UNODCC); second, in 2004 with the United Nations Development Program (UNDP) as Programme Advisor for Law and Order Trust Fund (LOFTA), based in the Ministry of the Interior, Kabul, working closely with the Deputy Minister and Minister, as well as with the Ministry of Finance; and, third, in 2007, based in Jalalabad as Conflict Mitigation Specialist, part of the Local Governance and Community Development Project (funded by USAID).

Deforestation, Community and Hunger

Over the years, I have visited 14 of the 34 provinces of Afghanistan, and have seen countless villages, many with distinct cultures and languages. One of these villages could only be reached after an eight-hour trek by donkey, or else on foot. If I may offer this humble advice to anyone who makes such a journey in the future: keep your pack on your donkey and your feet on the ground. I opted for the donkey at first, but after half an hour of dragging feet and encountering vertigo-inducing cliffs, I changed my mind. As I passed other villages on the way, I witnessed firsthand the extraordinary hospitality of the Afghan people. Steaming cups of tea were in abundance, made fresh after our arrival, and springs of water quenched our thirst on the way.

I was, in fact, the first "foreigner" ever to visit the village in question. It was home to about two thousand people, most of them farmers who were sustained almost entirely by the work of their hands. Their crops included potatoes and vegetables, which are preserved for the winter months, and some poppy cultivated for its seed, buds and stalks which are turned into oil, teas and fuel by women of the community. Irrigation, however, was increasingly a problem for the farmers, as it is for many across the region. Water was brought to the fields through irrigation canals, but these canals had become dilapidated and grossly inefficient so that much water is lost on its journey from source to fields. Pipes are not a realistic option in such areas, not only because of cost, but also because they burst when colder weather brings sub-zero temperatures.

There was a time when trees with strong root systems helped hold canal walls together, but as war and political unrest swept the country, trees were cut down to be used for fuel. As a result, the canal system is in ruins. In all the years since the Soviet invasion in the 1980s, there has been little or no replanting. New trees are desperately needed to reinforce crumbling river and creek banks and to provide shade and fuel for heating and cooking; but at present, and despite all the massive expenditure on Afghanistan by the international community, only *one* non-governmental organization is operating a tree nursery and experimental farm in the eastern part of the country. This project, which is so crucial to the future of the people, has struggled to find funding. It seems that the long-term lifecycle of trees does not coincide with the short-term goals of donor nations. Yet one of the most effective ways genuinely to help Afghanistan would be to invest in something as simple as reforestation.

During the years of post-invasion conflict, many villagers fled to neighbouring countries like Pakistan and Iran. Today, these people are returning as refugees—in addition to the return of internally displaced persons who went to camps inside the country—to find their old communities in ruins. Those who stayed have been unable to maintain canals, roads and other basic parts of the infrastructure. In order to build for the future, however, homes must be reconstructed, drinking water must be provided, and "community" must be re-established. Many of those now returning have spent years in refugee camps, where daily needs were met in however limited a way; back in their villages, unfortunately, support from international donors is limited at best, and in consequence, people are left floundering for resources.

To give some sense of the need, let me tell a story. When on another occasion I visited the village of Ishkashim (also Eshkashem) in northeastern Afghanistan, I stayed in the office of a local clinic attached to a small detoxification facility. The first morning after my arrival, I woke to the sound of babies crying—nothing out of the ordinary, one might think—except that I soon learned that these infants were crying for opium, not milk. They had been born to addicted mothers. Opium is commonly used to quell hunger. Given how often there is no food for either mother or child, it is no wonder that addiction is so prevalent, especially in villages in which the local economy has collapsed and where people rely almost entirely on the United Nations World Food Program for provisions.

While the security problems of Afghanistan are complex, some basic humanitarian and relief efforts are not so hard to conceive or even expensive to deliver. Reforestation, re-establishing irrigation, rebuilding community centres and communities for trade and food distribution, especially in light of the curse of opiate abuse due to the prevalence of hunger, can all be easily addressed on the ground in order to help people on an everyday level. None of these initiatives would be beyond the Afghan people, in co-operation with United Nations and international aid agencies, to implement. Indeed, the requirements are modest in comparison to the demands of other relief efforts elsewhere, and in comparison with the present expenditure on security in Afghanistan.

A Modest Proposal

There are currently nineteen United Nations agencies based in Afghanistan and coordinated by the UN Assistance Mission to Afghanistan (UNAMA).[2] The nature of much of the aid provided, however, is too often based on donor nations' perceptions of the people's needs rather than the reality of the situation, and often as such is missing the kind of "on the ground" perspective that I have experienced. Often, such assumptions are based on what is known of only a few geographic areas and a few social and political institutions. Rarely are the thousands of Afghan villages visited or their people themselves consulted on what is needed. This, however, is an approach that is doomed to failure, not least as it flies in the face of the traditional *shura* governance model used by the villages and districts of Afghanistan. In the traditional *shura* system, a decision is made

---

[2] UN Agencies based in Afghanistan include: UNDP (United Nations Development Program), UNAMA (United Nations Assistance Mission in Afghanistan), UN-HABITAT (United Nations Centre for Human Settlements), UNCTAD (United Nations Conference on Trade and Development), UNEP (United Nations Environment Programme), UNESCO (United Nations Educational, Scientific and Cultural Organization), UNFPA (United Nations Population Fund for Afghanistan), UNHCR (United Nations High Commission for Refugees), UNICEF (United Nations Children's Fund), UNIFEM (United Nations Development Fund for Women), UNODC (United Nations Office on Drugs and Crime). In addition there have been special initiatives such as those offering support for recent elections.

by the hereditary or elected leaders of a community, whose role is to act after community members have spoken. Consensus is actually required for change. "On the ground," *shura* communities would, I am suggesting, almost certainly ask that greater priority be given to reforestation, irrigation, and so to food production, so that agriculture can be revitalized and crops sold eventually in regional cities, since without this, all talk of security, education and so forth is at best partial and at worst a distraction. Attending to the former, however, could only enhance the latter. In my experience as a sojourner, this kind of aid is exactly what is needed in Afghanistan—yet it is very seldom provided.

Currently, international donors are seeking to strengthen or change governmental and commercial structures in the capital and in regional centres. The assumption seems to be that such forms of support will "trickle down" through these wealthier, more urban parts of the society to benefit the villagers. The truth, however, is that the approach taken to date has had very limited effect in the villages—except, perhaps, in fostering increased the numbers of "Anti-Government Elements" amid the widespread frustration among villagers who are simply not receiving the kinds of help that they really need.

Districts and villages, however, are the backbone of Afghanistan. It is here that attempts to generate real change should begin. Such change, however, requires contact and dialogue with the people concerned. Donor nations need to make decisions on what aid is to be made available in consultation with the people who will be receiving it. Respect needs to be paid to the cultural and tribal systems governing villagers, and to the needs and opinions of the villagers themselves.

Eight hours spent on or alongside a donkey may seem a poor solution to Afghanistan's woes, but many more of those hours need to be spent for the sake of the peaceful rebuilding of that shattered nation, and they would repay our investment handsomely.

Inculturation and Intervention in Afghanistan: Perspectives from Contextual Theology

Christopher Hrynkow

Inculturation and Particular Cultures

Inculturation falls into an interesting place within the emerging "new" contextual theologies. It is not so much a theological school, but is rather a contested term with deep significance for what it means to be Christian and be Church in the current phase of human intellectual and social being. Inculturation is so intimately connected to reading "the signs of the times"[1] that it is often referred to as contextualization. However, before offering a working definition of inculturation, it is important to touch upon a related concept from the disciplines of anthropology and sociology: enculturation.

The term enculturation attempts to name the phenomenon of established cultures being transmitted to new members. Working in this area, Peace and Conflict studies theorist Kevin Avruch, for instance, has commented that culture is dynamic and derivative of human experience. He therefore concludes that the transmission of culture is a key factor in the evolution of conflict.[2] It is therefore, also central to the transformation of conflict and the installation of forms of good governance. Culture can be learned through customs, practices, language, beliefs, symbols, social practices and (we should remember) institutions.[3] As such, culture's mean-

---

[1] See John XXIII, Encyclical letter *Pacem in Terris*, 127-129.
[2] See Kevin Avruch, *Culture and Conflict Resolution* (Washington, D.C.: United States Institute of Peace, 1998).
[3] Lisa Schirch, *Ritual and Symbol in Peacebuilding* (West Hartford, CT: Kumarian Press, 2004), and John Paul Lederach, *Preparing for Peace: Conflict Transformation Across Cultures* (Syracuse, NY: Syracuse University Press, 1995).

ing is often encoded in stories that provide intergenerational continuity, and explain the meaning of life.[4] Additionally, in the present sense, culture is a key means through which a group can shape its history, identity and ideology, as well as other elements of a worldview. These dynamics allow for dialogical processes of meaning making. Such processes in turn, allow a specific group to make sense of its milieu.[5] Consequently, life becomes predictable to the extent of allowing individuals to understand others in their own cultural group so that they can interact comfortably with each other.[6] It follows that when people move outside their own culture and continue to work from their own cultural lenses and cues, the result can be a state of culture shock when individuals have to adjust to unfamiliar socioeconomic, cultural, and political systems.[7] As will be shown more clearly below, if in Afghanistan we are looking to assist in establishing good governance we must also seek to avoid and mitigate the conflict-fostering outcome that can accompany severe culture shock precipitated by such dynamics.

Invoking similar sets of meanings, "inculturation" is used to refer to the interaction between Christianity and local cultures. The tensions associated with such interaction are not new; indeed, it can be easily read into the Council of Jerusalem's decision to allow non-Hebraic forms into the Jesus movement, as described in the New Testament Book of Acts.[8] However, a specific focus on these processes is evident from the use of "inculturation" in contemporary theology. Nonetheless, as Jesuit theologian Ary

---

[4] Jessica Senehi, "Constructive Storytelling: A Peace Process," in *Peace and Conflict Studies* 9 (2002): 41-63.; and Jessica Senehi, "Constructive Storytelling in Inter-communal Conflicts: Building Community, Building Peace," in *Reconcilable Differences: Turning Points in Ethnopolitical Conflict*, ed. Sean Byrne and Cynthia Irvin (West Hartford, CT: Kumarian, 2000), 96-115.
[5] Marc Howard Ross, *The Management of Conflicts: Interpretations and Interests in Comparative Perspectives* (New Haven, CT: Yale University Press, 1993).
[6] Raymond Cohen, *Negotiating Across Cultures: International Communication in an Interdependent World* (Washington DC: United States Institute of Peace Press, 1999); and Douglas Fry, *The Human Potential for Peace: An Anthropological Challenge to Assumptions about War and Violence* (Oxford: Oxford University Press, 2006).
[7] Hamdesa Tuso, "Indigenous Processes of Conflict Resolution in Oromo society," in *Traditional Cures for Modern African Conflicts: African Conflict Cedicine*, ed. William Zartman (Boulder, CO: Lynne Rienner Publishers, 2000), 79-94.
[8] A description of the retrospectively labelled "Council of Jerusalem" is found in Acts: 15. This passage depicts the decision made by the early followers of Jesus that one did not have to become culturally Jewish (*e.g.* keep kosher or, if male, be circumcised) to follow him.

Crollius points out, one of the major problems when dealing with the term's connotations is that "inculturation" is a neologism that has been used in multiple ways since being coined in the 1960s.[9] In the Roman Catholic tradition, an official definition of inculturation was offered by John Paul II via two papal encyclicals. For the sake of clarity, I will use these two selections as the basis for my working definition:

> a) The incarnation of the Gospel in native cultures and also the introduction of these cultures into the life of the church;[10] [and]
> b) [t]he intimate transformation of authentic cultural values through their integration in Christianity and the insertion of Christianity in the various cultures.[11]

At the outset, it should be noted that, at its centre, inculturation represents a tension. This tension is one of purpose and delineation; that is, one of boundaries. Such a tension is based in the fear of going too far in a direction set by the local culture. Although both terms are contested, syncretism (most especially in certain Protestant traditions) can often be considered in a negative light, while inculturation can denote a positive process. However, Jesuit theologian Carl Starkloff claimed that such a normative categorization is representative of a false dichotomy. Building on work of Eric Voegelin, Starkloff reforms this acute dichotomy between good inculturation and bad syncretism with his notion of "syncretic process", which he considered "a *de facto* human dynamism that is not going to be dismissed, however critical we may have to be in studying it. It is, in...[his] theological opinion, 'connatural' with, not the heritage of sin, but a laudable desire of humans for unity within diversity." [12]

---

[9] See Ary Ross Crollius, "What is so New about Inculturation?," *Gregorianum* 59 (1978): 721-738.
[10] John Paul II, Encyclical letter *Slavorum Aposotoli*, 21.
[11] John Paul II, Encyclical letter *Redemptoris Missio*, 52. Here, John Paul II is reworking the definition of inculturation offered in the final report of the extraordinary Synod of Bishops in 1985: "Because the Church is communion, which joins diversity and unity in being present throughout the world, it takes from every culture all that it encounters of positive value. Yet inculturation is different from a simple external adaptation, because it means the intimate transformation of authentic cultural values through their integration in Christianity in the various human cultures." (Extraordinary Synod of Bishops, "The Church, in the Word of God, Celebrates the Mysteries of Christ for the Salvation of the World," http://www.saintmike.org/Library/Synod_Bishops/Final_Report1985.html, 1985, II, C, 4.)
[12] Carl Starkloff, *A Theology of the In-Between: The Value of Syncretic Process* (Milwaukee: Marquette University Press, 2002), 11.

According to this reasoning, the syncretic process itself is neutral and the moral dimensions are infused by actors and interpreters. It follows that dichotomous comparisons will break down when it is understood that both inculturation and syncretism in fact refer to the same phenomenon.[13] Further, both syncretism and inculturation may either be positive or negative depending upon how the phenomenon is infused with value; the key is that both terms will always represent the tension that accompanies the syncretic process. This tension can be summed up in two questions: First, how much accommodation with the local culture is authentically possible when seeking to remain true to the Gospel message? And second, is there an irreducible core of Christianity that must be retained in every context for the result to be considered authentically Christian?

In this sense, inculturation is representative of what Starkloff labels "a theology of the in-between"; of what happens when a local culture meets a necessarily already inculturated form of Christianity. This concept can first be seen in St. Augustine's *The City of God*, where the "in-between" is the meeting place between the *civitas Dei* (the City of God) and the *civitas terrena* (the earthly city), or, in other words, the meeting place between the imminent and the transcendent. Practically speaking, the in-between can mean the place "where faith and culture interact to both contend and complement each other, and to join in a higher synthesis."[14] This meeting place inevitably becomes a source of tension through the dynamic, continuous and interactive process of communication between the two parties. In terms of this essay, the in-between is considered to be the space where, for example, the trans-cultural vision of Christianity is concretely expressed (incarnated, if you will) in a particular culture. Indeed, it may only be in such a specific contextual space that any trans-cultural vision can ultimately gain vital expression. Thankfully, however, resultant space can be potentially liberating and enriching for both Christianity and the local culture. As will be argued below, such a syncretic process may also be in operation when trans-contextual values of good governance take on vital forms in specific contexts.

Taking into consideration the above-mentioned information, in terms of a working definition, inculturation can thus be seen as signifying an open, mutually self-mediating[15] and symbiotic dialogue between Christianity and a local culture that changes each dialogue partner through a dy-

---

[13] Ibid.

[14] Ibid., 53.

[15] This borrows Jesuit philosopher and theologian Bernard Lonergan's term from another context. See Bernard Lonergan, "The Mediation of Christ in Prayer," *Method: Journal of Lonergan Studies* 2, no. 1 (1984): 1-20.

namic process. Inculturation conceived in this sense has the potential to save faith from imperialism because of its inherent respect for the local. Simultaneously, it can also serve to enrich the Christian tradition. The Jesuit missions to the native peoples in the Portuguese territories prior to the suppression of the order in the 18th Century or Mateo Ricci's Chinese Rites may been examples of such a symbiotic relationship.[16] In the present day, inculturation-type phenomena have proved immensely valuable for responding to the ecological crisis from a Christian point of view.[17] For instance, dialogue with indigenous and eastern religions has helped to reinforce and rediscover a strong basis for a necessarily emerging (given the realities of the ecological crisis) Christian ecological ethic that is engendering new ways of being in relation to the natural world.[18]

Inculturation, Peacebuilding and Good Governance

A major hope of an increasing number of people who work for an end to violent conflict around the world is that ways of co-existing together in peace can be found without cultural uniformity. As we saw above, through his experiences Karl Starfkloff was able to discern a laudable desire on the part of humans for unity in diversity. In the same vein, the Chief Rabbi of the Commonwealth, Jonathan Sacks, calls for tolerance in an age of extremism based on a recognition of "the dignity of difference."[19] One way to ground this type of hope is in the great potential that exists for a trans-contextual culture of peace to gain vital expression in particular cultures. By identifying common ideals in each culture, this trans-contextual vision proposes the existence of a broader ethic that can help shape what Quaker activist scholar Elise Boulding, following the lead of a United Nations Initiative, calls a culture of peace. As Boulding states, "the main point

---

[16] For a discussion of the Jesuit missions in the Portuguese territories during the 17th and 18th centuries see Clement J. McNaspy, *Lost Cities of Paraguay: Art and Architecture in the Jesuit Reductions 1607-1767* (Chicago: Loyola University Press, 1982). A substantive review of what is commonly referred to as the Chinese rites controversy can be found in Andrew C. Ross, *A Vision Betrayed: The Jesuits in China and Japan, 1542-1742* (Maryknoll, NY: Orbis, 1994).

[17] Thomas Berry's entire project can be seen in terms opening up Christian and Western ways of being to dialogue with cultures from both the past and present time that have ways of being which coalesce with integrated ecological ethics. See Thomas Berry, *The Dream of the Earth* (San Francisco: Sierra Club Books, 1990).

[18] See Thomas Berry, *The Great Work: Our Way into the Future* (New York: Bell Tower Press, 2000).

[19] Jonathan Sacks, *The Dignity of Difference: How to Avoid the Clash of Civilizations* (London: Continuum, 2003), vii.

about a culture of peace is that it deals creatively with difference and conflict."[20] Combining insights from Boulding's work and the concept of inculturation with this trans-contextual labelling, we can see a means through which substantive peace has the ability to be realized in different particularities. However, it is also noteworthy in this regard that due to a certain cosmopolitan quality, the trans-cultural vision itself, in a relevant sense, has a form of independent existence. It follows that, although necessarily realized in a particular culture, expressions of the trans-contextual culture of peace will share certain similarities.

A lively expression of syncretic process is generated when there is an authentic dialogue between the trans-contextual desire for peace and the local culture. This is something akin to what peace and conflict studies theorist Viktoria Hertling has labelled "countering a culture of violence."[21] Yet, notice the subtle but important distinction I am making here: it is not that a separate culture of peace needs to be established. Sequestration is not what I am advocating in relation to individuals embedded in their cultures. Rather, I am simply proposing what may be becoming increasingly obvious: that both good governance initiatives and peacebuilding work is more likely to be successful when people are given the option of living out key elements of their local culture while simultaneously expressing the trans-contextual vision of peace.

Such a statement recognizes that an authentic vision of peace can be separated from Western values. This is a way to move peacebuilding and good governance efforts beyond the sometimes quite legitimate accusations they face of being culturally imperialist. Within this movement, diversity and complexification are assets, not liabilities. In other words, the social organism will not be as healthy if it is reduced to a monoculture.[22] In short, I am suggesting that vital outworkings of the trans-contextual peace ethic will be advantaged when they can take on local forms of cultural expression. Dialogue and storytelling-based models of peacebuilding have implicitly recognized this truth for some time.[23] It is for this reason,

---

[20] Elise Boulding, "Building a Culture of Peace: Some Priorities," *National Women's Studies Association Journal*, 13, no. 2 (2001): 56.

[21] With this point I am simply exploring the value of imaging culture in a slightly different manner. This is not, of course, to say that I do not support Viktoria Hertling's laudable work in peace education. See Viktoria Hertling, "Countering a "Culture of Violence." Can it be Done?," *Peace and Change* 32, no.1 (January 2007): 78.

[22] See John Dear, *The God of Peace: Towards a Theology of Non-Violence* (Maryknoll, NY: Orbis, 1994), 99.

[23] See Dan Bar-On, *Bridging the Gap: Storytelling as A Way to Work Through Political and Collective Hostilities* (Hamburg: Köber-Stiftung, 2000); Jessica Se-

for example, that Jean Paul Lederach's "elicitive model" of conflict transformation is able to see the local culture as a resource, wherein "participants are capable of identifying and naming their own realities and tools."[24] The importance of tapping into this essential feature of the local context is further highlighted by considering anthropologist Clifford Gertz's discussion of "cultural patterns." According to Gertz's field-based analysis, '[c]ultural patterns—religious, philosophical, aesthetic, scientific, ideological—are "programs"; they provide a template or blueprint for the organization of social and psychological processes, much as genetic systems provide such a template for the organization of organic processes.'[25]

Ignoring these cultural patterns, realities and tools can be counterproductive and can generate grave results. This malaise is demonstrated by the tragedies that occurred at some Canadian "Indian" residential schools. As the resultant stories abuse make all too evident, when Christianity tries to impose another culture on vital peoples the results can be disastrous.[26] To counteract this tendency, Eboussis Boulagna, in his constructive study, *Christianity Without Fetishes*, recommends that Christianity be removed from its white middle-class expression when it is expressed in a tribal context. In this way, an authentically indigenous African Christianity would stand against the previously accepted notion that in order for one to become Christian, one would have to reject the entirety of one's former culture and embrace the white, middle-class Christian culture absolutely. This "necessary break" thesis assumed that the inescapable requirement of accepting Christianity was to take on the Western forms that the religion necessarily entailed (*i.e.* fetishes).[27] Boulanga rejects the imposed culture of white middle-class bourgeois Christianity. However, he is not arguing

---

nehi and Sean Byrne, "From Violence Toward Peace: The Role of Storytelling for Youth Healing and Political Empowerment after Social Conflict," in *Troublemakers or Peacemakers? Youth and Post-Accord Peacebuilding,* ed. Siobhan McEvoy-Levy (South Bend, IN: University of Notre Dame Press, 2006), 235-258; and Lisa Schirch, *Ritual And Symbol In Peacebuilding* (West Hartford, CT: Kumarian Press, 2004).

[24] Lederach, Preparing for Peace, 100.

[25] Clifford Geertz, *The Interpretation of Cultures* (New York: Basic Books, 1973), 216.

[26] In a report given to the author by a man who identified himself as a "residential school survivor," theologian Kevin Arnett discusses many mistakes made in terms of Christian cultural imperialism in the Canadian context. See Kevin D. Anett, *Hidden From History: The Canadian Holocaust* (The Truth Commission into Genocide in Canada, 2001).

[27] Boulaga is speaking about fetishes here in their anthropological (i.e. non-sexual) sense.

for the complete rejection of everything in the Western mentality and does not desire the "pristine restoration of ancient customs or traditional ways of thinking."[28] Rather, he seeks the transformation of existing relationships and the overcoming of this notion of the "necessary break," which would allow Africans space to "recapture" Christianity, potentially resulting in the integral renewal of the "tribal person" and the tribal relationships that were previously lost.[29]

Reconstituting trans-contextual ideas along lines that not only are responsive to but also shape the local culture in contextually more peaceful ways represents a difficult task. Here, theological thought can also be helpful. We might say, for instance, that a vocational level of commitment is necessary because peacebuilding and the establishment of good governance is difficult work.[30] Such integral thought also raises the possibility that sustainable peace can be achieved in situations where peacebuilders hold religious levels of commitment. In the peacebuilding context, such commitment requires understanding of and dialogue with the local culture. Peacebuilders working on this vocational level cannot just "parachute in" to a situation and be effective. An analogous situation can be found when Western middle-class conflict resolution practitioners encounter indigenous people and proceed on the assumption that there is little to no peacebuilding capacity present in the local culture or good governance capacity in the local. As I shall argue in reference to *Shura* system in what follows, such a perspective ignores a significant resource in particular cultures that emphasizes the resolution of conflicts amicably through customary institutions such as a council of elders, clan mothers, dialogue, or traditional cultural rituals like the *palaver*. The way that top-down approaches to ending violence often fail to appreciate or collaborate with these traditional mechanisms of resolving conflicts can only hamper their effectiveness.[31]

---

[28] F. Eboussi Boulaga, *Christianity Without Fetishes: An African Critique and Recapture of Christianity* (Maryknoll, NY: Orbis, 1984), 58.

[29] Ibid., 64.

[30] Lederach makes this vocation-related point with his concept of the moral imagination, which he describes as understanding relationships to be at "the centre and horizon the human community... [The moral imagination] therefore develops a vocation based on an unconditional commitment to build human relationships." John Paul Lederach, *The Moral Imagination: The Art and Soul of Building Peace* (New York: Oxford University Press, 2005), 61.

[31] For a discussion of such matters in an African context see Hamdesa Tuso, "Indigenous Processes of Conflict Resolution in Oromo Society" in *Traditional Cures for Modern Conflicts: African Conflict "Medicine"*, ed. William Zartman (Boulder, CO: Lynne Rienner, 1999).

Instead of always employing a top-down methodology, effective peacebuilders have to commit to walking peacefully with the local peoples (*i.e.* acting in solidarity). At the same time, those sent to help establish governance initiatives must interact with the local culture on a deep level to foster the growth of local capacity. Such holistic commitment to a vision of peace and good governance, in thought, heart and action, has the power to transform cultures toward more peaceful ways of being. To bring to mind some of the potential of vocational-type commitment in relation to peacebuilding and good governance along cross-cultural lines, consider Gertz's statement:

> as it moves beyond realities of everyday life the religious perspective differs from the common-sensical reality into wider ones which correct and complete them, and its defining concern is not action upon those wider realities but rather acceptance of them, faith in them. It differs from the scientific perspective in that it questions the realities of everyday life not out of an institutionalized scepticism which dissolves the world's givenness into a swirl of probabilistic hypotheses, but in terms of what it takes to be wider nonhypothetical truths. Rather, than detachment, its watchword is commitment; rather than analysis, encounter.[32]

When such an encounter is predicated upon religious-type vocational commitment, the results can be transformative. As Bernard Lonergan shapes it, herein we would be shifting the received idea of community and thus would be changing reality itself.[33] Gertz is also helpful in this area for reminding us of the power that religious thinking has to shape community:

> Religion is sociologically interesting not because, as vulgar positivism would have it, it describes the social order (which in so far as it does, it does not only vary obliquely but very incompletely), but because, like environment, political power, wealth, jural obligation, personal affection, and the sense of beauty, it shapes it.[34]

---

[32] Geertz, *Interpretation of Cultures,* 112.

[33] As the prelude to his 1992 essay *Bernard Lonergan and The Community of Canadians*, Frederick Crowe conducts a fictitious interview with the then deceased Lonergan. In this interview, based on past personal conversations, Crowe has Lonergan make the link between perception (in terms of the image of community) and reality with the following words, "[t]o change the received idea of the community is to change the reality itself." From Frederick E. Crowe, *Bernard Lonergan and the Community of Canadians: An Essay in Aid of Canadian Identity* (Toronto: Lonergan Research Institute and Canadian Institute of Jesuit Studies, 1992), 12.

[34] Geertz, *Interpretation of Cultures,* 119.

Additionally, this concept of dynamic inculturation informs the special tension for the human rights discourses within the peacebuilding and good governance paradigms, as represented in the question of how much accommodation is authentically possible within a local culture. In asserting that the gospel has a core that must be retained, inculturation shows us that there are some things which are absolutes. In a Christian framing, these absolutes may be reflected in a creedal statement; applied to areas of good governance and peacebuilding it would be difficult to see how a situation of substantive peace could coalesce with institutionalized slavery or organized killing of other humans. However, while making the case for a normative core in relation to the trans-contextual culture of peace, the concept of inculturation simultaneously challenges the human rights discourse to consider the possibly that some of these absolutes that form that core may lie outside individualist Western notions of right.

Yet, at the same time, these concepts serve to illustrate how the human rights methodology might also provide the best means of protecting the authentically-discerned core. Employed in this manner, they can help us to envision a situation where authentically constructed human rights provide a basis for family life and civil society.[35] Such a basis, almost necessarily, precedes a peaceful political society. In that abuses of human rights are symptomatic of violent tendencies in a culture, they would also provide a means to assess the health of the social organism. For instance, a substantively peaceful society is unlikely to engage in torture.[36] Additionally, basic economic rights are important in the sense that, as embodied beings, humans need a certain level of material wealth in order to function properly and to fulfil their moral commitments to the entire community. On this point, for example, it is evident that ecological conservation and biodiversity preservation become somewhat moot points when the last dodo bird is hopping along the beach in front of a mother wanting to feed her starving children. Basic economic human rights stand as a testament to the fact that it is better not to put people in such a difficult situation when there exists the means to feed everybody. Indeed, under conditions of ex-

---

[35] For a similar viewpoint, see Sally Engle Merry, *Human Rights and Gender Violence: Translating International Law into Local Justice* (Chicago, IL: University of Chicago Press 2005).

[36] For a discussion of the incompatibility of a peaceful society with the political use of torture, see Ezat Mossallanejed, *Torture in the Age of Fear* (Hamilton: Saraphim, 2005).

treme poverty or inequality, conflict and violence can only be encouraged.[37]

In the above example, we can see some evidence for the proposition that for peacebuilding to be sustainable it must address conflict on many levels (and, therefore, as I will argue below with reference to the work of Câmara, it also has to understand violence in a differentiated manner). As Lederach notes, sustainable reconciliation in divided societies is only possible when truth, mercy, forgiveness and peace meet and are balanced within an integrative peacebuilding framework that is aware of structural issues and takes a long-term view.[38] One image that can inform efforts to achieve this situation of integrative peace is mediated by the concept of inculturation. Such an image reminds us that the resulting peace will most sustainably be a peace of the in-between, wherein the trans-contextual vision of peace is authentically expressed in a particular culture. This integrative peace emerges in dialogue with the local culture. It follows that the prerequisite dialogical process of the in-between is not representative of relativism, but is, rather, a type of complexification producing dynamic results. It should be remembered that as a consequence of this totality and dynamism, the results of the process are unlikely to ever achieve closure.[39]

This dynamism, however, need not be viewed as problematic. Building on Lederach's family of peace analogy, in which "voices of Truth, Mercy, Justice, and Peace are imaged as social energies that are alive and present in any conflict",[40] this dynamism allows peace and conflict practitioners to harness these social energies and work towards a synergetic situation of ecological balance or health among the various objectives in view. Recalling Gertz's and Lonergan's thoughts presented above, such a dynamic balance would help move cultures towards what Lederach labels constructive social change, "the pursuit of moving relationships from fear, mutual

---

[37] Sean Byrne and Cynthia Irvin, "A Shared Common Sense: Perceptions of the Material Effects and Impacts of Economic Growth in Northern Ireland," *Civil Wars* 5 (2002): 55-86, and John Burton, ed., *Conflict: Human Needs Theory* (London: Macmillan, 1990).

[38] See John Paul Lederach, *Building Peace: Sustainable Reconciliation in Divided Societies* (Washington, D.C.: United States Institute of Peace, 1997).

[39] Carl Starkloff. *A Theology of the In-Between: The Value of Syncretic Process* (Milwaukee: Marquette University Press, 2002), 52.

[40] John Paul Lederach, "Civil Society and Reconciliation," in *Turbulent Peace: The Challenges of Managing International Conflict*, ed. Chester A. Crocker, Fen Osler Hampson and Pamela Aall (Washington, D.C.: United States Institute of Peace, 2001), 848.

recrimination and violence towards those characterized by love, mutual respect and proactive engagement."[41]

Peacebuilding and Good Governance Initiatives

Application of ideas and theory is a key part of contextual theology, peacebuilding and good governance methodologies. Theory in all three fields is concerned with effecting and facilitating tangible results. It is important that such a praxis-based application works towards "sustainable peace" in any given context. As I have suggested above, syncretic processes should be active when any a trans-contextual vision of peace receives expression in a given particular context. The recent history of Afghanistan demonstrates the importance of having syncretic processes mediated by a concern for authentic results. So the question becomes 'what would this process of the "in-between" look like in Afghanistan'? The implication of the theoretical considerations that have been presented above is, of course, that I cannot provide a complete answer to that question because I am not sufficiently embedded in the Afghan context. However, the truth is that part of the point of allowing the concept of inculturation to inform peacebuilding and good governance initiatives in Afghanistan is that it can help us to grasp that all the Western experts working together on the most cordial terms cannot come up with a complete answer to this inherently complex question.

So, in a real sense, all I can authentically suggest is that if we in the West are to continue to intervene for the purposes of peacebuilding and establishing good governance in Afghanistan, we might do well to undertake these interventions with a different emphasis than has occasionally been in evidence. That said, I realise the problem of ignoring the importance of the local is not universal—there are Western people who take the methodology for peacebuilding and good governance implied by the concept of inculturation quite seriously. Indeed, it was one of those individuals, the distinguished Canadian politician and humanitarian activist Flora MacDonald, who inspired the proposal for this particular paper.

In November of 2008, Ms. MacDonald delivered the 6th annual *Sol Kanee Lecture on Peace and Justice* in Winnipeg, Manitoba. That day, she spoke forcibly and eloquently about the "other Afghanistan."[42] In that fo-

---

[41] Lederach, The Moral Imagination, 42.
[42] Flora MacDonald. "Peacebuilding, Development, Hope... The Other Afghanistan," Nov. 19, 2008, *6th Annual Sol Kanee Lecture on Peace and Justice* (DVD recording held at the Arthur V. Mauro Centre for Peace and Justice, St. Paul's College, University of Manitoba).

rum and in her presentation to the parliamentary committee looking into the future of Canada's role in the present intervention,[43] Ms. MacDonald challenged the story that most of hear about Afghanistan. She did so by upholding the substantial progress made in terms of peacebuilding, development, good government and hope in Bamyan province. Stories from this part of Afghanistan fit well with the framework for this paper in numerous ways because Bamyan is a place of syncretism. Both presently (as I shall demonstrate below) and in the past, being the home of Greco-Buddhist art, processes of the in-between have been active in that province. Indeed, it was the showpiece destruction of such syncretic symbols from Bamyan province that brought Afghanistan to public attention when the Giant Buddha statues were demolished with explosives as part of a public spectacle by the Taliban government in March 2001.

In reference to the work of the NGO, Future Generations Canada (FGC), Ms. MacDonald raised several relevant points that accord with the general theme of this essay. Noteworthy is her explanation of the operating framework of the NGO in question. FGC, she asserted, recognises the complexity and difficulty of the Afghan context, including the fact that it is the third poorest nation in the world.[44] For this reason, FGC chooses to work with the local people in a spirit of what a Roman Catholic theology might label solidarity and subsidiarity. Thus, there is only one full time employee working for the NGO in Afghanistan, Abdula Barat, whom Ms. MacDonald convinced to leave a high paying job in Ottawa to return to his homeland in a facilitator and coordinator role for FGC.

It is especially noteworthy, in terms of this paper's theme that this NGO's main focus is on governance. Specifically, this focus on governance takes the form of support for renewal and revival of the *Shura* (local council) system.[45] Recognizing the fact that governance initiatives cannot take place in a vacuum, this basic focus has organically led on to work in other areas: help with schools, solar panels installed in family homes (for electric lighting, in partnership with Norwegian Church Aid), tree planting, health, clean water and cultural support. The beneficial results of the solar panel programming are obvious: "[t]he artificial light immediately

---

[43] Ms. MacDonald raised a similar set of points in her presentation to the Canadian House of Commons committee looking into the intervention in Afghanistan: Flora MacDonald, "Remarks by the Hon. Flora MacDonald to the Parliamentary Committee on Foreign Affairs—Afghanistan," from http://www.futuregen.ca/news_003.php.

[44] MacDonald, "Peacebuilding."

[45] Future Generations Canada Staff, "Our Projects: Governance," from http://www.futuregen.ca/governance.php.

transforms the lives of the villagers. Children are able to study in the evenings, women can do weaving, and men can attend to their many chores. Many tasks are simplified by the use of battery power."[46] Yet, the initiative was a simple one. This is in sharp contrast to imagery invoked by a photograph from *Time* magazine's April 20, 2009 issue, presented under the theme "how not to lose in Afghanistan" which depicts male U.S. solders eating with locals at night (undoubtedly a positive step), lighting the room, indeed, but with battery powered headlamps while their Afghan brethren sit in the shadows.[47] As will be more fully argued at the end of this section, the more emancipatory initiatives represented by the work of FCG are supported by, and in turn reinforce, a political climate that empowers women.

What Ms. MacDonald demonstrates poignantly is that the local capacity is present in Afghanistan to start to build up the trans-contextual culture of peace. It is, therefore, important that the intervention makes a concerted effort to foster these elements. However, this can be hard to accomplish. There are layers of cultural meaning invoked by both the "insurgency" and those who make up the foreign presence in Afghanistan. However, what else can Westerners in the conflict authentically do? Part of the issue here is that the West, often working with a national security frame of mind, has picked and chosen its "friends" before helping to build the military capacity of both Afghanistan and Pakistan, along with several other now less than friendly political actors in the region. Deliberation in a deeper sense would lead us to the conclusion that such examples of militaristic-styled "support" are instances of failed—or minimally of abortive—policy.

As a constructive alternative, we might give peacebuilding and good governance initiatives our support in a more sustainable manner by working from different framings. Christianity has always held a certain transnational character just given the fact that the content of faith implies that something matters beyond the dictates of the nation. Taking that insight and applying it to a global security framework, we might say in the present context that "in-between" forms of peace and good governance allow us to abandon concepts of national interest in favour of emphasizing the importance of Rabbi Sacks' "dignity of difference" in an intentional, integrated global sense. In short, a methodology of peacebuilding and good governance of in the in-between affirms, along with Sacks, that "[d]ifference

---

[46] MacDonald, "Remarks...to the Parliamentary Committee on Foreign Affairs—Afghanistan."
[47] This photograph, by Adam Ferguson, is reproduced on *Time's* website at http://www.time.com/time/photogallery/0,29307,1890204_1866751,00.html.

does not diminish; it enlarges the sphere of human possibilities."[48] The more the foreign presence in Afghanistan is concerned with good governance and peacebuilding referenced on this global communitarian level, the less valid the critique of the intervention as being only a matter of Western or in American self-interest becomes, and the stronger the prospects for a sustainable peace.

It follows that if we can participate as global (or cosmological) citizens in these interventions and allow peace and good governance to take on appropriate local forms (as suggested for the Christian by the dynamics of inculturation), then the intervention might cease to contribute to cycles of violence and begin to work in solidarity with the local culture. Reaching a critical mass in this regard will not come through military surges (or even "civilian surges"), but through drawn out processes that create space for local people to establish their own culturally appropriate means of good governance. To see how this transformation is possible we need only to look at the tenacity of the culture of peace in Afghanistan; for peaceful initiatives are able to take root despite everything that is going on around. It requires active deep listening to know what these initiatives need to continue to grow, the type of listening that can only be effected when "us and them" dichotomies are broken down and people are given space to form identities in relationship with each other, as an alternative to the foreign versus local identity that is encouraged by military engagement. As Flora MacDonald recognized, conflict pursued along militaristic lines often forces people to take unwelcome "sides."[49] Even unwelcome identities forged under such conditions may be difficult to break. In this sense, it is true that one of the best recruiting tools for the Taliban has been the foreign intervention.

In order to reverse such trends towards conflict-inducing forms of difference and violent identity formation, renewed efforts at substantive dialogue are necessary. Informed by the concept of inculturation, initial dialogues might focus on the question of human rights, held in tension with cultural and communitarian rights instruments (an area in which Canadians, among others, might have some skills to share). Further, the goal of such dialogue could be to help discern a core (roughly parallel to a creedal statement, explicitly crafted beyond existing constitutional arrangements) that can be invoked in trans-cultural terms to show a realm of common belief. The resultant mutually held and creed-like understanding of a shared core of human, cultural and communitarian rights could in turn be

---

[48] Jonathan Sacks, *The Dignity of Difference: How to Avoid the Clash of Civilizations* (London: Continuum, 2003), 209.
[49] MacDonald, "Peacebuilding."

used to foster a dynamic expression of the trans-contextual culture of peace. Perhaps, ritualizing these results in both our cultures would be helpful in terms of building a solidarist and subsidiarity-based framework of aid and intervention. Considering Canada's role in Afghanistan in particular, a deliberately and deliberatively enacted ritual performed in both countries could be helpful in this regard. If we accept Gregory Baum's argument that theology is increasingly peace and social justice oriented,[50] then local Canadian places of worship or schools might provide a link here. For instance, consider the proto-ritual (apparently motivated by a front page story in the local newspaper), at a Mass in which I was in attendance on April 25, 2009, where we were asked to pray for: (1) a 21 year old soldier, Karine Blais, who was killed in Afghanistan, (2) her family and (3) peace for the Afghan people and all peoples of the world.[51] This holistically solidarist petition might point the way forward for a future set of rituals that can help move the whole conflict toward conciliation.

As it stands, the story of Bamyan, as recounted by Flora McDonald, upholds the possibility that syncretic processes might be pointing the way forward in Afghanistan. Supported by the political climate in the province, wherein the people have a women governor (an appointee), female members of the *Loya Jirga* have been elected beyond the constitutionally set quota, the *Shura* in Bamyan town is headed by a woman and has 40 percent female representation, Flora MacDonald reminds us that one of things that makes Bamyan province different is the women.[52] These levels of governance also provide for important nonviolent conflict transformation mechanisms, where people can resolve their disputes at the local level and through enforceable regulatory frameworks without resorting to physical violence.[53] In this context, FGC seeks to learn from the Afghan people themselves, showing their commitment to what we might term a governance of the in-between. The prospects for the realisation of this governance of the in-between are buttressed as Afghans learn, as Ms. MacDonald phrases it, "to believe in themselves" as members of a fledgling democracy, despite the pull toward being a failed state in the current difficult situation.

---

[50] See Gregory Baum, *Amazing Church: A Catholic Theologian Remembers a Half-Century of Change* (Maryknoll, NY: Orbis Books, 2005).
[51] Andy Blatchford, "Funeral held for slain Trooper Karine Blais," April, 24, 2009, from http://cnews.canoe.ca/CNEWS/Canada/2009/04/24/9232591-cp.html.
[52] MacDonald, "Remarks…to the Parliamentary Committee on Foreign Affairs—Afghanistan."
[53] MacDonald, "Peacebuilding."

Recognizing the "Other Afghanistan"

As Flora MacDonald demonstrates, when we start our investigations from a place of reframing we can more fully grasp the fact that there are elements of the culture of peace present in the present day Afghanistan. Judging from most media reports we see in North America, one could be forgiven for thinking that these elements are not present at all. However, when we look more deeply for examples of local initiatives in peacebuilding and good governance, we can find them without difficulty.

From this place of re-imaging, and buttressed by the analysis of inculturation presented above, I would like to posit nine significant points that may (to use theological language) be proclaimed by the prophets of a culture of peace. This is not to suggest that these are the complete answers to the problem of Afghanistan, but merely that these are claims of the sort that need to be made (from a Western perspective informed by inculturation theory) in order to reframe the debate so that authentic dialogue might start within the local context in Afghanistan.

In invoking the language of prophetic witness, I am not attempting to assert a type of knowing that corresponds to a culture of the expert. Rather, what I am asserting, along with Flora MacDonald I believe, is that there organically arises from the situation of Afghanistan the need for prophetic voice amongst people who understand inculturation (and similar) processes. It follows that what I am speaking about here is something akin to the tradition of the reformist prophet. In a way, this tradition evokes prophetic voice that (1) may already ring true to hearer, but (2) nonetheless urge us to reconsider the function of our cultures, the organization of our societies and, when applied to this case, our normative methodologies for intervention.

Without in any way asserting divine sanction for them, I offer the following suggestions for "prophetic" consideration in this regard:

Governance exists outside of the central unitary state

This point should not be too difficult for Canadians (among others) to accept, given our federalist and multicultural (at the very least bi-cultural) system of government. The United States is also a federalist state, as are a range of our other NATO allies, yet perhaps too much of the "intervention energy" has focused on the establishment of a unitary state centred on Kabul.

Local power in Afghanistan does not exist only in militaristic forms

The case of the Shura demonstrates this truth. But, as in any society, there is more to the political arrangements of Afghanistan than is often assumed in the West. Also, in the absence of a belief in the value of a governance of the in-between, the distinction between militaristic and other forms of local governance may collapse. The key such a malaise may be to find ways for people to feel secure enough that they turn to local and national conflict resolution mechanisms. Only so will recourse to violence as a means to settle disputes be no longer normative within the borders of Afghanistan.

Expressions of the culture of peace do exist in Afghanistan.

Afghan culture and the local cultures in that country are not wholly violent. As implied above, the stories we tell ourselves about Afghanistan have the capacity to cloud our judgement in this regard. If we take the issue of framing seriously, these images may be unduly clouding the intervention and perhaps only lending force to a violent insurgency that responds to militarism and threat with physical violence and force.

The concept of subsidiarity as foundational

It is important to recognise how this principle works in Europe and can be helpful at multiple levels of governance. It is a principle that has allowed countries that were sworn enemies to agree to a host of collective conflict resolution and collective action programming that virtually guarantees that inter-European conflict between Great Britain and France or France and Germany is unlikely to result in war. I would argue that part of the reason subsidiarity has been so effective in the European Union is that is serves to reduce the propensity for the severe culture shock that might have accompanied integration.

As has been mentioned, in the case of Afghanistan, too much Western energy may have been focussed on propping up the central government. Such a focus may, in fact, have the effect of endangering Kabul's own legitimacy in the eyes of the Afghanis, and may have resulted in failure to foster more viable local initiatives. In relation to its culture shock reducing potential, subsidiarity also implies that it is inauthentic and disempowering in a significant sense for "higher" level political actors to invoke power if a more local level can handle the issue in accordance with the dictates of justice. Subsidiarity recognizes the need for central authority, but simultaneously questions the proposition that "the highest" authority should be a location of total power. In this manner, subsidiarity sets out spaces for authentic integration of peacebuilding and good governance initiatives.

Foster a culture of peace in authentic local expressions

The need for such space points to a role for aid not only in economic terms, but also in helping to establish secure conditions in Afghanistan. However, we have to recognize that long-term social development or any sustainable educational project needs local involvement. The commitment needed to build a culture of peace is on the vocational level. As such, fostering a culture of peace is a difficult task even over a lifetime of commitment aimed at fostering nonviolence in any given context. Therefore, such a culture is almost impossible to realise on any short-term "tour of duty" model. This is not to say that military tours of duty should be longer. It does indicate, however, that for any intervention to effective in the long term, a stable and principled commitment to local empowerment and ownership in the fullest senses of those terms must be assumed.

Remember the power of spirals of violence and help to break their hold

There is a Link to the work of Walter Wink and Dom Helder Câmara here, in that we need to see that conflict can take on a sort of spiritual life of its own.[54] In Câmara's thought, as in Wink's exegesis, violence is not conceived as being only related to phenomena such as the use of bombs and guns against each other. In this regard, Câmara, naming something highly relevant to the Afghanistan context, speaks of another destructive power plaguing the planet: the "poverty bomb."[55] Such language is of special value in present circumstances, since it helps to reveal how violence marks most forms of injustice.

Câmara distinguishes between three types of violence that mark the modern world (naming them merely violence no. 1, no. 2 and no. 3). Câmara's image of violence no. 1 is based on the simple truth that poverty kills as surely as the bloodiest war.[56] The mechanisms through which poverty wounds are not only physiological, but are also psychological and

---

[54] Walter Wink, *The Powers That Be: A Theology for the New Millennium* (New York: Galilee Doubleday, 1999), 7.

[55] Helder Câmara, *The Spiral of Violence* (Denville: Dimension Books, 1971), 29.

[56] Ibid., 25.

moral.[57] In this regard, the international structure of global inequality is a major cause of violence because it treats people as sub-human.[58] Viewing the world from this perspective, it becomes ridiculous to claim that any country is truly developed, because even the economically richest countries have internal inequalities supported by repressive systems, which in turn rest upon fractured relationships. Such fractured relationships lie at the centre of violence no. 1, and its presence is never far from the surface in the conflict in Afghanistan.

All too often, the result of this most basic form of violence is revolt. This response provides the nexus for violence no. 2.[59] When faced with injustice and a repressive system that fails to recognize their human dignity, young persons are particularly apt to take the option of violent revolt.[60] Like Wink, Câmara thinks the use of violence by those seeking social transformation to be folly. Specifically, Câmara argues that when violence is embraced as a means of liberation, it only gives the entrenched regime an excuse to use the coercive power of the state against the rebels. In this situation, we witness the emergence of violence no. 3, state-sanctioned violence which groups all dissidents together and provides an excuse for a wide range of repressive and dehumanizing acts, such as torture in the name of anti-communism.[61] Câmara viewed all three of these forms of violence as interconnected examples of violence begetting violence. The implicit danger of leaving the interplay between violence no. 1, no. 2 and no. 3 unchecked is that the entire world would fall into a spiral of violence.[62] It follows that to prevent these spirals from taking on a life of their own and getting out of control in Afghanistan or any other context, we must address the roots of violence at all three levels: poverty (no. 1), the "insurgency" (no. 2), and that perpetrated by the central government and its Western partners (no. 3).

Good government can exist apart from Western liberal models

Rather than using force, a role for Western governments might be to "be the change" they want to see. Particularly, we may wish to look at alternative forms of global, national and local governance as means of establishing a peaceful and tolerant world. The history and reality of present

---

[57] Ibid., 28.
[58] Ibid., 28-30.
[59] Ibid., 30.
[60] Ibid., 50.
[61] Ibid., 32-34.
[62] Ibid., 40.

day Afghanistan would seem to indicate that the establishment of government by outside force is hardly effective. Just as inculturation theory recognizes that there are diverse ways of being authentically Christian, we must more fully integrate the insight that good governance, inclusive of respect for the dignity of peoples and cultures, can exist outside of Western liberal models.

Remember the value of peace witness

In a point not unrelated to "being the change you seek" as mentioned above, the Canadian Mennonite scholar Harry Huebner writes of the arrogance of even the concept of peacebuilding, preferring to use the term "peace witness" from his perspective as a Christian Peace Ethicist.[63] His point concerning arrogance is especially important here, capturing as it does the manner in which we too often think in the West that we have all the answers. Hubris in this Huebnerian sense can severely damage the efficacy of good governance and peacebuilding initiatives.

The dynamic of invitation in Afghanistan

The majority of the population in Afghanistan continues to support a foreign presence in the country.[64] Perhaps, in the concept of inculturation, we might find a metaphor for how to channel this hope—without sending any of our dialogue partners into culture shock. We must look for ways to sustain this sense of invitation, which we are presently in danger of losing. Particular attention ought to be given, therefore, to the kind of ongoing nonviolent work being done by international agencies such as Future Generations Canada in partnership with the people of Bamyan province. If the people of central Afghanistan are to serve as a mimetic model of a governance of the in-between, then they need to know that they are not ignored, and that their example is valued.

Conclusion

It goes without saying that many of these suggestions are already being implemented in Afghanistan, since donors and intervening governments are slowly coming to similar conclusions.. This movement towards inte-

---

[63] Harry Huebner, *Echoes of the Word: Theological Ethics as Rhetorical Practice* (Kitchener: Pandora Press, 2005), 196.
[64] MacDonald, "Peacebuilding."

gration does not, however, detract from the prophetic point of this essay; indeed, it is part of the argument. Theological vision applied to the public sphere helps us see that much of how the future of Afghanistan unfolds will be related to how the values of peace and good governance are supported by and received into the local cultures. Participating in the processes associated with the culture of peace is about a basic choice everyone involved in the Afghanistan context (Canadians included) makes about what kind of world they would like to support. Stemming from a place of critical reflection associated with contextual theological method, this paper is premised on the idea that the choice advocated by Christians ought to be for the culture of peace and good governance against the forces of militarism and violence. If such positive choices parallel our ultimate eschatological or teleological goal for the world, and if we hold the view that human participation in such a reality is paramount, then we can legitimately evoke the language of calling or of vocation in our service in the realm of good governance and peacebuilding. For such reasons, inculturation theory might inform efforts to foster a culture of peace in Afghanistan. Sustainable peace and good government in Afghanistan can not be made to rest solely on establishment of a Weberian bureaucracy, the triumph of a rational-legal form of law, and the imposition of a highly centralized state.

In many Western countries themselves, indeed these very arrangements are being challenged by alternative political and conflict transformation arrangements. In the Canadian context, for instance, sentencing circles are being used with the sanction of the law to respond to transgressions in numerous contexts involving the administration of Aboriginal justice, wherein the dominant Canadian retributive system has proved dismally ineffective. This shift in ways of establishing justice involves a certain devolution of power to the local. The results have been a more effective (and it might be added less expensive) way of "doing justice." Additionally, we now have a situation in Canada whereby the cultural survival of the Cree and Ojibway cultures, for example, is being aided by many of the very Churches and government agencies that were complicit and often actively involved in the destruction of those cultures in generations past. That shift is remarkable. It is also representative of a certain "letting go" in the fostering of space for a certain amount of cultural autonomy. This is movement towards a culture of peace.

A hope-based dimension of social programming, so active in contextual theology, holds that similar movements towards the culture of peace, given adequate space and support, can be established in Afghanistan. Flora MacDonald's and Abdullah Barat's work in its educative and practical aspects points to this possibility. The hope found in Bamyan province can be a source of hope for the entire country. This is the latent potential of locally implemented and, in the terms of this essay, appropriately inculturated, forms of international aid. Such aid can help transform the difficult situation in Afghanistan by allowing for movement, based in solidarity and subsidiarity, towards sustainable peace.

DEATH, INTERPRETATION AND PROPHECY

HOWARD ADELMAN

On Death and Interpretation

On the 3rd of March 2009, three military deaths brought the total toll of Canadian soldiers lost in the Afghan War to 111.[1] Corporal Kenneth Chad O'Quinn (Happy Valley-Goose Bay, Labrador), Warrant Officer Dennis Raymond Brown (St. Catharines, Ontario) and Corporal Dany Olivier Fortin (Saguenay, Québec) were killed by an improvised explosive device while returning to base after helping defuse another improvised explosive device in the Arghandab district of Kandahar in Afghanistan. The three soldiers were members of a small quick-reaction force linked to a provincial reconstruction team. Brown left behind a wife and four children.

For the German philosopher, George Wilhelm Hegel, death is a necessary step in the development of Spirit that brings about the next dialectical phase. When that death is the product of terror, we learn that the route to securing freedom requires the death of self-conscious individuals who give their lives for a cause. Death is the universal work of the march of freedom. "In this its characteristic *work* [namely death], absolute freedom becomes explicitly objective to itself, and self-consciousness learns what absolute freedom in effect is"[2] -- dying for the sake of freedom to confront terror determined to obliterate the essence of what self-conscious freedom is.

That terror was committed on a national scale during the French Revolution and that terror is committed by the Taliban in far off Afghanistan when the fight for freedom operates on a global scale. Death through terror and the terror of death become one. *Terror* is the transition through which the very idea of the Enlightenment is embodied when an abstract idea becomes concrete and material. Death teaches us through the erasure of all

---

[1] In the year that has passed since writing this paper, total Canadian casualties have gone up to 148.
[2] G.W.H. Hegel, *Phenomenology of Spirit*, tr. A.V. Miller (Oxford: Oxford University Press, 1977), §592, pp. 360-361.

distinctions that, although we all must die, there is a difference between self-conscious freedom merely as an abstraction and freedom lived and expressed as self-sacrifice for the right to express one's individual personality.

For the French Jewish philosopher and Talmudist, Emmanuel Levinas, the more significant moment of death is not as a necessary stage of progress, but the moment when death as the moment of progress turns into the impossibility of leading us to the next stage. Instead of positive change, one faces ruin. Instead of work that repairs the world, one faces "unwork" and destruction. Instead of a turning point, we are confronted with wasted time that is trumpeted as "down time" but is really "dead time".[3] Since Judaism is a religion that emphasizes the importance of this life rather than any after life, destruction and death in life assume much greater significance. Talmudic Judaism is a historical rather than a transcendental religion with mystery relegated to the background.[4] God has become a transcendent entity beyond the understanding of anyone.[5]

Religion does have a transcendent horizon but consists of set practices that qualify and modify human conduct within a practical world. There are no ahistorical lessons or guides to conduct that can be derived from the religion even though there are legal and ethical norms that have to be applied to different times and different places. When certain times and places face us with the contradiction between our ideals and the reality that confronts us, when the reality that confronts us threatens to shatter our ideals, we are asked to make decisions and forge new strategies using our ethical norms. However, the application of those guides are not derived from the guides themselves but, in one Talmudic tradition of commentary, are akin to the modern legal method drawn from precedents themselves embodied in historical cases.[6] One applies those guides making peace in Afghanistan after first understanding the current situation in the country and the region as well as the options available, given current debates, for dealing with the war.

---

[3] Cf. Dennis King Keenan, *Death and Responsibility: The "Work" of Levinas* (Albany: State University of New York Press, 1999), 1-2.

[4] Cf. Jacob Neusner, "Explaining the Great Schism: History versus Theology," *Religion* 28 (1998): 139-153.

[5] Avi Sagi, "Yeshayahu Leibowitz—A Breakthrough in Jewish Philosophy: Religion Without Metaphysics," *Religious Studies* 33 (1997): 203-316.

[6] "Chakira" is one method of studying Talmud through analyzing cases and through observing which laws are applicable, arriving at generalities applicable to a new case.

A choice had been made by the polis though the people's representatives in the government of Canada in Parliament to join in the fight against Islamic extremism that had sent 20 Muslim martyrs to crash four airplanes into the World Trade Towers in New York and the Pentagon and White House in Washington, for New York and Washington were regarded as the twin satanic centres of global economic, political and military power. In a moment that joined the deaths of individuals to a greater whole, the three Canadian soldiers who sacrificed their lives seven-and-a-half years later chose to join the military, the second Canadian Mechanized Brigade Group Headquarters and Signals Squadron in Petawawa, ON, the Lincoln and Welland regiment in St. Catharines, ON, and the 425 Tactical Fighter Squadron based in Bagotville, Québec. Perhaps driven by a sense of adventure and looking forward to the camaraderie of their fellow soldiers, they gained recognition for their individuality and their contributions to the mission.

O'Quinn, a soldier of deep faith unafraid to display that faith to others, gained recognition as a "consummate professional" always willing to challenge himself and others in the belief that "he could accomplish anything". He clearly had faith in himself and faith in a Transcendent Other that earned his fellow soldier's faith in him. Brown wore a constant infectious smile on his face as he demonstrated his proficiency as "an extremely dedicated and hard-working soldier." Fortin, an avid Montreal Canadians fan with a comic timing always able to stir a laugh from his comrades in arms, served as an "intelligent, sincere and upright soldier" in the Canadian forces posted to that tragic mission in Afghanistan.[7] There are not hagiographies but attempts, however feeble, to provide a glimpse into the individual personalities of the soldiers who died.

The contradiction of personal pleasure serving a higher abstract cause in an act of great personal self-sacrifice is the ultimate concrete act in which the quest for personal pleasure and satisfaction became a shared *unity* of Spirit. That happiness turned to *disaster*. However, through that disaster, the three soldiers gain distinction and recognition throughout Canada. We as fellow-Canadians, through their deaths, become gut-wrenchingly *connected* to this abstract cause as we shed tears over the loss, though at almost all other times the cause and the self-sacrifice required evades us. Through their deaths, the abstract becomes real.

What a horrific reality! Three rational individuals in plunging into life at the edge of greatest risk find only death. The necessity behind those deaths in the movement of Spirit is inscrutable. Abstract reason in service

---

[7] Mike Blanchfield and Archie McLean, "3 Canadian soldiers killed in Afghanistan," Canwest News Service, 5 March, 2009.

to a cause becomes joined to that necessity, but we are unable to recognize the equation. The identity of cause and necessity seems empty of meaning. Our hearts wrench as we see only a meaningless loss of life and cry for the parents, the brothers and sisters, the wives and girlfriends, the children—and also the grandparents—of those men who sacrificed their lives. This effect becomes doubly tragic if we begin to recognize that their sacrifice for the cause of freedom was wasted if what we are witnessing instead is the advance of authoritarianism and dogmatism rather than the cause of freedom.

As Queen Hecuba laments in Euripedes' *Trojan Women*:

That mortal is a fool who, prospering, thinks his life
Has any strong foundation; since our fortune's course
Of action is the reeling way a madman takes,
And no one person is happy all the time. (1200-1207)

Parents and wives and siblings love their children. Husbands and wives, fathers and mothers who serve also love their country which has asked for this sacrifice. Duty to family requires courage to allow those soldiers to leave for battle, but duty to country requires an even greater courage when their bodies return in wooden caskets. For what loyalty do you owe the state when it has taken from you your loved one? In a pious service wrapped in the maple leaf, they are buried and one knows not why. It takes courage to attend that burial and not scream: Why mine? Why him? Why?

Canadians through their sacrifice are joined in the Faustian bargain as love's highest happiness wrought through the bonding of men, as rage is harnessed and disciplined in its only worthy purpose in the heroic warrior to serve a common cause, as much for the soldiers in Kandahar as for Achilles who met the Trojan King, Priam, on the sand strip before Troy. That bargain is brought to grief in the most concrete of ways. As the disciplined *thumos*, the anger that must be captured and trained, is transformed in the sacrifice of military heroes in such an ignominious and depersonalized way, our shared sorrow, our shared pity, returns us to the most central issue for the polis. For in Greek terms, the competitive virtues of *arêté* must be transformed into the cooperative spirit of *phusis*. Justice, no longer simply as a discussion over the equitable division of goods and services among citizens or the legal justice dispensed by its courts, becomes a higher, historical justice in determining the worth of the cause that demands of necessity the self-sacrifice of our soldiers. What cause is worth such sacrifice?[8] In harnessing the rage of unmanageable passion to the purposes of the state, in moving beyond interests and the rule of law, beyond questions of distributive justice and equality before the law, into questions of historical justice in the face of an implacable enemy when we, unlike they, no longer believe in either natural or supernatural justice, we as citizens are obligated to provide an answer. We are not concerned merely with the moral ordering of personal lives. We become preoccupied with the greatest ethical question—the purpose of and service of our collective existence that requires and demands self-sacrifice.

In the Biblical Garden of Eden story, G-D tells Adam and Eve that if they eat of the Tree of Knowledge of Good and Evil, they will surely die. But they are mortal anyway, so what is the big deal? They do eat of the tree of knowledge of good and evil, they do have sex, and they are mortified. Ashamed and humiliated, they experience death in life. Why? Instead of desire rising to love—love of the other, love of country—desire is recognized as lust. For they entered into the passionate embrace because "the devil made me do it," because the *homos erectus* as the snake seduced Eve with his words and Adam refused to acknowledge that erectile function as his own but detached his penis from himself and refused to take responsibility. This is the shame. This is the humiliation. This is the mortification. It is the failure to take responsibility. This is the great sin—not our passion driven desires and certainly not our disobedience. It is the refusal to take responsibility before we acted and after we acted so that action itself is reduced to compulsion by another.[9]

Action is Janus-faced. On the one hand, we think, weigh values and consequences, conditions and expectations, and do our best in ordering means and ends. But we do so in a context of the unknowable, in a context of what is ultimately incomprehensible, when forces are in play that we can neither comprehend nor control and cannot tell whether we are headed for success or disaster. But we take responsibility for our individual and collective lives lest we suffer Adam's fate of mortification. And the beginning of that assumption of responsibility starts when we leave behind our lives as isolated individuals for the sake of an Other.

---

[8] This was a central question for Plato's transformation of the Homeric exaltation through poetry of the heroic cult of sacrifice into the question of justice. See Barbara Koziak, *Retrieving Political Emotion: Thumos, Aristotle, and Gender* (University Park: Pennsylvania University Press, 2000), 39.

[9] Howard Adelman, "Of Human Bondage: Labour, Bondage and Freedom in the *Phenomenology*," in Jon Stewart, ed., *Essays on Hegel's Phenomenology of Spirit* (Albany: SUNY Press, 1997), 155-171.

That, however, is not an answer but only the beginning of questioning. Which Other? What do we do? When do we do it? How do we act? Most critically, why do we act? The answers are not self-evident. They require interpretation, especially of sacred texts wherein answers are supposedly found but where mythology provides an icing that must be demythologized, where layers of meaning abide that need to be deciphered, where the first thing that must be sacrificed is any adherence to literalness. However, that truth must weigh insights from texts against the reality that confronts us. For in our desire to see our quest for freedom objectified, in our desire to see the world as a reflection of our own sense of who we are as self-conscious beings, we encounter the world that we have made and it barely resembles the fruit of our desires. The objective world is harsh and alien. Instead of finding the victory of freedom, we face the tragic likelihood of defeat. Instead of the spread of a self-governing communities that foster respect for individuals and the freedom and dignity of the individual, we find a world of corruption and intimidation, of tribal loyalties that insist upon death of the Other and theological dictatorship that insists on sacrificing deviants in the quest to extend their authority and control over the waywardness of individuals. Thus, the world as we would like it to be and as it "ought" to be, the world as a projection and development of our ideals, stands in sharp contrast to world as it is.

In interpreting that world as we confront it, it is insufficient to describe what is "out there' without at the same time depicting the way we have tried and continue to try to objectify those ideals. In this respect, there has been a sea change in the transition from the Bush administration to the Obama administration. Whereas Bush saw only black and white, the evil Taliban and the saintly Americans, Obama expressed his willingness to engage the Taliban and view them in terms of various shades of grey.[10] The "Axis of Evil" has broken and the disabled vehicle that carried so much of foreign policy has been towed away. Instead of lofty dreams that repressed the reality that stared the Bush administration in the face as the administration pursued the birth of additional free nations out of the authoritarian old ones, the reality that faces us has to confront our contradictory desires. Obama, as a believing Christian, pursues these compromises out of a particular prophetic rather than a Christological "born again" tradition. That prophetic tradition must be interpreted in comparison to the

---

[10] As well as these differences when avoiding the language of spreading democracy and freedom as we war against terrorism in general, as well as changes in dealing with Taliban, this shift is taking place in the way Obama has set the tome for handling Putin's revisionist steps towards a resurrection of Stalin, opening up to the Syrians and, significantly, in early efforts to talk to Iran.

one rooted in reborn gods and dreams of resurrection of the old in new forms as well as against the backdrop of more pessimistic prophetic voices. That prophetic tradition requires our understanding in relationship to the real world we confront. But we begin with the subjective, for even though the self consciousness of the Subject has changed, the desire to project the dreams of that Subject onto the world is still there.

A Prophetic Voice

The most sacred text of America is undoubtedly its constitution. The U.S.A. also has a number of secondary sacred texts that include the inaugural addresses of each of its successive presidents. Barack Obama both mined and undermined[11] those texts. On the 20th of January 2009, Obama gave his inaugural speech as the 44th president of the United States. The substantive content of the speech was compelling though its rhetoric rarely soared. In rhythms of American Black preachers, the speech began with death and the ghosts of the past—for Obama's mind was full of the memories and thoughts of "the sacrifices borne by our ancestors" whose spirit does and "must inhabit us all". Obama was not speaking of a prospect of death or death as an immanent danger or death as a moment of revelation. He was speaking of the deaths of others in the past raised by memory into spirit so that the natural life cycle becomes not just a material matter but a moment of self-conscious development through history even though the future is literally "embodied" in the past. Obama was speaking of the legacy of the past and the responsibility we in the present bear to carry out the promises and ideals of those who came before.

The speech contrasted the still waters of peace and rising tides of prosperity with those interruptive moments of gathering storms and clouds. According to Obama, *Sturm und Drang* characterize the present moment. Obama himself embodies the still waters. Obama is cool. He exhibits great depths beneath a calm exterior and an ability to retreat within his inner silence. Barack Obama is the Black voice resonant of the Kool Kat and Ralph Ellison's invisible man. He cited the most famous of Biblical psalms, the 23rd, and the role of the Lord as the shepherd of his flock "who leadeth me *beside* [my italics] still waters" and then "*through* [my italics] the valley of the shadow of death" into a future of hope and a capacity to confront evil and taste the abundance that life has to offer.

---

[11] He specifically, even if implicitly, rejected the Bush doctrines of exceptionalism, of preventive war and of the message in George Bush's second inaugural address that "the survival of liberty in our land increasingly depends on the success of liberty in other lands" as stated in Bush's "Freedom Agenda."

At least one-third of Americans would instantly and subconsciously recognize the reference to the past containing the message of how one travels into the promise of the future and a guarantee of eternal life. Further, although we may think of the phrase, "leading me beside still waters" as an overused expression that has lost the force of the original meaning, it must be remembered that the root of the word "cliché" comes from stereotype, the casting of a repeatedly used phrase as a single slug for printing. In his rhetoric, Obama recovers the deep structure of the origins of the cliché to restore "the remembrance of timeless words." Obama used another apparent cliché -"the rising tides of prosperity" that immediately evokes its opposite—the rising tides of Hurricane Katrina "when the levees broke" that reminded us of the future of rising tides brought by climate change that threaten to inundate the populous coastal cities of the world. Katrina provided the turning point in President Bush's downward spiral to an ignominious end. So the rising tides of prosperity hid the near death of America's most joyful city as the surge of waters covered the Black sections of the city that reminded us that what lay ahead is the prospect of the death of civilization in the future. Neither still waters nor rising tides of prosperity are what they appear to be.

The issue and challenge for a president as the shepherd of his nation is now to guide his flock through the valley of death, not as in a horror movie, but as an inspiration as long as God's chosen remain faithful to the ideals of their forebears and the founding documents and institutions of the state. At a time of peace when the waters were still, the leader, instead of indulging in cynicism under the mask of a charming smile, should have provided a guide for the flock *beside* those waters to make the hard choices for the coming radical disruptions in the course of history instead of wallowing in the waters of greed, corruption and irresponsibility, instead of standing pat rather than moving forward, instead of protecting special interests rather than serving all the citizens of the U.S.A. This was not a speech of clichés, for the vision was opposed to worn-out and stale dogmas (the false past), petty grievances (the misguided present) and false promises (the illusionary future). Barack Obama was offering a past immanent in the present turmoil that guaranteed hope and an unwavering spirit to tackle evil in the future. What a different sense of evil and goodness Barack offered in contrast to George Dubya.

"(I)n the words of Scripture, the time has come to set aside childish things...to reaffirm our enduring spirit; to choose our better history; to carry forward that precious gift, that noble idea, passed on from generation to generation," *l'dor v'dor*. America is a young nation, but it is time it grew up and became a mature adult. It is time for the American nation to accept its full responsibilities to its own citizens, all of its citizens, to the world and first and foremost to the ideals of its forefathers. But this isn't what Paul meant in 1 Corinthians 13:11 when he asked the followers of Jesus to set aside childish talk, thought and reason and simply accept the message of love. It is clear in what Barack does and in what he says that he is a 'thinking and reasoning' man as well as a man of talk who can give old meanings to new words. That is why he is a man of what Christians call the Old Testament. Though he offers hope as a universal unifier directed at the future, he does not put forth love as the panacea for our troubles, let alone love for the reborn Greek Christos. Instead, deeds, work and self-sacrifice in honouring one's forefathers provide the path of righteousness and truth rather than the sacrifice of the Other so that you too may be saved.

For the promise of freedom from slavery and the equality and dignity of all is God-given but man-made: "that all are equal, all are free, and all deserve a chance to pursue their full measure of happiness." Obama's rephrasing of Thomas Jefferson's words in the Declaration of Independence affirming the rights of everyone to "life, liberty and the pursuit of happiness" echoed Abraham Lincoln's 1857 speech criticizing the Supreme Court's decision in the Dred Scott case and Senator Stephen A. Douglas' defence of that decision in which Chief Justice Roger Taney excluded Blacks from the protection of the American Constitution. All are equal not as a matter of reality, for we are different sizes and different weights and have different countenances. All are equal in terms of rights and opportunities so that the Declaration of Independence provides the rationale for why a constitution and institutions are needed to enforce and deliver rights and why rights need to be married to the rule of law and enduring convictions married to sturdy alliances.

And who are the carriers of that sense of sacrifice and of dedication to that message? Not philosophers who enjoy the leisure of critical reflection. The carriers of the past are the doers, the risk takers, the workers, the soldiers who sacrificed their lives at Concord and Khe Sahn and who lie in the graves of Arlington, but nevertheless manage as good ghosts to "whisper through the ages" with their spirit of service and sacrifice to carry the past into the future as a promise for generations to come. How did the "bitter pill" become transformed in his speech into the "bitter swill of civil war and segregation"? Those words certainly evoked something very different than swallowing something that tasted horrible for one's long term health and benefit. Instead "swill" connoted something filthy, like the waters that covered New Orleans that we wallow in at our peril—divisions, strife, civil war, segregation—versus the unity and common purpose that

Barack Obama invoked. Swill is what is fed to pigs. In black homes it was usually the ends, scraps and leftovers dumped in a big bucket that became sour and rancid when fermented in the sun. How do we escape from that swill? By echoing the opening words of one of America's greatest musicals, South Pacific, the 1949 Rogers and Hammerstein tale of racial prejudice—by picking ourselves up and washing "that man (who was sitting right there on the stage as Barack Obama raked his record with biting language) right outta our hair" and the rest of the others who sow conflict and discord, whether they be terrorists in the caves of Pakistan or knaves in the caves of Washington who "cling to power through corruption and deceit" like Karl Rove in what Brian Urquart described as the "fog of know-nothing ideology, anti-intellectualism, cronyism, incompetence, and cynicism"[12].

The values Obama invoked at the foundation of America were not based on neo-con self-interest, but "the values upon which our success depends—hard work and honesty, courage and fair play, tolerance and curiosity, loyalty and patriotism—these things are old. These things are true." "What is demanded is a return to these truths" in "God's call on us to shape an uncertain destiny." And with whose words did he end his speech—a quote from George Washington: "let it be told to the future world…in the depth of the winter, when nothing but hope and virtue could survive…that the city and the country, alarmed at one common danger, came forth to meet (it)." The remembrance of timeless words provides the foundation for a future resurrection to enable the flame of freedom to be passed on to future generations sensible of the limits of our finitude and modest about our virtues, power and wisdom. How do those values deal with the disaster facing America and the West in Afghanistan?

---

[12] Brian Urquart, "What You Can Learn from Reinhold Niebuhr," *New York Review of Books*, LVI:5, 26 March, 2009, p. 22. Obama wrote a back cover blurb for the republished edition of Reinhold Niebuhr's *The Irony of American History*, describing him as one of his favourite philosophers, from whom he learned "the compelling idea that there's a serious evil in the world, and hardship and pain. And we should be humble and modest in our belief we can eliminate those things. But we shouldn't use that as an excuse for cynicism and inaction." As Niebuhr pointed out so well, as we travel the historical pathway from necessity to freedom, we must not delude ourselves, as the Soviet masters did, that we have achieved Absolute Freedom and are no longer subject to the limitations of nature and history, a mindset that percolated up from America's messianic beginnings into the neo-con conceits of the Bush era.

Prophecy and the Reality on the Ground

In the face of rising casualty rates in Afghanistan, Gordon Brown in his March 2009 Congressional address[13] referred to his father who was a minister who taught him that "judgment is a summary court is perpetual session". Brown saw the United States as not only the indispensable nation but as the irrepressible nation with Obama articulating the modernist enlightenment vision of a "faith in the future" as the path for curing past ills. Will faith in the future work? At least in the military sphere, the war is not going well[14] to say the least. The Afghanistan War possibly passed the tipping point of reversal as far back as early 2007.[15] The war has gone awry as the insurgency increases in strength.[16] More and more areas of the country have fallen back under Taliban control.[17]

---

[13] Gordon Brown, "PM Gordon Brown's Address to Congress, 4 March, 2009, http://www.realclearworld.com/articles/2009/03/gordon_brown_congress_address.html.

[14] James L. Jones, currently national security adviser to President Obama, in a report that he directed of the Atlantic Council, concluded unequivocally that the West was "not winning in Afghanistan." That same report concluded that Pakistan is "on a rapid trajectory toward becoming a failing or failed state." Cf. Ann Scott Dyson, "NATO's Not Winning in Afghanistan, Report Says," *Washington Post*, 21 January, 2008, A18. See the Afghanistan Study Group and the Atlantic Council of the U.S., "Saving Afghanistan: An Appeal and Plan for Urgent Action," 30 January, 2008. The Afghanistan Study Group (ASG) Report faulted the United States and the international community for having tried to "win the struggle in Afghanistan with too few military forces, insufficient economic aid, and without a clear and consistent comprehensive strategy." http://www.embassyofafghanistan.org/documents/01.30.2008AtlanticCounciloftheUS.pdf.

[15] Laura King and David Holley, "Afghanistan War Nears 'Tipping Point': Government support is flagging, NATO is split on strategy, and Taliban fighters are revitalized," *Los Angeles Times*, 9 December, 2006.

[16] Normally referred to as a Taliban insurgency, its sources of support are much broader and the name does not reflect the variety of differences among the Taliban. Ahmed Rajid has called the Taliban a lumpen proletariat of Pashtuns made up of the unemployed and the unemployable graduates of militarized madrassas, alienated from both the state and traditional society. Ahmed Rashid, *Descent into Chaos: How the War against Islamic Extremism is Being Lost in Pakistan, Afghanistan and Central Asia* (London: Allen Lane, 2008), 401.

[17] By the end of November 2007, more than half of Afghanistan had been put back under Taliban control. Subsequently, that area had expanded considerably. See Kim Sengupta, "More than half of Afghanistan 'under Taliban'," *The Independent*, 22 November, 2007. Cf. also the work of the Senlis Council, a Paris-based international drug policy think-tank now re-labelled as the International Council on Secu-

Multiple reasons are offered in explanation: insufficient numbers of ground troops to conduct a counter-insurgency war, the conflict among different strategic approaches, the balkanization of the command and control structure, the inability to distinguish locals from those who employ arms against the coalition, the radically different goals and perceived appropriate means of the coalition, and the weakness and corruption of the installed government in Kabul. After seven years the number of casualties absorbed by Operation Enduring Freedom (OEF) and by IFOR (and probably the Afghan army) has increased.[18] Many more Canadians have suffered serious injuries, ignoring for the moment the traumatic stress disorder from which many returning combat forces suffer upon their return.[19] And this is out of a total military strength of about 2400 deployed by the Canadians.[20]

Over seven years ago, an alliance of 88 countries[21] rallied around the United States after the terrorist attacks of 11 September 2001 (9/11) and supported the United States in its determination to defeat the militant al-Qaeda and the Taliban Islamicists[22] who controlled Afghanistan and

---

rity and Development (ICOS), in three of its reports: "Senlis Recommendations for US Policy in Afghanistan," February, 2008 (http://www.icosgroup.net/modules/publications/us_policy_recom-mendations); "Afghanistan: Decision Point, 2008" February, 2008 (http://www.icosgroup.net/modules/publications/Decision_Point), and "Recommendations to the Independent Panel on Canada's Future Role in Afghanistan," December, 2007 (http://icosgroup.net/modules/public-cations/manley_report).

[18] According to http://www.icasualties.org/oef/, fatalities increased each year from 57 in 2003 to 295 in 2008, with the upward rate undoubtedly being set to continue.

[19] A Rand Corporation study indicated that in the US 300,000 veterans suffer from post-traumatic stress disorder and that suicides among soldiers continue to rise. Terri Tanielian and Lisa H. Jaycox, eds., "Invisible Wounds of War: Psychological and Cognitive Injuries, Their Consequences, and Services to Assist Recovery," RAND Corporation, April, 2008, http://www.rand.org/multi/military/veterans/.

[20] Originally, 1800 troops were deployed for a six-month tour of duty "to stabilize Kabul and protect the interim government of President Hamid Karzai. By 2006, Canada assumed responsibility for the dangerous southern part of the country as part of the NATO-led International Security Assistance Force (ISAF), with a battle group of more than 2,000 Canadian soldiers based around Kandahar.

[21] By 2008, 32 countries were providing troops to ISAF.

[22] There are very different kinds of Taliban: Taliban-e- Jangi (also known as Taliban-e shuri)—the fighting or insurgent Taliban; Taliban-e darsi—the madrassa students; Taliban-e alsi (also Taliba-e pak—the real or clean Taliban); Taliban-e Pakistani versus Taliban-e mahdi (local Taliban); Taliban-e duzd—thieves who joined the Taliban to save their hides; and Taliban-e Khana neshin (Taliban who have retired from the conflict and now sit at home). There is also the division be-

served as host for the al-Qaeda terrorists. The Taliban were easily routed[23] but have clearly not been defeated. Further, as Prime Minister Stephen Harper opined in a CNN interview on 1 March 2009, "Frankly, we are not going to ever defeat the insurgency."[24]

Further, the debate over the effectiveness of air power that played such an important part in the initial and quick defeat of the Taliban has resumed. The 22 August 2008 air bombing of 33 civilians incurred the wrath of the Karzai government, and shamed the West, as all countries recognized how counter-productive such incidents are, quite aside from the moral distress at the death of innocent civilians in what is known as an unintended consequence of a military attack in which there is "collateral damage". Yet President Obama ran on a platform of not only increasing the strength of troops on the ground that was followed by a commitment after he assumed office to send 17,000 more troops to Afghanistan,[25] but to a renewed effort to use air power to attack the havens for the Taliban in the northern territories of Pakistan. As the new CIA Director Leon Panetta

---

tween those who were forced to join (the majpur) and those joined because they were dissatisfied with the way power was exercised and benefits were distributed. I am grateful to Martine van Biljert, a Dutch expert on Afghanistan, who provided me with this nomenclature in an unpublished paper, "Unruly Commanders and Violent Power Struggles: Taliban Networks in Uruzgan." Uruzgan is the province north of Kandahar patrolled by Dutch troops.

[23] Cf. Michael Griffin, "Reaping the Whirlwind: The Taliban Movement in Afghanistan," *The Progressive*, 1 December 2001, subsequently included in his book, *Reaping the Whirlwind: Afghanistan, Al Qa'ida and the Holy War*, rev. ed. (London: Pluto Press, 2002). See also Ahmed Rashid, *Taliban: Militant Islam, Oil & Fundamentalism in Central Asia* (New Haven: Yale University Press, 2000). Both books were reviewed by Jamal Hanifi in *The Middle East Journal*, LVI:2, 1 April, 2002, 329-331.

[24] Peter Wilson in *The Weekend Australian* ("Situation normal, all fouled up," 1-2 November, 2008, 29) echoed this view and wrote that "a military solution appears impossible."

[25] Troops deployed in Afghanistan are now approaching the troop strength deployed by the Soviet Union before it decided to leave Afghanistan, a move when completed in January 1989 that was followed by its own collapse. Yet US Defense Secretary Robert Gates acknowledged that strategic purpose of this escalation was not at all clear (Bob Herbert, "Wars, Endless Wars," *The New York Times*, 2 March, 2009). General David Petraeus insisted that the 17,000 troops would allow control of that 10% of the territory where 80% of the military threat originates. Other areas would be controlled by local militias supplied by the Americans with rapid reaction forces able to reinforce them in times of challenge. The reality is that the US in escalating the troop strength still lacked not only an exit strategy but even an escalation strategy.

promised. "US aerial attacks against al-Qaeda and other extremist strongholds inside Afghanistan would continue, despite concerns about a popular Pakistani backlash."[26]

This was just after the Pakistan Government arrived at an agreement in the Swat valley of the northern territories to withdraw the Pakistani army and allow the Islamicists who burn down girl's schools to run the region in accordance with their interpretation of Sharia law.[27] The move has to be grasped by understanding first the strategic background against which the initiative was taken. From the Taliban side, Mullah Mohammed Omar, the leader of the Afghan Taliban, urged the Taliban in Pakistan to make the deal and concentrate efforts on attacking the foreign troops in Afghanistan. This move coincided with an effort to unite the Pakistani Taliban by Jalaluddin Haqqani which resulted in the warlords, Baitullah Meshsud, Maulvi Nazir and Hafiz Gul, to set aside their rivalry and create a new alliance, the Shura-e-Ittehad ul Mujahadeen of Council of the United Holy Warriors, though this unification effort took place after the Pakistanis made the Swat deal with the radical cleric, Maulana Sufi Mohammed whose son-in-law is Maulana Fazlullah, allied with al-Qaeda and leader of the Swati Taliban. After all, the deal was really an acknowledgement of defeat of the Pakistani army by Fazlullah who succeeded in driving the army out of Swat and then followed his victory by setting up Sharia courts, hanging teachers and policemen as 350,000 internally displaced people fled their homes out of a 1.5 million population.

---

[26] Karen De Young and Joby Warrick, *Washington Post*, 26 February, 2009, A10. Panetta was referring to the CIA missile attacks launched from unmanned Predator aircraft against ostensible Taliban and Islamicist targets in Pakistan. Panetta claimed that these efforts to destabilize al-Qaeda and destroy its leadership "have been successful," but it is difficult to discern how Panetta derived that conclusion given the course of the war. Further, in the interviews the journalists held with Afghan and Pakistan leaders, Pakistani Foreign Minister Shah Mahmood Qureshi, while applauding the Obama willingness to listen in contrast to the previous administration, noted that Pakistan objected to Predator strikes and, instead, requested that the US supply Pakistan with its own drones, Cobra attack helicopters, sophisticated communication and night vision equipment to improve Pakistan capabilities. For a thorough pre-9/11 history of the CIA role in Afghanistan, see Steve Coll, *Ghost Wars: The Secret History of the CIA, Afghanistan, and Bin Laden, from the Soviet Invasion to September 10, 2001* (New York: Penguin Press, 2004).

[27] Panetta, in the 26 February *Washington Post* interview cited above, was very sceptical of the Swat agreement and continued to believe that such agreements only allowed al-Qaeda and the extremists to strengthen their base. Cf. "Fareed Zakaria: Learning to Live with Radical Islam," *Newsweek*, 9 March, 2009.

The deal was just recognition of the *de facto* situation, but the formal surrender is symbolic of a much larger retreat. Further, it sets a dangerous precedent given the widespread sympathy among Pashtuns for withdrawal of western troops and the prominent role Pashtuns play in both the Pakistani army and the Frontier Corps and their knee-jerk opposition to imposing central state authority in Pakistan over Pashtun dominated areas.[28] That is why the enhanced focus on unilateral bombing of Taliban and al-Qaeda targets in Pakistan is bound to enhance anti-American feeling. At the same time as there was a renewed use of air power when its utility and ethical foundation were once again increasingly coming into question, a troop surge is underway. There is also a new emphasis by both the Afghan and U.S. governments on understanding and utilizing knowledge of local social structures in the conduct of thee war. More specifically, the U.S. and the Afghan governments at the end of 2008 agreed to initiate community outreach programs and to specifically make use of traditional community shirias and local councils to advance the war aims.[29] Further, the two governments also agreed to strengthen local security capacities by enhancing community guard programs and the ability of the local tribes to protect themselves and their traditional structures and institutions.[30]

---

[28] See Ahmed Rashid, "Slide toward anarchy," The Globe and Mail, 28 February, 2009, A19, and his latest book, Descent into Chaos: The United States and the Failure of Nation Building in Pakistan, Afghanistan and Central Asia (New York: Penguin, 2008).

[29] The war aim had shifted from defeating the Taliban and extremists to ensuring that, "Afghanistan cannot be used as a base for launching terrorist attacks" against the United States. Henry Kissinger, in a *Washington Post* article entitled, "A Strategy for Afghanistan," 26 February 2009, A19, supported this shift in emphasis when he insisted that, "military strategy should concentrate on preventing the emergence of a coherent contiguous state within the state controlled by jihadists. In practice, this would mean control of Kabul and the Pashtun area."

[30] Sarah Sewall, who collaborated with Gen. Petraeus on the US counter-insurgency field guide in John A. Nagl, James F. Amos, Sarah Sewall, and David H. Petraeus, *The U.S. Army/Marine Corps Counterinsurgency Field Manual* (Chicago: University of Chicago Press, 2007), recommended integrating with the local population, assuming more field risk, emphasizing protecting civilians rather than killing adversaries, supporting humanitarian assistance and construction projects and clearly delineating military and civilian responsibilities in nation building during a counter-insurgency campaign. Counter-insurgency warfare is based on a number of premises, but two are specifically important: strengthening the organs of the central state in its governance of the population and the territory; and an emphasis on protecting civilian populations rather than killing adversaries, thereby requiring high force levels. For older versions of the updated Petraeus doctrine, see David Galla, *Counterinsurgency Warfare: Theory and Practice* (London: Pall Mall

The question is how the troop surge fits in with Lakhadar Brahimi's original emphasis that the international military presence in Afghanistan carry a light footprint.[31] Is this an interim effort until the Afghan army strength doubles from 65,000 to 130,000 and until local militias can be armed and trained? How does the troop surge fit in with the reduced war aim of simply ensuring that Afghanistan cannot be a training base for anti-Western terrorists rather than their defeat? Since the correlate of the light footprint was an enhanced reliance on air power, how does an increased use of air power against Taliban bases in Pakistan coexist with an increased use of ground troops? These questions are critical in the renewed debate over the function of NATO given that NATO in the past has a record of success, even in its role in Kosovo and the Balkans left many questions about the nature of that "success" unanswered. Afghanistan was NATO's first foreign war under the doctrine that an attack on one was an attack on them all. Serious reservations about this foreign adventure now run through all member states as public support for the war withered.[32] NATO is determined not to leave Afghanistan with its tail between its legs at the same time as it is increasingly determined to leave Afghanistan.

Thus, just as Europe and the U.S. are enjoying a renewed faith in multilateralism, when Prime Minister Gordon Brown in an address to Congress declared that never before had the U.S. enjoyed a more pro-American leadership in Europe eager to partner with the United States in renewal[33], just when the view of the U.S. as preponderant in a unipolar world is being put on the back burner—the aims of the war are being reconfigured. Is the aim in Afghanistan stabilization or is it creating a liberal

---

Press, 1964), and Robert Thompson, *Defeating Communist Insurgency: Experiences from Malaya and Vietnam* (London: Chatto & Windus, 1966).

[31] Brahimi was the UN Secretary-General's special representative for Afghanistan. See UN Security Council 4469th meeting, 6 February, 2002, UN doc.S/PV.4469, 6.

[32] Though two thirds of Americans support President Obama's decision to send an additional 17,000 troops to Afghanistan, half of America does not believe the war was worth the cost, and half again (as opposed to 41%) believe that it is essential to win in Afghanistan in the broader battle against terrorism. Joe Cohen, "Majority of Americans Back President on Afghanistan," *Washington Post*, 28 February, 2009. Part of the disillusion with these military efforts has not only been the weak foundation for justifying the wars in Iraq and Afghanistan and the extremely flawed execution, but the simplification of terrorism itself into a war of the "good" against powerful satanic forces, thereby paradoxically adopting the crude dichotomies of the Islamicists themselves.

[33] Prime Minister of Great Britain, Gordon Brown's Address to the U.S. Congress, 4 March 2009, http://www.realclearworld.com/articles/2009/03/gordon_brown_congress_address.html.

democracy in the Bush neo-con mission of state building in Afghanistan? Clearly, the former is emerging as the preferred policy as even Henry Kissinger, the master of a political and exit strategy to end an unwinnable war, recommends a multilateral initiative involving Pakistan, India and other permanent members of the Security Council to assist in the reconstruction and reform of Afghanistan while opposing the use of Afghanistan as a terrorist base.[34]

Further, in contrast to the beginning of the Afghan War when the emphasis was on *global* legitimation, there is a renewed effort at *local* legitimation on the premise that legitimacy starts from the ground up. Instead of concentrating on legitimizing the state as a source of central authority when it now has a record of widespread corruption[35] and ineffectuality, the new emphasis is on local leadership. However, if the shift in Afghanistan can be from nation building towards stabilization, from global and state legitimacy to local legitimacy, why is such a policy agreed in Afghanistan but wrong in Pakistan, where the new civilian Pakistani government initially surrendered its efforts to control Swat? If the U.S. can follow the lead of the Afghanistan government and distinguish not only between Pashtun and Taliban, but many different variety of Taliban, so that the war aims are only directed at the Taliban solidly allied with al-Qaeda, why cannot the Pakistani government consistently follow in that path? Is it because of different beliefs about the character of the Taliban that controls Swat?

All of these debates take place in a context of fears about Pakistan as a nuclear power becoming a failed state with the Taliban at the control of the nuclear triggers and the immanence of Iran, Afghanistan's other neighbour, becoming itself a nuclear power. All of these debates take place in the long durée of the four century old effort to build modern nation-states based on respect for autonomous individuals and the rights of nations to self-determination and governance according to the rule of law in order to organize and manage a material world rather than a nation dedicated to the service of a divine vision for a nation and a polity. How does the war in Afghanistan fit into the modern enlightenment vision?

---

[34] Kissinger, *op. cit.*, also does not include Iran or even Tajikistan, Uzbekistan or Turkmenistan, each of which has legitimate interests in Afghanistan.

[35] To take one prominent example, the "warlord" Ahmed Wali Karzai is also allegedly implicated in drugs dealing. In fact, the fundamental weakness behind that corruption is seen to be the absence of a real and effective central state which exists primarily as a virtual entity with very fragile institutional foundations on which to base its authority.

Canadian Policy in Kandahar

Given this overall framework for examining the situation, what is the situation in Kandahar where Canada faces such difficult issues? I will not and cannot provide a thorough description on the ground in whole or in part in Kandahar. What I can do is offer a glimpse of the complexity, overlapping and contradictory loyalties that make it so difficult to forge an effective policy for Kandahar.

Greater Kandahar includes not only the province of Kandahar but Helmand (the British zone immediately west of Kandahar), Zabol (northeast of Kandahar with a major U.S. base) and Uruzgan (the Dutch zone north of Kandahar). I will focus only on Kandahar, the most turbulent of the tumultuous southern arc of Afghanistan where the Canadians have been stationed in the effort to bring peace to Afghanistan. The total population consists of just under 900,000, with one-third of that population located in the city of Kandahar founded by no less than Alexander the Great. Kandahar is the epicentre of the Pashtun tribe, particularly since Ahmad Shah Durrani founded modern Afghanistan in 1747 and made Kandahar the capital of his Pashtun Afghan Kingdom until the capital was moved to Kabul in the 1780s.

The population is divided into ethnic groups, tribes and sub-tribes, the latter providing the main solidarity group to which the greatest fealty is attached. But on top of these loyalties are new military loyalties to specific commanders (usually but not always from the same sub-tribe), and those political loyalties forged in the decades of struggle between political parties and that are the historic product of struggles for power and status within sub-tribes. Tribal membership, past conflicts and sleights, and promises of patronage and goods from foreign sponsors all play a part in establishing loyalties.

Calculations about the future power order seems to be as important on the collective level as the past history of loyalties and grievances, especially when, instead of allowing former Taliban to retire from the field, they were hunted down propelled by the Bush doctrine of punishment as well as the determination of those now in power to ensure their positions as well as exact revenge on their former foes. Tajik, Hazara, Aimak, Baluchi and Uzbek are all minorities in Kandahar; the major small minority consists of Hazaras who carry a long antipathy to the Taliban ever since the Taliban pushed their leader, Ali Mazari, out of a helicopter. The main fight is between other Pashtun tribes and the Durrani Zeerak tribe of Pashtuns that control the government.

The Pashtuns are divided as follows[36]: Durrani Zeerak (sub-tribe Popalzai, President Hamid Karzai's tribe); Barakzai; Achekzai; Mohammadzai; Alikozai; Panjpai (sub-tribe Noorzai); Kogyani; Ghilzai (sub-tribe Tokhi); Hotak; Niazi; Kakar; Taraki; Wardak; Suleimankheil; and Mullahkheil. According to a *Globe and Mail* report on Taliban insurgents, other than a few Durrani Zeerek fighters who have personal resentments— in one case, his family home was destroyed in a bombing raid and, in another case, his opium fields were destroyed without paying compensation—overwhelmingly the fighters come from tribes outside of the Durrani Zeerak Popalzai and Barakzai sub-tribes that control the government. The largest numbers come from the Noorzai sub-tribe of Panjpai and Ashekzai sub-tribe of Durrani Zeerak.[37] These insurgents provide the major attack force against the beleaguered Canadian forces. As Jeffrey Simpson writes, Canadian soldiers died and continue to die, "in an ill-defined mission that defied all the rules of counterinsurgency, sent by an enthusiastic general who has curiously become a kind of media hero, and by gullible politicians who did not ask the right questions, did not know the country, the nature of the war, the precise aims, the equipment required to fight it, and how to define success."[38]

In a society where the values of honour and shame, acknowledgement of status and revenge, prestige and saving face are so important, a new regime of predation and humiliation only perpetuates old conflicts in new variations. This was as true of the rulers who took over under the communists, of the Taliban period and of its successor Karzai regime, in which rule by consent is the rare exception and instead one finds, threats and punishments, levies and patronage rewards, immobility and forced movement. When predation is compounded by bombs that fall from the sky and kill civilians, when intrusive home searches by international forces breed resentment, disaffection grows. The Taliban is in many ways is a mirror image of government petty power struggles, but one in which debates over ideology have a more prominent place and in which a far more ruthless policy in imposing discipline is pursued. In many places where the Taliban do not exercise power, they furthermore constitute a shadow government.

---

[36] Here again, I am indebted to van Bijlert, *op. cit.*, for her guide to the tribes and sub-tribes as well as her various groups of Taliban.

[37] Doug Saunders, "Afghans rejecting Canadian troops for Taliban, survey finds," *Globe and Mail*, 19 March, 2007. See also: http://www.liveleak.com/view?i=913_1214670100.

[38] Jeffrey Simpson, "Yes, the Afghan mission is 'failing' and, yes, the rituals continue," *Globe and Mail*, 11 March, 2009.

Though affiliations seem to be determined more by strategic calculations than by ideology, neither of these generally trumps sub-tribe loyalties.

The Canadians are far too few in number to serve as a counterweight in a province the size of Texas when the insurgency is fuelled by the narcotics trade, the central government is corrupt and weak, and the insurgents enjoy a safe retreat across Pakistan's porous borders. The January 2008 Report of the Independent Panel on Canada's Future Role in Afghanistan[39] made up of John Manley, Derek Burney, Jake Epp, Paul Tellier and Pamela Wallin stressed the importance of the Canadian mission in Afghanistan in terms of "global and Canadian security, Canada's international reputation, and the well-being of some of the world's most impoverished and vulnerable people." (p. 6) The Panel concluded "that with patience, commitment, financial and other forms of assistance, there is a reasonable prospect that its people will be able to live together in relative peace and security, while living standards slowly improve," (p. 8) and defined the problem as moving from a military to a civilian role as the former role is transferred to the Afghan army.

The basic premises of the modestly optimistic scenario according to its own report need to be clearly stated for the Manley scenario depends on: 1) doubling the size of the Afghan army and training it to be an effective fighting force; 2) transforming the poppy fields back to regular agricultural production; 3) uprooting the corruption of the Karzai government; and 4) significant expanded infrastructure development. While the Panel viewed the prospects as an opportunity for Canada to bring a level of commitment to an international problem that gives the nation weight and credibility, I, coming from a prophetic tradition of pessimism rather than Obama's prophetic tradition of hope[40], view the prospects as almost totally bleak, as not one of the four premises has much chance. Infrastructure cannot be built because, without security, contractors[41] abandon their projects. With only

---

[39] The Queen's Printer, No. FR5-20/1-2008, http://dsp-psd.pwgsc.gc.ca/collection_ 2008/dfait-maeci/FR5-20-1-2008E.pdf.

[40] Chaplain (Capt.) Buddy Hammil in a piece called, "When God seems distant," (in the Canadian military magazine, *The Outlook,* 2 August, 2005, p. 2) quoted Isaiah 8:17: "The Lord has hidden himself from his people, but I trust him and place my hope in him." The Chaplain advised the soldiers that when they feel forlorn and abandoned, trust that God is there and that you will not be abandoned no matter how you feel.

[41] At the beginning of December 2006, in the sixth attack in ten days, two American contractors were killed in a suicide bombing in Kandahar with a subsequent detrimental effect on development projects. On 28 November 2005, the Canadian embassy in Afghanistan reported that the Taliban had "attacked construction and

a fraction of the troops required, road travel and cooperation with the West invites retaliation from the Taliban who control the countryside.[42] No sooner was the Report tabled than the Poles announced that they would *not* be sending 1200 troops to Kandahar to reinforce the Canadians. Until recently, not one ally from NATO has stepped up to the plate to risk its soldiers in Afghanistan and assist the Canadians. Without security, how can critical infrastructure such as the Dahla Dam possibly be repaired?

On 30 January 2009, *Time* magazine asked rhetorically, "Will the U.S. Stick By Karzai in Afghanistan?" in the light of warnings by U.S. and NATO commanders "that the rampant corruption and inefficiency of the Karzai government are undermining the war effort." This was the major theme of the Afghan donor's conference in Paris in June 2008 when Karzai asked for another £12.5 billion in Western aid. It is a drum beat that

---

military vehicles with machine-gun fire and rocket-propelled grenades, killing a number of Afghan workers and causing five contractors to quit" (http://www.afghanemb-canada.net/en/news_bulletin/2005/november/28/index.php).

[42] It is difficult enough to get the supplies in to reinforce the military, let alone construct new infrastructure projects. On 18 October 2008, Tom Blackwell wrote in the *National Post* ("Private security a necessity in Kandahar province") about the private security firms required to protect the supply convoys and even the military bases themselves. Mohammed Salim, a leader with Rozi Mohammed's employer, Commando Security, noted that since he took his job four to five years ago, he had lost 500 men. This is one security team of only 200 men for just one security firm. "During the last 10 days," said Mr. Salim, "there was not one day we did not fight." 22% of the Canadian mission's costs (an accumulated total of $1.34 billion until 1 October 2006 had been spent on private security contractors. Cf. Mission Costs for Operation Athena, Department of National Defence," and "Incremental costs of the Canadian Forces Deployment for Op. Apollo, Athena and Archer," October 1, 2006, Access to Information Request A-2006-00756, p. 2, footnote 56 on p. 20 of David Perry, "Contractors in Kandahar, eh? Canada's 'Real' Commitment to Kandahar," *Journal of Military and Strategic Studies* 9:4 (2007): 1-23. Perry quoted Jack Granatstein and opined that the Canadian mission was underfunded by $1B a year. On 4 April 2008, a report noted that a contractor was even accidently killed by Canadian troops (http://www.closeprotectionworld.co.uk/close-protection-forum/3052-contractor-accidently-killed-afghanistan-canadian-troops.html). On 1 November, Elissa Golberg, the Canadian government representative in Kandahar, announced a signature $50 million project—a contractor had been hired to repair the Dhala dam on the Arghandab River in northern Kandahar Province but the contractor would have to provide his own security. (*Globe and Mail*, 15 July, 2008) SNC-Lavalin/Hydrosult was awarded the contract on 9 January, 2009.

repeats and repeats ever since Karzai took office, but the situation only gets worse not better.

As far as the drug problem, Sean Maloney in the September 2005 issue of *The Walrus* ("Poppy Fields Forever?") described booming opium production as potentially the greatest threat. However, ever since 2004 when U.S. contracted aircraft began spraying poppy fields to destroy crops and bombing Taliban strongholds, the effect has been to rally more farmers to the Taliban side. The Taliban force farmers to grow poppies[43] Canadian Foreign Minister David Emerson in 2008 acknowledged that burning Afghan poppy fields is not the best tactic; Emerson emphasized interdiction. However, when the Canadian troops cannot control the main roads, such efforts are fruitless. Powerful warlords and tribal chiefs protect their own controlled fields under threat that they will defect to the Taliban side. That is why only 20% (and not 100%) of the fields are destroyed and why what is destroyed is so quickly replaced.

However, progress on tackling the drug trade has been reported. The government of Afghanistan launched an anti-drug campaign to destroy poppy-fields in Helmand province that produces 67% of the whole poppy harvest that supplies 90% of the world heroin supply. Poppy production dropped by 20% in Helmand and just over 2,000 hectares of poppy fields were destroyed in 2008. However, over 100,000 hectares are devoted to poppy cultivation so this is at best a 2% decline.[44]

Further, the decline in production has been attributed not so much to the eradication program as an overabundance of supply. Unfortunately, as the supply diminishes, the prices go back up and the incentive to grow opium once again returns. The main factors behind the decline in poppy production from the oversupply of the 2007-08 peak years has been market forces and weather that cut opium production by 6% in 2008 to 7,000 tonnes, though overproduction still produced a decline in the opium price by 20% and by 45% percent from its peak 2007 price of over $100 a kilogram. (The average price in November 2008 was $55 a kilogram.) At the same time, the price of wheat and maize has risen nearly 50%, in part because of a global wheat shortage. Thus, one can anticipate a short term decline but no significant dent in poppy production.[45]

---

[43] "Plymouth people in poppy fields—the future of war in Afghanistan," *The Herald*, 8 January, 2007.

[44] Chinese Xinhua News Agency on 22 February 2009, http://news.xinhuanet.com/english/2009-02/22/content_10870903.htm.

[45] Cf. the UNODC annual winter survey of poppy production carried out in 484 villages of Afghanistan. The United Nations Office of Drugs and Crime December 2008 report on opium/heroin production in Afghanistan for 2009 concluded that

On the fourth assumption of the Manley report, what is the likelihood of the Afghan army being doubled by the 2011 Canadian armed forces withdrawal in 2011? On 28 January 2009, Mike Blanchfield reported in the *Calgary Herald*: "Americans to double Afghan force" and quoted U.S. Defense Secretary Robert Gates that these expectations were 'realistic and limited'. In fact, the plans were to grow the force from 80,000 to 134,000 troops by 2011. *The Economist* received the news with great scepticism and quoted critics who claim that, "President Barack Obama is now reinforcing failure by sending thousands more troops to confront an insurgency organised from across the border in Pakistan."[46] In any case, the enhanced deployment of American forces and the prospective increase in the Afghan army may dampen down the success of the insurgency, but it will certainly not defeat the Taliban. At best, the increase will prolong the war and delay the day of reckoning. More Canadian soldiers will die in the effort to ensure a credible exit strategy.

President Obama recognizes the sacrifice of Canadians and does not unduly press them to stay beyond 2011. Just days after Obama gave his inaugural address, he also took action to attack Taliban bases in Pakistan as he fulfilled his promise to take direct action against insurgents in Pakistan who threatened U.S. security if Pakistani security forces did not act.[47] The U.S. military bombed the redoubts of the terrorists using two remotely controlled missiles in strikes three hours apart against compounds in northwestern Pakistan without the Pakistani government's consent or even involvement.[48]

Although its policy subsequently changed, how did the Pakistani government initially respond to these threats to its sovereign territory, and to the insistence that the government take greater military action to undermine al-Qaeda and the Taliban lest the U.S. curtail military aid? Husain Haqqani, Pakistan's ambassador to Washington, had warned the U.S. that Pakistan would "review all options" if the U.S. ignored Pakistani concerns and interests. Partly in response to Obama's actions, and totally ignoring

---

"there are no [Afghan] provinces which are likely to show an increase in opium cultivation" and that "overall, the cultivation of opium in Afghanistan is likely to decrease in 2009."

[46] "Boots on the ground," *The Economist*, 19 February, 2009.

[47] Though, as in Iraq, the US initially met quick and outstanding success, Obama in his election campaign kept reiterating that the command cell of al-Qaeda had escaped and has never been captured. Further, though diminished, the Taliban were not a spent force but had regrouped and gradually *expanded* their areas of control.

[48] R. Jeffrey Smith, Candace Rondeaux and Joby Warrick, "2 U.S. Airstrikes Offer a Concrete Sign of Obama's Pakistan Policy," *Washington Post*, 24 January, 2009, A01.

the threats, a month later the Pakistan government under Asif Ali Zardawi announced a deal with the Taliban in Swat, the long valley effectively controlled by the Islamicists north of Islamabad, to withdraw the army and allow the Islamicists to enforce their interpretation of Islamic law. Though Obama's special envoy to the region, Richard Holbrooke, stated in an interview on CNN that Zardawi had reassured him that the truce was temporary and that the President of Pakistan knew full well that the Islamicists were "murderous thugs and militants,"[49] it seemed that the increased use of airpower inside Pakistan without coordination and consent of the Government of Pakistan[50] had provoked retreat rather than a more intensive campaign.

Obama's new strategic option is based on the following premises:

Afghanistan and Pakistan are the central focus of the war on terrorism since terrorists found sanctuary under the Taliban leaders in Afghanistan supported by the Pakistani Inter-Services Intelligence (ISI).

More troops and resources are needed in Afghanistan since enough troops had only been inserted to hold the cities and conduct sporadic offensive operations but not enough to defeat either al-Qaeda or the Taliban.

The Taliban and al-Qaeda are one and the same even though the past goal had been to defeat al-Qaeda and simply keep the Taliban from returning to power.[51]

Since the Northwest Province serves as a sanctuary for the terrorists, one has to be ready to attack the sanctuaries if Pakistan will not do the job—unilateralism while ostensibly emphasizing re-engaging America's allies.

Support the democratic forces in Pakistan for it was a mistake to coddle Mussharaf and supply him with 11 billion dollars just because he was 'our' dictator.

---

[49] "U.S. envoy calls Pakistani's Zardawi over Swat deal," Reuters, 19 February, 2009.

[50] One hundred and thirty-two people had been killed in 38 CIA missile strikes inside Pakistan by the Bush administration in the previous six months.

[51] In 2005, the Canadian goal according to the Canada/Afghan Agreement (Canada-Afghanistan Detainee Agreement, December 2005) was to "eliminate al-Qaeda, the Taliban, anti-coalition armed groups, and any other insurgents threatening the security and Stability of Afghanistan or international peace and security." Cf. *Toronto Star* editorial, 10 March, 2009.

The fifth strategic element meant a government more responsive to domestic interests and less compliant in following the American lead. The fourth element had also backfired as indicated above. The third foundation ignores the reality that not only are the Taliban (who are essentially Afghan Islamic religious fundamentalists) and al-Qaeda (as leaders in global Islamism and terrorism) quite different, but the Taliban itself is varied. The second element of defeating the Taliban had already been conceded openly by the Canadian Prime Minister as a chimera as well as by the American leadership,[52] and, in any case, 17,000 troops are not nearly sufficient to defeat the Taliban according to U.S. counterinsurgency doctrine. The first proposition yokes two traditional rivals and antagonists in a concerted effort that neither is willing to undertake since both states want to negotiate with the Taliban. The only agreement the two countries have is their disagreement with American policy.

Canada itself is not even in the same ballpark as the Americans. Canada faces two bad options: the more Canadian soldiers die, the more domestic support declines; the more Canada fights a detached war and allows civilians to die in Afghanistan, the more hearts and minds are lost risking further destabilization of a nuclear power. Canada cannot fight a three block war (a 3D strategy of a robust military effort in addition to diplomacy and economic aid) without the fourth block of public support and a communications strategy to gain that support. But as the coffins kept mounting and returning home, as the financial costs grew to exceed eight billion dollars[53], Canadians began to avert their eyes and withdraw from any emotional and intellectual engagement. When that happened, any effort at counter-insurgency war was lost. Canada plans to complete a *total* military pullout from Afghanistan by 2011 at the latest. Clearly, there will be pressure on Canada to stay in Afghanistan as well as up the ante between now and the end of 2011.[54]

---

[52] The war aim had shifted from defeating the Taliban and extremists to ensuring that, "Afghanistan cannot be used as a base for launching terrorist attacks" against the United States. ("Drone Attacks Inside Pakistan Will Continue, CIA Chief Says," *Washington Post,* 26 February, 2009.)

[53] Kevin Page, the Canadian Parliamentary budget watchdog, released a report just prior to the October federal election that costs to date were actually at least $10.5 billion. He estimated the total cost of the war at between $14 and $18 billion dollars, $1500 for every single Canadian, from Canada's initial involvement in 2002 to the end of 2011 when Canadians are scheduled to leave Afghanistan. These estimates exclude salaries and do not take into account the increase in the numbers deployed from 2500 to 2850.

[54] Canada will have great difficulty doing so. The very deployment to Afghanistan has sapped Canada's ability to train more soldiers and in 2008, the armed forces

A Third Option to Bush and Obama

There is a third option to the Bush and Obama administration strategies. The U.S. is attempting to secure a regional concert of interests involving Pakistan, India, Iran and Russia based on a multilateral diplomatic effort complemented the military effort in Afghanistan. There is little evidence this can be successful given the wide divergence of views and the extant mutual mistrust. Fen Osler Hampson urged a third option—peace from the ground up and not the military strategy from the top (Bush) or the sideways multilateral political effort conjoined with enhanced military action. Hampson argued that we "need to launch a process of constructive dialogue that engages local actors (and not just national political elites) and in such a way that they begin to consider their political—as opposed to military options—and also take some real ownership over their future and that of their people".[55]

The bottom-up option can be best understood in the comparison and contrast with the other two. All three options, however overlapping and unclear at the periphery, have been enunciated in dealing with the Afghan War. They are:

> A top-down conservative Hobbesian reliance on force and the primacy of a unipolar power can be used to ensure the authority and the legitimacy of the central state through its monopoly of coercion and its ability to impose its will over the territory it governs—the Bush strategy.[56]

---

were increased by only 628 when the Canadian forces need to be increased from 64,400 to 90,000. Currently, Canada can only deploy 1000 combat troops at any one time. Colin Kenny, "We need people," *National Post*, 12 March 2009, A17.

[55] Fen Osler Hampson, "We need super ideas, not a super envoy," *National Post*, 10 March, 2009, A15. Hampson is the Director of the Norman Paterson School of International Affairs at Carleton University.

[56] As Henry Kissinger, *op. cit.*, described this policy under Bush, "America pursued traditional anti-insurgency tactics to create a central government, help extend its authority over the entire country and, in the process, bring about a modern and democratic state." However, Kissinger, the normally traditional realist, declared that, "This strategy cannot succeed in Afghanistan—especially not as an essentially solitary effort. The country is too large, the territory too forbidding, the ethnic population too varied, the population too heavily armed." Afghanistan has never been colonized because the country has a common dedication to independence but not a common dedication to supporting a strong centralized government and lacks a democratic tradition. Kissinger opted to support the new emphasis on strengthening local and regional entities using aid to strengthen security, the middle option above negating the assumption of the first option that one begins with a

A Lockean liberal internationalism can be attempted, one that sees the military as primarily a device to provide room for economic development as the state ensures stability and security and an international partnership works with local political and economic forces to being that state into the modern international regime—the Obama strategy.

Finally, and in contrast to the above top-down and side approaches, there is a bottom-up approach that emphasizes, on the one hand, the independence, dignity and rights of individuals in the pursuit of freedom and equality under the law, while also stressing the use of traditional non-individualistic constituencies, such as local tribal leaders and new groupings of women and youth, to forge networks operating from the local level. This places the emphasis neither on state government nor on securing civil society space, defined as the room for economic entrepreneurship, but upon expanding the realm of civil society with a stress on civility and society rather than individual acquisitiveness. Here peacebuilding begins at the grass roots in a tense symbiotic relationship with central political authority, the tension increasing in proportion to the reliance of the central authority on the use of its control of violence, and to the extent that entrepreneurship is advanced through corrupt means. A bottom-up approach requires language mastery of those who come from outside the country and a commitment in time well beyond the six month rotation cycles of military troops. As the latter serve not simply as advocates for human rights, and are no longer content to serve just a humanitarian role,[57] especially in the context of political corruption, they move into information gathering and independent political analysis. They adopt peacebuilding roles through the use of instruments of persuasion using authoritative knowledge and a demonstrated long term commitment to the people at the ground level to serve as facilitators, mediators and mobilizers who use advocacy, training, and confidence-building measures between and among various communities at the local level.

---

tabula rasa and an uncommitted population whereas the war is being fought in an arena where each citizen has a myriad of overlapping and tension-ridden loyalties.

[57] In the nine months between January and September of 2008, Ban-Ki-Moon, the UN Secretary-General, reported to the Security Council on 23 September, 2008 that 30 aid workers and had been killed and 92 abducted by the Taliban and that 90 of 400 districts were areas of extreme risk with almost 50% of the country inaccessible to the UN. If UN personnel rely on the security forces to protect themselves, they are cut off from local society. If they ignore that protection, those UN workers are exposed to high risk. Cf. Marens Sack, GTZ Security Adviser on Afghanistan, "Afghanistan: Aid agencies call on Taliban to back new humanitarian agenda," http://www.alertnet.org/thenews/newsdesk/IRIN/3b129b44abcf23ecded051ee4fca60c0.htm. Negotiations by Pakistan and the UN with the Taliban are bound to increase.

There is only one major difficulty. Given the ruthless and determined effort of the Taliban leadership, such a strategy has no chance of success without an honest central government that can provide security. It is a utopian idealist strategy but one with minimal cost that could be used to secure our moral capital even if unlikely to be effective, especially in the rough and tumble of Afghanistan politics.

The Future Though the Valley of Death

The valleys of death in Afghanistan, whether the Shinkay Valley in Zabol or the Arghandab Valley northwest of Kandahar City, are planted with improvised explosive devices, as one comes face to face with suicide bombers, attacks against Western convoys, and assassinations of government officials and police. In 2005, Maj. Greg Harkins, the operations officer for the U.S. paratroop battalion in Zabol, described the Taliban as cornered rather than resurgent and continued to see the war aim as defeating the Taliban, though he was unwilling to set a date for that defeat.[58] However, the Prime Minister of Canada in 2009 conceded that defeat of the Taliban is not possible in the face of the continuing growing strength in the insurgency. Thus, we have a recipe for interminable war and the assurance that Afghanistan will continue to be made up of very many death valleys.

Promises of solar lights and roads and building schools and dams do influence support for the Karzai government. However, fear of retaliation from the Taliban may be even more persuasive. So what do Westerners do? If the war cannot be won, why continue to sacrifice troops? To allow for a dignified exit? What about the betrayal of all of those who cast their lot with Western forces? What about the government officials who will be tortured and killed? What about the tens—no hundreds of thousands who will flee rather than live under Taliban tyranny? As Afghans see projects stopped because of security fears, as they scent abandonment, as they sense the likelihood of the Taliban prevailing, the less likely they are to risk supporting the Karzai government.

Do we interpret the glass as three-quarters empty or one-quarter full? Is the West facing an apocalyptic disaster in Afghanistan? Let me offer an attempt at a "prophetic" Jewish response to this question.

In Judaism, there came a point when the voice of living prophecy was replaced by scribes and interpretive scholars dealing with a textual inheri-

---

[58] John Lancaster, "U.S. Tries to Boost Authority of Shaky Afghan Government: Forces Engage Villagers to Turn Tide Against the Taliban," *Washington Post*, 27 November, 2005.

tance—the Owl of Minerva first takes flight with the twilight closing in. Jews raised on the written word and the silencing of prophecy were resigned to only applying the insights of wisdom to looking backwards. John the Baptist, however, revived living prophecy. Unlike the Jewish prophets who always, even in the apocryphal writings, anticipated the future as arriving out of the patterns and lessons of the past by linking the present to a result brought about by past history, for Christianity the dominant narrative is a story of new beginnings without the need to track the future as a continuation of the past. Redemption is immanent.

Whether a Hobbesian top-down Bush model, or a Lockean Obama template is adopted which appropriates the voice of the old prophets, or whether naïve innocent voices of grass roots organizers offer a third option to join the fray, all three efforts are variations of Christian revelation and belief in a new born day at odds with the evidence and the past. All are based on hopes for a miracle or a divine helping hand and are not the products of an autopsy. In contrast, Jewish visions are pessimistic, not only about the ultimate course of history, but also about contemporary possibilities of one group of humans coming to the rescue of another group. For the messianic age when G-d's redemptive purposes will consummate history is not here or even just around the corner. It is a distant dream. And in the meantime, we wait news each morning to see if another Canadian soldier will be returning in a coffin in a war which our own Prime Minister has declared we cannot win.

Should I offer inspiration and hope or should I serve as a purveyor of doom and gloom? When G-d withdrew from the world, when we can no longer hear a voice that will foretell the future, then an analysis of history rather than hope must be relied on for an answer. And the answer is that the glass is three quarters empty and no deliverance can be expected in the present situation. After the Babylonian captivity, G-d withdrew and Enoch foresaw seventy corrupt shepherds delivering the future of his nation into the hands of satanic evil claiming to speak in G-d's name. G-d saw but did not intervene and remained cold and aloof, unmoved by the suffering of the people. And any feeling, empathetic person has to feel despair and deep pain and compassion for those who suffer, including those who come from abroad, from our own lands, to die futile deaths. The Christian leadership of various stripes of the Western states, whether driven by a powerful faith in themselves and their prowess, or by a prophetic hope as if they could hear a divine voice and the voice alone could defeat evil, or even by a deep sense of service to those who suffer, takes its lessons and guide to conduct from one version of hope or another—*and not from history*. Christians believe we can open the scrolls, assuage our grief and break the seventh seal. For the first seal demands applying faith in scripture to the present, whereas, for Jews, the first seal itself is the evil naïvité of innocence.

Immanuel Kant began his *Foundation of the Metaphysics of Morals* with the first categorical imperative that nothing can possibly be conceived which can be called good without qualification, except a *good will*. Whereas for Jews, good intentions constitute the first seal of evil that must be broken open, in the old cliché, to discover that the road to hell is paved with the flat rocks we pay Afghan labourers $3 to $7 a day to build new roads through Kandahar, and with the good intentions behind those payments. So it is incumbent to say No in a different prophetic voice, a voice that challenges habits and false assumptions that are the symbiotic partners of a complacent public unwilling to make the deep sacrifices required if they are truly determined to confront evil. For a prophet is a watchman (Ezekiel 3:15), not a fortune teller or a seer, and a trumpeter rather than a soldier blowing "Taps" on his bugle as one more soldier is buried.

No Choice but to Confront Afghanistan: Theological Reflections on the Impasse between Policy and Theology[1]

Darren C. Marks

I steal my title from Yitzhak Greenberg's reflections on the Holocaust in his *Cloud of Smoke, Pillar of Fire* in which Greenberg raises the question of the impact, role and future of the Holocaust for Western Abrahamic religions. We shall have cause to return to Greenberg later, but for the present, what he asks is an essential series of questions embedded in a real historical event that revealed the shallowness of many Christian and Jewish theologies as played out in the *Realpolitik* of history. These ideas run from the nature of Jewish-Christian history and relationship, to Jewish-Christian passivity towards the Holocaust, to what are the standing effects of failing to deal with those questions, and finally to what resources in the Jewish and Christian traditions of theology might help prevent such terror, malaise and evil ever again. What Greenberg does for the Holocaust, I hope to begin to do in connection with Canada's war in Afghanistan. Obviously, the sense of scale between the Holocaust and Afghanistan is not the same (although I do think if one expands ideas to the "war on terror" and its shaping of the last decade in our global psyche there may indeed be a case for some such claim). What I am arguing, however, is that the Canadian Abrahamic religions and even liberalism's view of salvation must confront Afghanistan as a crucible of how our theology fares in terms of that *Realpolitik*. Furthermore, our Canadian mythos or identity and the future of Canada as a middle power is at stake in these issues.

Afghanistan, in short, reveals our strengths and weaknesses as a people invested in a particular vision, even a vision of God, tested in real terms of

---

[1] Thanks is due to my research assistant for this paper, Ms. Courtney Spence. She proofed, researched and filled out some areas of the work, particularly the section on *Tikkun Olam's* intellectual history.

our responsibility as peoples of salvation. As Greenberg argues in his works in reference to the Holocaust, our real historical and positive activity, multiplex and multifaceted, reveals our true theological foundations and commitments rather more honestly than does our rhetoric or imagined self-image. Afghanistan, in short, asks Canadians, secular and sacred, basic questions that are deeply foundational and that need to be faced. At the heart of all these questions is this simple question: "Who is the 'responsible human'?" I will argue that this is both a theological question and a matter of theological mission or *Tikkun Olam* which is shared by Jews and Christians in terms of living responsibility under the idea of the image of God. This then involves advocacy, witness, and deeds. I will argue that the *Tikkun* demands that the Abrahamic religions confront Afghanistan.

The manner by which I expand this idea will be first to explore the history and applications of Canadian public policy makers in order to place what motives drove the escalation of Canada's role in Afghanistan. I then ask whether there has been a transmutation of that vision. All I am doing in this historical rehearsal is to attempt to understand what values seem to be in play in our application of responsibility. Then I will read against this the notion of responsibility as found in the largely Christian tradition, bringing to the stand Jean Bethke Elshtain and her readings of Bonhoeffer and Niebuhr on the notion of the "responsible human," and by implication "responsible [sic] Christian society." As a foil for Elshtain, I will read Jean Amery's reflections on the "first blow" and "resentment" within the Holocaust as a way to help us reassess how we might not fuel Islamic fundamentalist reaction to Western presence in Afghanistan and further afield. Améry, I hope, deepens our sense of responsibility to the future. Finally, I reassess the notion of "responsible humanity" in terms of the *Tikkun Olam* for faith communities which, I hope, avoids playing shill for Taliban and al-Qaeda spindoctors,[2] eschews Islamophobia and neo-Imperialism and

---

[2]In 2003 and then again in 2008, the sobering charge has been made that both Taliban and al-Qaeda media gurus have actively sought to exploit left media and academics in order to create a fog of war doubting Canadian and Western roles in Afghanistan and further in the war on terror. Jean Bethke Elshtain and Sean Maloney both note that such "fixers" exploit media and academy in such a way as to exaggerate loss and minimize impact in order to force policy makers to reduce responsible actions in Afghanistan, Iraq and other places. Elshtain is more extreme arguing that, by definition, the academy is a "negator" to most governmental interventions in foreign climes since the Second World War. Maloney, on the other hand, notes the sophistication of hard Taliban and al-Qaeda media fixers who have perceived in the Western media a fear of loss, both military and civilian, which can be exploited to sway public opinion and galvanize desired action when, in fact, Afghanistan is indeed albeit slowly moving to a more stable state. See, Jean

brings together Abrahamic communities with secular policy makers in such a manner that Afghanistan has a future. In short, I hope to remind us to confront Afghanistan, reassess our commitment to the *Tikkun Olam* and be responsible humans before God and to each other. This then is not merely, contra Elshtain, naïve academic negation, moral purism and handwringing, victimizing truth in the face of totalitarianism, but the deepest affirmation of the responsible human as working against symbols of death/terror in order to think and act in terms of absolute value.[3]

I begin with an analysis by a hapless theologian on policy and history.

Imperialism and Deterrence in Light of Failed and Failing States[4]

The doctrine of "failed and failing states" has been around a long time, perhaps as long as there have been nation-states.[5] The doctrine of failed and failing states, however, assumed prominence in the months and year after 9/11 as a reason for Western intervention in Iraq and Afghanistan. Perhaps the most famous articulation was given in a speech by Jack Straw, British Foreign Secretary, on 6th September, 2002 at the European Research Institute in Birmingham, England. Here, Straw, wedged between the invasion of Afghanistan (October 2001) and the American preparation to invade Iraq (March 2003), gives voice to the responsibility of powerful nations as understood in the failed and failing state model:

Bethke Elshtain, *Just War Against Terror: The Burden of American Power in a Violent World* (New York: Basic Books), 71ff., and Sean Maloney, "A Violent Impediment: Evolution of Insurgent Operations in Kandahar Province 2003-07," *Small Wars and Insurgencies* 19, no. 2 (2008): 207-215.

[3] Elshtain argues all the above as failures of the academy in its response to terrorism and, by implication, as the rationale for a neo-Imperialism of the one remaining Superpower. Ibid., 71-106, 166ff.

[4] I borrow this phrase from Elshtain: "Rather, the sort if imperialism that commentators like Sebastian Mallaby and Michael Ignatieff are groping toward is an image of the world's great superpower taking on an enormous burden and doing so with a relatively, though not entirely, selfless intent. The imperialism they suggest is not one of colonial states dominated by provincial governors, but rather a form of nation building that is primarily concerned with a new version of deterrence. What is being deterred or forestalled are failed states ....." Ibid., 166

[5] See, for example, Michael Drolet (2007), "Failed states and modern empires: Gustave de Beaumont's *Ireland* and French Algeria," *History of European Ideas* 33, no.4, (2007): 502-24.

> Yet the events of 11 September devastatingly illustrated a more particular and direct reason for our concern. For it dramatically showed how a state's disintegration can impact on the lives of people many thousands of miles away, even at the heart of the most powerful democracy in the world. The shocking events of that day were planned, plotted and directed by a group which exploited domestic chaos to commit the most heinous international crime. So as we approach the first anniversary of the attacks, we need to remind ourselves that turning a blind eye to the breakdown of order in any part of the world, however distant, invites direct threats to our national security and well-being.
>
> I believe therefore that preventing states from failing and resuscitating those that fail is one of the strategic imperatives of our times.[6]

Straw further articulates the view that the failed and failing state model is both a *new* policy for his office, and a new manner for *ranking* concerns of government foreign policy. Straw observes that "history shows that governments have largely been unable to summon the collective will to intervene in the collapse of a state,"[7] and therefore, however good in theory an international vision of law might be, it may ultimately fall to a powerful few to take responsibility. The powerful few may "[have] strong reasons for wishing to prevent state failure; or particularly effective tools at [their] disposal. Why should [they] not then take the lead?" In short, the doctrine of failing or failed states is a manifestation of the highest kind of collective responsible civic and political action.

What is the doctrine of failed and failing states if it is to be used as a criterion for responsible action? Classically (as again is reflected in Straw's stump speech) the Weberian definition is that if a legitimate government fails to maintain an exclusive monopoly of (legitimate) force within its borders then the state is failed. Further development expands Weber's problematic definition (since say, in theory, a totalitarian government could thus be deemed a successful government) into a dozen or so indicators of social, economic and political vitality. These include the question of displaced peoples, human flight, inability to meet basic human needs, continued conflict, economic chaos, corruption and other criminalized normalities, human rights abuses, identity politics and irredentism and so on. What does seem new in the present invocation of the failed state doctrine is the very point that Straw makes central, namely the probability of threat to the *security* of not only near neighbours but to distant superpowers: "the dreadful events of 11 September have given us a vision of

---

[6] Jack Straw, "Failed and Failing States," given at European Research Institute on 6 September, 2002, http://www.mafhoum.com/press3/111P3.htm.
[7] Ibid.

one possible future. A future in which unspeakably evil acts are committed against us, coordinated from failed states in distant parts of the world. If we are to avoid a recurrence, then international action to prevent state failure is a challenge today and for the ages."

It then follows, as has been articulated by Elshtain and many others[8]—and ironically invoked also by Straw, that to avoid a Hobbesian future of life brutish, chaotic and short, it falls to the powerful few to be responsible to remedy failed and failing states in order to seek a future for those persons within and for us without. To fail to do this is to take leave of politics, humanity, God and justice.

So, before we enter into an analysis of this position of "groping towards imperialism" we must ask a basic series of foundational questions of Canada and of our policy makers. Was this *responsible* action our motivation for entering into Afghanistan? And further, if it was not, then has Canada in either decision or execution *abrogated* that responsibility in any manner that may compromise justice? And finally, if we have failed to act responsibly, then what kind of role might people of faith carry in assisting Canadian policy makers to ensure that the doctrine of failed and failing states should not be used merely to buttress what Noam Chomsky charges is merely a neo-Imperialism?[9] This last possibility raises a significant challenge to Elshtain's assertion that democratic "habits of the heart"—which she roots in the Enlightened ideal of the equality of all before God—are in themselves really what is formative or foundational in our response to failed states.[10]

I think it fair to say that by all accounts, the doctrine of failed and failing states and its subsequent stress on some kind of humanitarian response came late to Canada, perhaps as late as 2005 (although Canada's allies in Europe had been long appealing to it as the reason for Iraq and Afghanistan). Janice Stein and Eugene Lang, relying on interviews with the primary players from 9/11 to the present (including John Manley, Bill Graham, and former Prime Ministers Jean Chrétien and Paul Martin), give an excellent account in their *The Unexpected War: Canada in Kandahar*. In fact, as reported by Bill Graham, it was only in the summer of 2005 that Canada used, culled to bring the Pearsonian peacekeeper Canadian to mind of "warrior diplomat," language which referenced the failed state model itself and its obligation to human rights in particular. While it had a new name in Canadian parlance the three Ds of "defence, development

---

[8] Elshtain, *Just War*, 169.
[9] Noam Chomsky, Failed States: The Abuse of Power and Democracy (New York: Holt, 2007).
[10] Elshtain, *Just War*, 33ff.

and diplomacy"—the heart of the public case made was pure failed state doctrine married with democratic protection of human rights. It was Canada's role, amongst others, to reconstruct a war-torn Afghanistan in order to give "hope for the future of a long suffering people as an expression of our Canadian values at work."[11] As Graham commented, this was not a war, not a part of the "war on terror," but purely a matter of "bringing stability to the region."[12] Perhaps more to the point, however, is the fact that the failed state doctrine also developed in Canadian rhetoric in a distinctly new direction, for as was publicly declared by then Chief of Defence Staff General Rick Hillier, the goal was one of getting at "'detestable murderers and scumbags' who inhabited Kandahar province and threatened Western societies"; the end effect was that the "Kandahar mission was now defined as an operation to root out terrorists who might someday, somehow, again do violence to North America."[13] "Peacekeeping heavy" became the new failed state doctrine heavily imbued with a recognizably Canadian focus on human rights which fit with the common Canadian self-image of the peacekeeper par excellence. The Afghanistan war, in other words, became "The Mission." This language, for example, is to be found throughout the 2008 Manley Report.

So, if the doctrine of failed states arrives late on the scene in Canadian thinking about Afghanistan, then the natural question concerns what motivated Canada's involvement in the first instance? By most accounts, what preoccupied Canadian policy makers from 2001 to 2005 was a complex of motivations and *Realpolitik*. These ranged from the ongoing inter-party leadership squabbles of the day between Jean Chrétien and rival Paul Martin,; the ruling Liberal Party of Canada's preoccupation with Québec polls which historically have been suspicious of war; public doubts about the role of the Canadian military within NATO; the charismatic and very public personality of General Rick Hillier, who wished to bring the Canadian Forces to international prominence as "warriors" rather than as "bluehelmeted" peacekeepers; to finally the complex relationship Canada has to the United States in terms of the "war on terror," the war in Iraq and ultimately the ballistic missile defence program.[14] It is not my purpose to rehearse these factors but merely to draw attention to one simple and glaring fact: Canada from its initial deployment and for nearly four years was not overly concerned with responsibility as evidenced in the failed state doc-

---

[11] Janice Stein and Eugene Lang, *The Unexpected War: Canada in Kandahar* (Toronto: Viking, 2007), 198-99.
[12] Ibid., 199.
[13] Ibid., 200-01.
[14] See, Ibid., 1-198.

trine as a primary or even major motivation in its decision-making. The question then is what changed in those four years or so of activity, and will the change in question help or detract from the stated goal of the "mission" as envisaged in the Manley Report: "to make a difference in Afghanistan—to contribute to a more stable and peaceful, better governed and developing Afghanistan" which "will directly affect Canada's security, our reputation in the world, and our future ability to engage the international community in achieving objectives of peace, security and shared prosperity."[15]

The First Blow: the Principle of Hope and the Reign of Fear[16]

In his 1964 work, *At the Mind's Limits*, Holocaust survivor and Jewish philosopher/thinker Jean Améry points us to two important ideas that I think are important if the failed state doctrine is to work. These two ideas are not found in any book on international relations but were forged, in Améry's case, in the context of history and personal experience. Améry reminds us in particular of the unspeakable assault on his humanity that took place in the camps. This assault, which occurred in the name of state ideology and presumably security, had certain devastating effects beyond what was purely physical. Améry describes the response of the tortured in disarming terms:

> I am certain that with the very first blow that descends on him he loses something we will perhaps temporarily call "trust in the world." Trust in the world includes all sorts of things; the irrational and logically justifiable belief in absolute causality perhaps or the likewise blind belief in the validity of the inductive inference. But more important as an element of trust in the world, and in our context what is solely relevant, is the certainty that by reason of written or unwritten social contracts the other person will spare me—more precisely stated, that he will respect my physical and with it my metaphysical, being.[17]

Two immediate points jump from Améry's work. The first is that the policy of torture, as represented by the Nazis, was legitimated from the

---

[15] *Independent Panel on Canada's Future Role in Afghanistan* (commonly called *The Manley Report*), p 12, http://www.dsp-psd.pwgsc.gc.ca/collection_2008/dfait-maeci/FR5-20-1-2008E.pdf.

[16] Jean Améry, *At the Mind's Limits*, trans. S. Rosenfield (Bloomington: Indiana University Press, 1980 [1964]), 40.

[17] Ibid., 28.

point of view of their concerns for security or "for information important for national policy." It was therefore carried out in "good conscience." The second is that, by placing torture in their service, they made torture their own master and so destabilized all hope for a truly human future.[18] Torture, for Améry, is not merely the absolute abrogation of human dignity, but it creates in both the tortured and the torturer the end of hope, while begetting fear and ultimately resentment.[19] Resentment is key.

Améry tells us that having had his trust in the world shattered by being tortured he is forever without a home, uncomfortable in the "peaceful lovely land" promised in the post-war reconstruction of Europe in which there is tacit agreement that Nazism was a one off mistake of history.[20] Instead of the dream forged in the war and in the new European peace, Améry lives sick, terminally ill, because he cannot legitimize the rhetoric amid the reality of what happened to him. Instead of being easily placed in the new vision of liberal European society where collective guilt is parsed, tamed, reified and explained so that the victims and perpetrators alike can forget and forgive, Améry claims and holds resentment because as an *individual* he was assaulted and because he cannot be reduced to a principle or point of necessity. As an *individual*, he now knows something more sinister concerning the nature of human politics and life, and as such he cannot hope but lives in resentful fear. His answer is that if collective guilt is to be addressed with any hope for restitution, it must first be freed from "myth and mystification" by allowing the victim to speak of their burden.[21] It is not those in power who need to be heard. For Améry, however beautifully paved are the Autobahns, or reconciliatory the words of government, there can never be peace for the victim because it was precisely that world of promise that betrayed and tortured him. The betrayal was not merely one undertaken by individual actors, but it was implied by the promise itself which sought prosperity and peace. The greater good was the goal of Axis and Allied alike, but the individual human was very often left in the dust amid the grand vision underwriting the war's prosecution and even the reconstruction that followed.

I bring Améry to the stand for a particular reason. If, as Elshtain holds, it is a *religious* obligation to uphold the dignity of the human person, rooted in the image of God written into human nature and in the nature of the justice of God, then human rights at every point in the conduct of a just war must be protected. One would expect this to apply particularly in the

---

[18] Ibid., 31.
[19] Ibid., 40.
[20] Ibid., 63.
[21] Ibid., 73-5,

neo-liberal agenda, for which individual human rights are sacrosanct. Even admitting that civilian deaths might be an unfortunate result of the prosecution of a war, for instance, there must surely be off-limit actions, determined by the concept of human rights and so extending beyond Elshtain's own reinvented law of proportionality of nuclear, biological and biochemical means.[22] Given the fact that both NATO and American use of airstrikes have actually increased since 2006, causing the Afghanistan government itself to pass a resolution limiting them by NATO forces, and given the rate of civilian casualties resulting from some, at least, of these airstrikes, this has become a pressing issue both in Afghanistan and in the Muslim world in general. One further taboo, however, must be torture. It is now indisputable, not least as it has been revealed by the Obama administration, that the American military and security services have engaged in the use of torture in the quest, not merely for security, but specifically in enforcement of the failed state doctrine. It is also possible that the Canadian military and security services have both knowingly handed over captured or suspected insurgents to state authorities worldwide that use the practice of torture. However much it may have sought to avoid such abuse, the sheer fact that it has trained and aided such a government in the case of Afghanistan itself makes it indirectly complicit in torture. "Those vexatious detainees" alarmed Bill Graham from as early as 2002 in terms of the American rendition practice, but it continued all the way to 2005 when General Hillier, on his own initiative, signed an agreement with the Afghanistan government for the transfer of captured insurgents to the Afghanistan police without any protections therein, as won by Britain and Denmark, that those given over would be granted basic human rights and excluded in particular from torture. Seventeen months later, in 2007, it became public knowledge that Afghan authorities "routinely torture and abuse detainees" and that perhaps Hillier's signing of the transfer agreement was in fact both non-binding and perhaps an usurpation of political authority by a martial authority.[23] Only in May of 2007, nearly six years after the prosecution of the war, did Canada formally create a new document of transfer which stopped the potential and reality of abuse for prisoners.

So, we are left with this question, whether in Canada's haste and the "fog of war" we have effectively created Améry's resentment within Afghanistan? Have we participated in the abrogation of something so precious and so essential to the winning of peace that Afghanistan is doomed

---

[22] Elshtain, *Just War*, 69. Surely human distress caused by failure of basic medical needs and services and poverty is a form of biochemical-biological warfare?
[23] Stein and Lang, *Unexpected War*, 247-55.

to a kind of fear and displacement, as evidenced in its colonial and Soviet history, to be a society that holds no promise for its peoples? Can the failed state doctrine work if it tramples upon something so essential and therefore creates the possibility that our "habits of the heart" are in themselves problematic for those on whom our power imposes? Success in the Afghanistan mission is not merely a case of whether we are better than warlords, ethnic rivalries, or Taliban rule, but of whether our vision of society can ever be trusted by those who have felt our "first blow" in the name of our security. Améry is important because he reminds us that responsibility must involve decisions concerning the one human being as well as the many. This means that not only must we probe the question of the collective good, which is itself a mark of just war, but that we need also to secure the future of the individual. Responsible humanity must hold this thought.

Who is Responsible? Taking Note of Politics[24]

Perhaps the most substantial defence of the kind of activity engaged post-9/11 comes from the pens of Jean Bethke Elshtain and her group of 60 or so scholars who signed the document, "What we are fighting for: Letter from America."[25] Elshtain rehabilitates Augustinian just war theory and blends it with Niebuhrian Christian realism in order to argue that it is not merely in American self-interest to wage the "war of Terror" post 9/11 but that it is both the loving and Christian response to a group of individuals and rogue nation-states who have "taken leave of politics" and therefore cannot be treated with the juridical instruments of international law; the United Nations, while promising this, fails to deliver.[26] Instead of juridical and incremental movement through deterrents, interdictions and the host of other measures that the United Nations might impose (and presumably fail to enforce or be shown to be ignored), Elshtain argues that it falls to a (sic) Christian nation to enforce politically God's justice.[27] She accordingly nuances by stating that the goal is peaceable kingdoms, restraint of sinful wills (including that of the U.S. and the West) and argues that this is not vengeance but justice; therefore the bedrock must be the basic, naturally evident truth of human worth, equality and freedom.[28] Both terrorists and fascistic religious fundamentalists, and by extension,

---

[24] Elshtain, *Just War*, 19.
[25] Reprinted in ibid., 182-208.
[26] Ibid., 9-26.
[27] Ibid., 46-59.
[28] Ibid., 34.

any state that hosts, fosters, or gives succour to those two sorts of unnatural humanity must be met with justice in order to foster peaceable common life.[29] This would, in the face of 9/11, be the action of a responsible human and by extension of a responsible society.

Along the way, Elshtain dismantles conceptions that Christianity is a radical peace movement in essence, that Christianity is essentially pietistic and therefore not politically engaged and that the one to one match of American culture and Christianity is not true.[30] Her primary dialogue partner is Augustine, although she certainly has Reinhold Neibuhr and a kind of Dietrich Bonhoeffer in mind who both advocated the need for Christians to get themselves dirty in worldly affairs rather than sit with a kind of pious eschatological detachment while the innocent suffer.[31] In short, utopian projects, including those of NGOS and even the United Nations, insofar as they operate with a misty kind of human progressivism, must be countered by the Augustinian view of human sinfulness and politics as a necessary curb (see the Hobbesian quote in Straw) to human sinfulness. Thus a nation-state or kingdom which has cultivated a habit and dialogue of the heart towards justice, peace and security (now detached from peace ironically) can legitimately use military means or other force to secure peace.

What I wish to focus on here in particular is Elshtain's understanding of responsibility, but I cannot leave alone several other deeply problematic ideas in her ethics. This will necessarily be staccato-like, as each could be developed at length in principle. First, is whether terrorists, by definition, qualify for the "two kingdoms in conflict" model that Augustine seems to intimate in his just war thought. Can just war in the Augustinian sense be applied to terrorism and specifically to the "war on terror," especially when the condition for terrorism's survival is exactly the kind of displacement that a prolonged war cultivates? For example, research on the backgrounds of captured al-Qaeda members reveals that one quarter of them come from Western countries and youth substantially impacted by economic and societal displacement. Of the remaining two thirds, the vast majority are recruited from dispossessed populations in camps or in other forms of exile.[32] Clearly the seedbed for terrorism is related to societal ills not necessarily fuelled by Islamic "law based religion."[33] In other words,

---

[29] Ibid., 143.
[30] Ibid., 102ff.
[31] Ibid., 25.
[32] Seem Peter Bergen, "Al-Qaeda: The Organization. A Five year forecast," *Annals of the AAPSS* 618 (2008): 14-28.
[33] Elshtain, *Just War*, 29.

is the type of sinfulness in question here more akin to Augustine's famous pirate than to that of a nation or kingdom? The second problem is whether there is enough space for redemption, surely the goal of Augustine's model, in the prosecution of such a war when it is not justice or peace *per se* that is sought but security. Security is a shifty concept—for example, is it the same as Augustine's ontology of peace or different?—And what kind of scale does one use in order to measure either concept? What seems implicit in Elshtain is that security—protection from crimes against liberty—is the same as peaceable living. But at what point in human and Christian history has there been, apart from the kind of theocracy that Elshtain eschews as idolatry,[34] such a conflation between crime and peace? Terrorism seems to be criminal given its scale and occasion. It is terrible, but is it ever proportionate to the ills of war which is indeed sin? In Elshtain's own words, in a theocracy "there is no difference between sin and crime."[35] A third issue is the kind of Islamophobia she creates with comments such as those concerning Islam as a "law-based" religion over against Christianity's grace orientation, or concerning the notion that the evils of theocracy, the very thing many litigious Christians advocate daily in the U.S., never took root in the West.[36] Surely, this kind of conversation can only fuel conflict? And what of other "law based religions" such as Judaism? Finally, there is a terrible unreflectivity in her thinking which refuses to ask whether it is our actions that have, in small or large part, created the conditions for the situation we face. At no time does Elshtain nuance her thoughts by reference to the role of history, our history, in assisting in the production of the world that faces us in the twenty-first century. At least for Augustine there was a sense that indeed *Christian times* were terrible times in his *City of God* and that it is imperative for any Christian statecraft to begin with difficult and hard introspection before action towards the other city. Another way of understanding this is to say that Augustine's just war theory must be read alongside his two kingdom theology, even the bits we don't want to ponder which may be that the city of humanity is indeed a sword in the hand of God. But, enough here, let us return to the claim that it is responsible for us to engage with the world in this way.

---

[34] Ibid., 30.
[35] Ibid., 41.
[36] Ibid., 29.

Two Witnesses: Neibuhr and Bonhoeffer

Certainly it is well known that recent, or near contemporary just war theologies share much with Augustine. However, many argue that the primary differences between Augustine and near contemporary just war apologists are rooted in the latter's more pessimistic view of the church and its involvement in the crucible of history. The line of argument is that Augustine(or more accurately, perhaps, the tradition of Augustine's as mediated in the natural law theology of Aquinas) simply assumes too much in his theology of misplaced and corrected loves between the two cities and therefore conflates the two rather too easily. Thus the door is opened for a kingdom or ruler to assume that God is "on our side," and to move with justice *sicut Deus*, proofed by some version of natural law theology supposedly evident to all. There is, however, and other and more subtle reading of Augustine available to us. Thus Reinhold Neibuhr, for example, argues that this reading of the Augustinian just war tradition is too simplistic and that the strength of Augustine is indeed his acknowledgment of the complex of human motivations, even within the church itself, combined with a strong measure of eschatological reserve. In this case, it is not so much justice and competing loves that drive the engine of Christian political theology but rather that the Christian kingdom, which is without absolute certainty in these matters for the most part, should nevertheless endeavour to act responsibly or in love towards even the unjust other. That, of course, may include use of the sword. To act responsibly then is the key to Augustine's just war theology and his understanding of the two cities. Both cities are equally gifted with freedom and burdened with encultured sin, and both are pervaded by grace despite sinful loves (although one may in fact be more aware of this shortcoming due to Christian habits), but finally it falls to the city of God and to the Christian state alike to act in that freedom to love the other as best it can but with grave circumspection. To love the other is to act, as in Michael Ramsey, to protect the innocent as well as to chastise the wicked. For Niebuhr, in the same trajectory, to act responsibly is to act politically, for the city of God which is to engage in agapic responsibility to the world, to the other, the innocent and the wicked alike, cannot evade its political responsibilities. Responsibility then seems to be the commission to engage in dialogue and action. Action may be merely testimony to the eschatological goal or it may take shape in decidedly political and military forms of action which may involve force. But the emphasis is important—it is to act in responsibility.

Bonhoeffer adds to our understanding of responsibility. In her work, Elshtain has herself argued that Bonhoeffer is important due to his "chart[ing] a course between corrupt inaction and action motivated by revenge rather than a call to responsibility."[37] What she grievously fails to plot, nonetheless, is not only that Bonhoeffer worries of a much deeper problem than inaction but that he tempers his idea of responsibility with a theological notion of God loving the *individual* sinner. But before I turn to what the mature Bonhoeffer means by that, we need to understand how in fact the more grievous issue that vexed Bonhoeffer was not inactivity *per se* but rather Christian *folly*. Bonhoeffer, as Elshtain notes correctly, is not an advocate of pacifism and laments the lack of "civil courage" by Christians in light of human evil. This is for him the very problematic nature of German Protestantism with its pietistic emphasis on the self, and its Lutheran concession to the secular city as God's hand; the resulting situation, for Bonhoeffer, is "irresponsible." To counter it, Bonhoeffer argues that Christians are neither privately reasonable nor inwardly focused but that they must in their vocation be responsible to resist evil as an exercise of freedom. This freedom, however, is circumscribed by God: "It depends on God who demands responsible action in a bold venture of faith, and who promises forgiveness and consolation to the man who becomes a sinner in that venture."[38] This seemingly echoes Elshtain's comment that Christian responsibility is invariably a "contamination." It can be read out of this that Bonhoeffer argues that responsibility means becoming active, that activity may be messy morally but that God forgives and sustains the venture because it is God who has made/makes us morally free agents in the drama of redemption. But Bonhoeffer is no fool, and his worth is not whether we are active but *how* we are active: "The ultimate question for a responsible man to ask is not how is he going to extricate himself from the affair, but how the coming generation is to live. It is *only* from this question, with its responsibility to history, that fruitful solutions can come, even if for the time being they are very humiliating."[39] Bonhoeffer asks us a better question of responsibility than does Elshtain. His approach is not merely pragmatism but the enduring of responsibility for the sake of the coming generations and for the sake of its witness to God. To fail in this is *folly* for Bonhoeffer.

Folly, then, is more to be avoided than irresponsible inaction: "Folly is more dangerous enemy to the good than evil. One can protest against evil;

---

[37] Ibid., 25.
[38] Dietrich Bonhoeffer, *Letters and Papers from Prison* ed. Eberhard Bethge and trans. Reginald Fuller *et al.* (New York: Macmillian, 1971 [1953]), 3-5.
[39] Ibid., 7. Emphasis mine.

it can be unmasked and, if need be, prevented by force. Evil always carries the seeds of its own destruction, as it makes people, at the least uncomfortable. Against folly we have no defense."[40] The reason, he notes, that folly is so dangerous is that it cannot be argued against, protested or forced away through coercion. It remains anti-God because at its root, folly assumes that God is not. A fool is a person who thinks he is above God, independent in his actions and unaccountable to God for what he does, even in the pursuit of justice. This, then, tips us to the most central idea in Bonhoeffer's notion of responsibility—the belief that God *is*. What does this mean for Bonhoeffer, and then for us?

First, it means that responsible action must take into account that what we do is *before* God rather than *against* evil; accordingly: "...we must learn to regard people less in the light of what they do or omit to do, and more in the light of what they suffer."[41] Can we envision a terrorist as a person who suffers as well as a person who inflicts suffering? Second, the "view from below" means that like God we too must be prepared to suffer in order to be of use for God in the future. We cannot "become suspicious of others and kept from being truthful and open" in light of our "intolerable conflicts" but need to be ready to suffer in order that the future is not closed off for others by our need for peace or security in the present.[42] In short, in our responsibility we need—including in the cause of our strife— to hold but one responsibility which is "one of love...as God did not despise humanity but became man for men's sake."[43] It is this last point that I want to spend some time thinking on lest it become susceptible to Neibuhr's complaint of pious sentimentality in too much of Christian thought.

At the heart of Bonhoeffer's insight I think is his most central idea in the area of ethics. This is the idea that God knows humans *only* as sinners and as individual sinners at that. This may seem trite but it is deeply rooted in his Christology and describes for us perfectly something integral to the concept of responsible action. What is proposed is a theological anthropology in which emphasis is placed on Christ/God and specifically on the notion of the human person as sinner but nonetheless made whole by God's summoning in Christ, or "vocation." Bonhoeffer's ethical theory, and his commitment to responsibility for others, is based squarely on the notion that freedom, and therefore true identity, is only found in responsibility or in conformation to what has already been declared and enabled by

---

[40] Ibid., 8.
[41] Ibid., 10.
[42] Ibid., 16.
[43] Ibid., 10.

God in Christ. Bonhoeffer is clear that what results from this vision is not an idealized person or state polity but an understanding of humanity as humanity really is—namely as constituted by its essential and irreducible relationship to God and therefore to "reality" as it really is.[44] In short, when we see ourselves before God, we see ourselves and the world correctly for the first time because in that moment, sustained by God's graciousness to us, we are free in our vocations as people of God to "help our neighbor [and creation itself] to [likewise] be a person before God."[45] It follows from Bonhoeffer's thought that the real human, and real foundation of reality itself, is Christ: for in Christ "there is a place at which God and cosmic reality are reconciled, a place at which God and human have become one."[46]

Now foundational to this idea is something largely repugnant to moderns—the claim that only as sinner is humanity constituted—and an idea largely repugnant to ethicists—that individuals matter. However, before moving to explore this idea more deeply, we must be careful to realize that this is not primarily a *moral* issue for Bonhoeffer—a description of a Kantian universal moral imperative or worth, soundness or reasonableness—but rather an affirmation of the action of God in which what humans offer towards God is judged, renewed and annexed into the divine. There is a motif from the Lutheran *theologia crucis* operative here: that in the sentence/ judgement of God on the individual human sinner one finds instead the presence of the crucified God or a willingness, in the parlance of modern theological themes, to embrace the other despite human folly, whether personal moral or systemic, and to establish *that* person as a person called by God. It then is the *fate* of sinful humanity, and so of individuals, to be taken up by God, to be executed on the cross in order to find their truest nature which is in concord with God as revealed in the Godman (and Torah for Jews). It is not the notion of the sinner as pariah, nor of the righteous as beloved, that determines human worth, but rather our "acceptance of the sentence passed…by Divine love."[47] This is the glorious "yes" of grace in which we learn to unlearn what the world teaches and instead are called or summoned to something else. It is this notion of summons, call or conformation that I wish now to address.

First, we must note that summons, call or conformation is not a call to morality *per se* but instead a call to what Bonhoeffer calls "responsibility." The "responsible human" is not responsible in the usual moralistic sense,

---

[44] Ibid., 9.
[45] Ibid., 22.
[46] Ibid., 8.
[47] Ibid., 16.

but is in reality a sinner, one who knows the need and effect of grace, who realizes that only Christ is the form of humanity and *therefore* one who takes seriously the call of God to foster *that* love of God and for God in the other:

> Every day a [Christian] person dies the death of a sinner. He humbly bears the scars of his body and soul, the marks of the wounds which sin inflicts on him. He cannot raise himself up above any other man or set himself before another as a model, for he knows himself to be the greatest of all sinners. He can excuse the sin of another, but never his own.... He does not attach importance to distinguishing himself but only to distinguishing [witnessing] Christ for the sake of others.[48]

But is this not an abstract concept, capable of being reduced to a principle of inclusion, Christological imperative or ecclesial virtue as in much of contemporary "mainline" religion?

Were Bonhoeffer to end on this note, then I think the answer would be yes. But he adds more to his Christological suppositions. To distinguish from "how can I be good" to "what is the will of God" is a theological move, involving reference to the theological concept of vocation.. Vocation is, for Bonhoeffer, the problem of realization among God's creatures of the revelational reality of God, or in another sense the question of the "good" is really a question of *participation* in the divine reality.[49] Vocation is not a correspondence to an "order of reality or mandate"[50] or even a kind of polity but it is the call of God alone to *this* sinner so that *this* sinner encounters God-in-the-world or the reality of the world as already sustained, accepted and reconciled.[51] Vocation is theological existence and this Bonhoeffer notes is a "proving" the will of God (Rom 12:2).

---

[48] Ibid., 19.

[49] Ibid., 57.

[50] Bonhoeffer makes an interesting argument on the orders of creation or mandates of labour, marriage, government and Church. In each of these, it is not a natural right per se that is espoused but how each of these human socialities functions in order to evoke the "law of love" of witness to God's grace. As such, for example, in marriage it is not procreation or divine institution of sexual production that is important but rather how in the issue (or restriction thereof) of children or spousal relationship one points to the reality of God in the life of the other. Thus, Bonhoeffer concludes that marriage is a contract between two persons to uphold certain "rights" namely protection of life but that the foundation of those rights is that all life is sacred to God because of Jesus Christ in whom God bonds to created life. Ibid., 73-131.

[51] Ibid., 61.

Proving the will of God for Bonhoeffer is living in response to new questions and issues—the problem of sinful people and sin-vitiated creation—each day. It is a humble and trustworthy exercise that presupposes *unity* with its origin and expects to find unity because of the simplicity of the ever one word of God:

Possibilities and consequences must be carefully assessed. In other words the whole apparatus of human powers must be set in motion when it is a matter of proving what the will of God is. But in all this there will be no room for the torment of being confronted with insoluble conflicts, or for the arrogant notions that one can master every conflict, or even for the enthusiastic expectation and assertion of direct inspiration. There *will* be belief that if a person *asks* [note prayer and worship] humbly God will give certain knowledge of God's will...and then freedom to make a real decision....[52]

But underscoring this is the recognition of ourselves as sinners and subsequently the knowledge that "Jesus Christ is in us," for it is foundational that Jesus Christ lives for us and in us, and that God occupies within us the same space previously occupied by idols of our own making in the knowledge of good and evil and God's will: "Christian self-proving is possible only on the basis of foreknowledge that Jesus Christ is within us."[53] This means, for Bonhoeffer, to love as a *response* to divine call by the sinner as "love is always the revelation of God."[54] What for Christians is Christ, is for Jews above at every point, the Torah shaped life. It then is to call others to God, to recognize God in them and, above all else, to never transform the gospel that exists for the sinner into a commendation of sin or a justification of the wicked. But is that last point not exactly what the liberal West can often be guilty of? Do we in our seeking responsibility and condemnation not pay enough attention to our own role in enabling that which we condemn?

For Bonhoeffer, the place of responsibility for the Christian in vocation as sinner is to heed the one who calls. It is neither what Bonhoeffer so acutely notes as the secular Protestant virtue of loyal discharge of human mandates of good citizen, spouse-parent, labourer and church-goer, nor the monastic or Augustinian "struggle" against the world.[55] It is a simple responsibility towards God first and foremost, and in witness to this idea Bonhoeffer calls to his defence the master of suspicion, Friedrich Nietzsche, and his criticism of mere inclusion:

---

[52] Ibid., 164.
[53] Ibid., 165.
[54] Ibid., 174.
[55] Ibid., 222-25.

> You are assiduous in your attentions to your neighbor and you find beautiful words to describe your assiduity. But I tell you that your love for neighbor is a worthless love for yourselves. You go to your neighbor to seek refuge for yourselves and then you try to make a virtue of it, but I see through your "unselfishness."[56]

Here Bonhoeffer crystallizes the importance of love for theological anthropology. Love is not mere inclusion, for that can work as an idol in which we cement our commitment to ourselves or some other power which enthrals us. Instead, to show genuine love is, as in the case of God, to love whomever is furthest from us as a single person. As sinners, we know that we who were far off have been brought near, and we, who were unlovely, have been loved because of God in Christ. The Christian gospel proclaims that this is the human story because it is God's story. The human responsibility that arises from it and that corresponds to it, for Bonhoeffer, is to act as if God *is*, to act as if God is even for our enemy. The human story is that story, and human responsibility is not security or peace but to act for God as if God is. There are immediate and instructive ramifications of this idea: in loving those farthest away, we love a singular and a plural simultaneously. We love the individual by seeking to be responsible to this particular sinner, but we love the collective by establishing boundary conditions which, in all cases, serve as a check against any denigration of their essential humanity as given by God. They are not opposites, even when they are our enemies, since the stance that we assume must work as the grace of God does towards us. The fallout of this last point in terms of polity is again simple: there are not one size fits all off the rack solutions in a place such as Afghanistan. Our responsibility is not to engage in casuistic ethics but rather to show a willingness to tailor our responsibility to the need of the other.

This introduces our final thought. The *Tikkun Olam* of God's people.

Tikkun Olam[57]

Generally translated as "repairing the world," *Tikkun Olam* is the belief within Judaism that the world matters to God and that human responsibility before God does not involve the destruction of other belief systems or social structures per se but rather the establishment and recognition of God's intentions for a humane humanity.

---

[56] Ibid., 227.
[57] For this section, I am grateful to Ms. Courtney Spence for her research on this area.

As a concept, *Tikkun Olam* has gone through many metamorphoses since first appearing during the 2nd century. It does not appear explicitly in the Bible, but is referred to several times in the Talmud. It fell out of general use in both its legalistic and spiritual connotations (both of which can be seen in the use of the term in the Talmud) after the third century, with the notable exception of the *Aleinu* prayer. During the 16th century the concept is renewed and revised in Rabbi Isaac Luria and Kabbalism. By the 18th century Hasidics claim *Tikkun* in a more personalistic and universal way in order to help bring about the coming of the messiah.[58] The concept continues to be both a personal and a public instruction in being responsible for making the world a better place, with the current focus being close to the original Talmudic intention of improving all of society, and the world, through correct public policy, social action, and the pursuit of social justice, but with shades of the Kabbalistic idea that the world is broken in such a way that it cannot indeed be fixed by human activity alone. It is both for God and humanity, and in particular, God's people to live as communities of responsibility.

Emil Fackenheim did much to bring the concept of *Tikkun Olam* back into current Jewish theology. For Fackenheim, the modern move towards humanism was not successful at recognizing the worth of people or at finding ways to positively move the world forward, so he introduced a different form of *Tikkun Olam* which focused on a realistic, as opposed to a utopian, view of the nature of man and the nature of the world. He attempted to avoid human apathy by emphasizing balance and solidarity as the focus of human behaviour.[59]

Yitzhak Greenberg has made significant recent contributions to the concept of *Tikkun Olam*. In *Living in the Image of God* he defines *Tikkun Olam* as "the arrival of the messianic kingdom—when the actual legal, political, social institutions in the world will be structured so that each human being will be sustained and treated as if he or she is an image of God."[60] The first step for Greenberg is the improvement of humanity in *real history* for the specific individual human being, and this will lead to a place where the world can then be made whole as an act of Ha-Shem. The

---

[58] Gilbert S. Rosenthal, "Tikkun ha-Olam: The Metamorphosis of a Concept," *Journal of Religion* 85, no. 2 (2005): 214-240.

[59] Eliezer. Schweid, "Does the Idea of Jewish Election Have Any Meaning after the Holocaust?" in *Wrestling with God: Jewish Theological Responses during and after the Holocaust*, ed. S. Katz, S. Shlomo Biderman, and G. Greenberg. (New York: Oxford University Press, 2006), 229-43.

[60] Irving Greenberg, *Living in the Image of God* (Northvale, NJ: Jason Aaronson, 1998), 70.

fullness of life of all people must be the goal for all, and especially for the people of Abraham in their historical situation. We are not consigned to fate but actors as a people of faith in understanding our responsibility for the mending of the world. As Greenberg argues, for the people of God, this is by definition not mere liberalism, democracy, internationalism or any other human ideology, nor is it even the secular absolute, but it is rather something deeply rooted in God's commanding voice. Like Bonhoeffer, it is call and command, non-negotiable and irreducible. In light of Auschwitz, Greenberg argues, the secular is not worth our ultimate loyalty as it is an idol. The *Tikkun* is not speaking for God on principle, but speaking about what God is for in *this* moment of history.[61] Greenberg calls this "the critical religious act" and this is belief in God, despite human folly, because God is for life, not pragmatism or mere utility, and is certainly not for the hopelessness of death.[62] Life is the reality of redemption, and redemption for Greenberg, like Bonhoeffer, is God's alone—but humans are permitted to see the "matrix for existence as an image of God."[63] God gives life, God redeems despite our fears, God alone gives the "indivisibility of human dignity," and this is the work of creation and the testimony of the people of God. Our responsibility is to live this central religious act as a matter of faith, recognizing that each human is the image of God, and to work in real history in obedience to that simple commanding voice.[64] This, he argues, is not simple hope: "Any hope must be sober, and built on the sands of despair, free from illusions."[65] However, the worst of all for Greenberg, as in Bonhoeffer, and as is proved by Auschwitz, is silence by the people of God. Greenberg, speaking of the Shoah, could well be speaking of our role in Afghanistan when he writes: "Whoever consistently holds back from murder or human exploitation when he could perpetrate it with immunity—or any person who unswervingly devotes himself to reverence, care and protection of the divine image which is man...reveals the presence within of a primordial awe—fear of God."[66] This is the mending of the world, and the avoidance of folly, because it assumes that God is, and involves Abrahamic responsibility.

---

[61] Irving Greenberg, "Cloud of Smoke, Pillar of Fire," in *Contemporary Jewish Theology*, ed. E Dorff and L Newman (Oxford: Oxford University Press, 1999), 396-404.
[62] Ibid.,, 402-3.
[63] Ibid., 406-407.
[64] Ibid., 408-9.
[65] Ibid., 413.
[66] Ibid., 408.

The *Tikkun* in Practice

The heart of what I have argued concerning the Abrahamic *Tikkun* is simple: it is to bless the nations/peoples of the earth in the light of the simple yet profound idea that God *is* (Gen 12). For people of faith, this is a call to responsibility because each and every human being is in the image of God. That means, regardless of situation, the each human being is loved by God even in the most distant possible configuration to us. Therefore, we should behave as God has behaved towards us, giving promise or covenant in order to be near. To be in the image of God is not merely a consideration of a human capacity, a definition of uniqueness or a claim of "otherness" or alterity as in Levinas, although even that would be a beginning. It is to call the people of God to be responsible and act as if God is for the person, people or situation that we confront. It is to avoid folly, which is to act without that consideration, and to find what is best in order to testify to God's care and stamp it, as it were, on each person, people and place. It is to see all as in the penumbra of God's care and to seek theological vocation to that situation, not as a type but as a call to the *Tikkun Olam*.

For the secular-minded, the *Tikkun Olam* can be a de-centring exercise, for the foundation of human responsibility enshrined in liberalism (and whether it can hold this with consistency is another matter) is as David Hume argued "humane empathy."[67] More popularly, this might be boiled down to "walking in another's shoes," in which the goal is to see the essential worth of another because of common humanity, and therefore in action to regard that other as one regards oneself. Thus responsibility is alterity, seeing "face-to-face" and acting thus in order to benefit from and create a different kind of society that embraces difference, distance and allows for diversity.

What then might this *Tikkun Olam* look like if both the Abrahamic and secular traditions come together in a vision of seeing the other as essential? And in particular, what might it mean for Abrahamic religious traditions and secularists in terms of Afghanistan?

In the most broad sense, at the very least, both should be engaged in a sustained and deeply commitment dialogue with policy makers and governments, a dialogue which espouses a *responsibility* towards Afghanistan's peoples as well as towards Western security and interests. Careful public, visible and loud scrutiny should be part and parcel of each Abrahamic community and secular body as to how we are doing in terms of this

---

[67] David Hume, *Dialogues Concerning Natural Religion*, ed. R Popkin (Indianapolis: Hackett, 1980), 84.

basic responsibility. For example, Henry Giroux notes that there has been post-9/11, particularly in the U.S., an "imposition of war as an organizing principle" in the academy and popular culture.[68] An increasingly martial imposition on the symbols that once belonged to the academy and Abrahamic traditions is evident. All one needs to do is look at the transposition of the word "mission"; Canada is not fighting a war or counter-insurgency, it would appear, but Canada now has a "mission." Further evidences include the increased work of the academy and think-tanks for the prosecution of the "war on terror," the disproportionate spending on the "war(s) on terror" as opposed to other development projects (only 8%, for example of Canada's spending on Afghanistan is explicitly budgeted for development purposes),[69] and in the American situation, we have witnessed the downloading even of much of the military work to private security firms.[70] Elke Krahmann asks an important question concerning this relatively new reality of private actors in state-motivated security concerns, as to whether the classic ideas of deterrence, removal of threat and peace (just war) can adequately coexist with firms that operate in a commercial way.[71] In other words, in the classic sense of just war the state intervenes for collective interests, but in the new neo-liberal military polity of state-employed private security firms, there are ultimately only individuals who operate to maximize profit. In the classic just war theory the state seeks peace for all, and in theory, its peace does not diminish the "good" won by peace for any of the peoples concerned. In the new world of private security firms involved in theatres of war, any peace won would actually diminish a "good" of market share for the private firms in question. This pushes, in principle if not reality, against the idea of universal enjoyment of peace by all in all areas. In short, there is, for many, no good reason to think that peace as a non-rivalled and non-excludable good is actually something to which we are really committed.

However, lest that critique be read as the ravings of one of Elshtain's egghead leftist negators, allow me to sharpen the point by returning to Améry. Améry is called to attention as a reminder that there are indeed places to which we cannot go in responsibility to the image of God in humanity, or lines which cannot be crossed without signalling that we are no longer responsible and that in fact we act in folly, as if God is not. To draw

---

[68] Henry Giroux, "Militarization of US Higher Education after 9/11," *Theory, Culture and Society* 25, no. 5 (2008): 58-60.
[69] Stein and Lang, *Unexpected War*, 266.
[70] Elke Krahmann, "Security: Collective Good or Commodity," *European Journal of International Relations* 14, no. 3 (2008): 380.
[71] Ibid., 379.

on another of our sources, there are actions that we can take that jeopardize the future as a place of God's action. One such place, or line, or action, according to Améry, is torture. Torture, he reminds us, is both the first blow and the creator of resentment which makes the future for the tortured a place without hope. It creates a displaced humanity in them and therefore creates an impediment to the prospect of a peaceable future. As seen in revelations concerning Western policy in this area, and even in such cases as that of the Syrian-Canadian Maher Arar, there has been use of torture in the "war against terror," and Canada has been a part of that in some form. Further, this is not merely a matter of the proverbial "few bad eggs" such as in Somalia in 1993; it is rather a strategy known and authorized at the highest level of American government, to which NATO allies and too many international agencies have turned a blind eye. And yet, for both secularists and Abrahamic religions, there has been a terrible silence concerning this assault on humanity and a failure to give voice to the *Tikkun Olam*. We have robbed the world accordingly of a peaceable future. We have thus failed to be responsible in holding our policy makers to our common vision and have instead helped to sustain the kind of hopelessness that folly creates. And still we wonder why those outside our circle of concern cannot find our reason?

I have suggested two specific areas in which we have failed to be responsible and need still to actualize our responsibility: consenting to cultural militarization and tolerating security at the expense of the first blow. I would like to conclude with some areas of positive engagement, areas in which Abrahamic religions and secularists can assist policy makers in seeking to be responsible to the image of God or our common humanity in order to heal the world of violent extremism. I propose three areas: a renewed commitment to a different model of statecraft than is implicit in the "failed state" model; a renewed commitment to interreligious dialogue in order to avoid Islamophobia and cultivate Islamic responsibility; and finally, a renewed commitment to understanding our own culture. Surprisingly, these do correspond roughly to what Sean Maloney notes is going on in Afghanistan internally as the "wars of schools, mosques" and implicitly of hearts and minds.[72]

Maloney notes that within Afghanistan there is a war of schools in which hard Talibans target education as a place of threat to the narrow version of Islam they espouse.[73] Through intimidation, assassination and strong arm tactics, the Taliban seeks to destroy conversation and to prevent the transformation of Afghan society from within. I propose that the

---

[72] Maloney, "A Violent Impediment," 201-20.
[73] Ibid., 207.

Abrahamic traditions and secularists resist the same kind of rigid doctrine here in the West and begin to offer critical engagement on the neo-liberal agenda as well. The rise of private military and security forces both home and abroad, the loss of human and civil rights in the name of security, and the rise of a doctrine of statecraft in the failed and failing state doctrine which assumes a neo-Imperial form needs to be criticized, not least as it has been used largely without critique by a powerful few and because it must be deemed to stand outside the boundaries of any doctrine of just war. In short, we need to wage our own battle of the schools.

Maloney notes further that within Afghanistan there is a war of mosques in which hard Talibans target any forms, teachers and embodiments of Islam that would predispose to another kind of Muslim life.[74] In fact, he and others advocate the strengthening of the national and provincial Ulema Shura as a means forward, in light of increased Muslim deaths at the hands of the Taliban.[75] The making of martyrs is a risky business. I propose that the Abrahamic traditions and secularists resist the same kind of ignorance of the power of Islam to heal its own theological excesses by working against Islamophobia in the media and popular culture which present Islam as *de facto* some kind of fundamentalist anti-human/woman religion—and by asking representatives of Islam to explain how it is possible, if there are indeed anti-human theologies within it, that this can be of God. If we can begin the deep process of inter-faith dialogue rather than some superficial appearance of it, we must encourage Islam to be an equal *and* responsible at the table. If we are capable of treating Islam as an equal and allowing Islamic nations to work alongside the West in its statecraft, then we will do what is needful in Afghanistan—allow a healthy Islam to produce in its people a vision of peace without violence.

Implied in Maloney's analysis is a battle for the hearts and minds of the Afghan people. I would suggest that this same battle needs to be fought in the West once more when the Abrahamic traditions and secularists look at what we are and ask the necessary, hard questions. The problem is not merely that we have a socio-economic system in which banks are not people-worthy, governments are seemingly preoccupied with pork belly no bid contracts and political posturing, or that there is a growing disparity within our own culture between the rich and poor, but also that much of what is found elsewhere in the world and that terrifies us is also in our own history and experience, as we disenfranchise the alien amongst us. Somewhere in the twentieth century, the Western Abrahamic traditions tacitly agreed to civil religion and in doing so left the hearts and minds of

---

[74] Ibid., 214-15.
[75] Bergen, "Al-Qaeda," 28.

the community in order to treat a warped individual concept, devoid of context. Even our so-called "resistance-movements" of liberation theology, feminist theology and other forms of "contextual theology" seem increasingly marginal and unable to speak to the powers of this world. Whether it be the fault of theological education or a matter of ecclesiastical complicity, it remains true that in the West there is a kind of anthropological and creation impoverishment that makes it difficult to speak of God (or the human) in the context of inhumanity.[76] We must, however, as Bonhoeffer argued, love those furthest from us, which includes loving them through our own polity. To do this is to be responsible, and for us to be responsible, it is time for Abrahamic traditions once more to turn to cultural engagement at the deepest levels, devoting our best minds to questions of the day, and tithing time and money accordingly. The great rabbinic mind of the past century, Joseph Soloveitchik, speaks of the Halakhic or religious mind as one having epistemological pluralism because it seeks to live God's will, and therefore allows itself to be questioned by possibilities that exist outside of the self. The thrust, whether you agree with "the Rav" or not, is simple: One who follows God must consider that God's purposes stand beyond the status quo and outside the norm, religiously but certainly also socio-politically, as God is wholly Other.[77]

Our relevance is perhaps our irrelevance? Yet by taking our theological claims seriously, there may yet be something that we can say. Each of the Abrahamic traditions, I would think, would subscribe to my boundary conditions on the theological nature of the human person, and allow for the intrusion of God in disrupting our distorted vision, allowing for a better and richer vision which is the future of God for all of God's people.

In Place of a Conclusion

It is deeply Canadian to see ourselves as pluralist but also deeply Canadian to be religiously quietist in order to tend, as George Rawlyk famously commented, "God's perfect garden in our lives" so as to "fulfill our Christian duties in Wilderness lands."[78] The Afghanistan war is an objection to our double mythos of being pluralist and quietist. This is a

---

[76] See, for this, my essay, "Living in a Global World and in a Global Theological World," in *Shaping a Global Theological Mind*, ed. Darren C Marks (Burlington: Ashgate, 2008), 1-9.

[77] Joseph B Soloveitchik, *The Halakhic Mind* (Tampa: Free Press, 1986).

[78] See, my article, "Canadian Protestantism to the Present day," in *The Blackwell Companion to Protestantism*, ed. Alister McGrath and Darren C Marks (Boston: Blackwell, 2004), 189-201.

moment in Canadian history in which our pluralism is challenged as there is a kind of martial cultural universality imposed from which no dissent can be voiced without being trumped as leftist, irresponsible or some other blight. It is a moment in Canadian history in which our quietism is being exposed as nakedly shameful, a movement away from responsibility towards folly, because we refuse to truly take that responsibility to tend, in part, God's garden (rather than merely our own) as our mission of *Tikkun Olam*. Canadian Churches and synagogues, have, by and large, not fulfilled their duties in wilderness lands in the present circumstance because they have not engaged Afghanistan in such a way that asks of the humane in the midst of the prosecution of the war.

I have tried, with the exception of the difficult doctrine of "failed states" and the absolute prohibition on torture, to avoid prescription in how one must conduct the war. I sincerely believe that Canada must remain deeply committed to Afghanistan and that much of that commitment must be worked out in terms of military force. But most importantly, I believe that the Abrahamic traditions and the secularist alike must help our policy makers to establish boundary conditions and to work towards a truly positive vision, inspired perhaps by the *Tikkun* itself, or by a theological vision of the humanity of God and of the responsible human, of what the conflict in Afghanistan is about.

I end with a modified quote from my starting point and inspiration in this essay, Yishak Greenberg:

> Whoever consistently holds back from murder or human exploitation when he could perpetrate it with immunity in Afghanistan for *the sake of our security or another secular value*—or any person who unswervingly devotes himself to reverence, care and protection of the divine image which is man...reveals the presence within of a primordial awe—fear of God.

That is the responsible human.

REASON, THE MORAL ORDER AND INTER-RELIGIOUS DIALOGUE: POPE BENEDICT XVI'S REGENSBURG LECTURE

CRAIG A. CARTER

Introduction: The Setting of the Regensburg Address

Samuel Huntington, in his famous 1993 article "The Clash of Civilizations?" warned that the future of the world might very well include major wars along the fault lines between major world civilizations.[1] Since September 11, 2001, no one needs to be convinced that the dangers Huntington warned of are very real. As the now outdated "secularization thesis"[2] gradually loses its grip on the Western mind, Westerners are coming to acknowledge, albeit with some reluctance, the fact that religion will play a major part in the future of the world and that inter-religious dialogue will be a key to world peace. The hope that secularization will spread around the globe and that the resulting decline of religion will then lead to a utopian world of peaceful co-existence and toleration is increasingly seen as a "beautiful myth" that bears no relationship to the realities we face in the twenty-first century. So what can be done to promote the dialogue that we all know is necessary to establishing peaceful relations between the world's great cultures?

This was the question taken up by Pope Benedict XVI in one of the most important lectures of his pontificate at the University of Regensburg on September 12, 2006. It was a university lecture, not a papal pro-

---

[1] Samuel P. Huntington, "The Clash of Civilizations?" *Foreign Affairs* (Summer) 1993. This article was later expanded into the book: *The Clash of Civilizations: Remaking of World Order* (New York: Touchstone, 1996).

[2] Richard John Neuhaus. *American Babylon: Notes of a Christian in Exile* (New York: Basic Books, 2009): 89-90. See also Peter Berger, *The Sacred Canopy: Elements of a Sociological Theory of Religion* (New York: Anchor Books, 1990) and "Secularization Falsified," *First Things*, no. 180 (February 2008): 23-27.

nouncement *ex cathedra*, infallibly defining dogma. Benedict XVI, like the professor he once was, made an argument in a public forum and invited comment, disagreement, debate and discussion. His thesis was meant to make its own way in the world of academic debate on its own merits; the Pope did not expect anyone to accept it just because the Pope said so. Public reaction to this lecture was, to put it mildly, considerably more widespread and vociferous than is the reaction to most university lectures. There were two main sources of reaction: first, the angry and at times even violent reaction from various Muslim individuals and groups who felt that their religion had been insulted and, secondly, from the mainly Western media, which utterly failed to grasp the meaning and import of the lecture and tended to reduce it to the familiar but misleading story of a politician issuing a "sound bite," which contained an unfortunate "gaffe." Most initial reaction, whether Muslim or Western, tended to reduce the lecture and its academic argument to a political event. While it is true that everything a Pope says or does is indeed "political" in a certain sense, this particular lecture was not primarily intended as a political statement; it was a philosophical argument. Not only that, but the philosophical argument put forward in this lecture is of immense importance to the future of the relationship between the world's religions and the great civilizations that contain and are animated by those religions.

The argument that Benedict XVI advanced in this lecture, however, is directed as much at Western civilization as at any other. In fact, his treatment of Islam actually is a side glance and not central to his main argument. The irony is that Muslim opinion was inflamed against the Pope as a result of one part of his lecture that contained an unfortunate quotation, while the major thrust of the lecture, which was a critique of, and challenge to, modern, Western philosophy, was ignored. Reading the media coverage of the event, it would be easy to get the impression that the Pope was castigating irrational Islam in the name of Western reason and thereby proclaiming the need for all non-Western religions to submit to Western standards of rationality and to historicist and positivist methods of scholarly investigation. This could not even be called a caricature of the Pope's thesis; it is not even close to his meaning. In fact, the Pope was extremely critical of modern, Western philosophy and it is no exaggeration, I would suggest, to claim that the clear implication of his lecture is that the dominant cultural relativism of the modern Western academy is itself the single greatest obstacle to peace in the world today. This last statement is my interpretation of the implications of what is said in Benedict's Regensburg lecture and this essay is an attempt to defend this interpretation and to explore some of its implications. Ironically, if I am right, one implication is that there may be, in fact, more common ground between the Pope and much of Islam, than between contemporary Western culture in general and Islam. Perhaps the upsurge in Muslim-Christian dialogue in the immediate aftermath of the Pope's lecture may be viewed as confirming this view.

The bulk of this essay will be devoted to an exposition of the argument of the lecture.[3] Although only some 4000 words in length, it is densely packed with ideas and historical interpretation. However, it is also extremely clear and concise and, therefore, accessible to even the general reader who is willing to do a bit of work. I will try to explain why I interpret his argument as being not only a challenge to the cultural relativism of the West, which it clearly is, but also as an implicit indictment of the West for making genuine inter-religious dialogue all but impossible.

The Argument

After some reminiscences and preliminaries the Pope tells a joke that leads directly into his topic. At the University of Bonn, where he taught beginning in 1959, there were two faculties of theology: one Protestant and one Catholic. He says that these faculties were a legitimate part of the university by virtue of the fact that they investigated faith using reason, "even if not everyone could share the faith which theologians seek to correlate with reason as a whole." (5) He recalls that this sense was not troubled even by a colleague who once stated that it was odd for the university to have two whole faculties devoted to the study of something that did not even exist, namely God! Benedict's point is that, even in a context in which scepticism is welcome and even prevalent, it is nonetheless appropriate to study theology. Why? In a sense the entire lecture is the response to this question, but the short answer is that the study of theology in the university is appropriate because this inquiry is undertaken through the use of reason (6). We should note that this issue of the place of theology in the university is raised at the start of the lecture and is a constant theme throughout. The very last paragraph sums up the theme by saying: "It is to this great *logos*, to this breadth of reason, that we invite our partners in the dialogue of cultures. To rediscover it constantly is the great task of the university." (63)

---

[3] I am using the text of the Lecture as printed as "Appendix I" in James V. Schall *The Regensburg Lecture* (South Bend, IN: St. Augustine's Press, 2007), 130-48. The text, including the section numbers, is taken from the official translation on the Vatican website. References from this point on will be to sections and will be given in the text rather than in footnotes. Schall's book is a commentary on the text and offers an excellent introduction to it.

Having stated the theme of his lecture as the legitimate place of theology in the university because it is a branch of knowledge that proceeds according to reason, the Pope now turns to the most controversial part of his lecture through the next eight paragraphs. Here he mentions a book edited by Professor Theodore Khoury containing some dialogues between Manuel II Paleologus and a well-educated Persian interlocutor on the subject of the truth of Islam and Christianity. These dialogues took place between 1394 and 1402 and were presumably written down by the Emperor. The Pope quotes from the seventh controversy or dialectic (Gr. *dialexis*), which deals with holy war. Pope Benedict remarks that the Emperor must have known that Surah 2, 256 reads: "There is no compulsion in religion" and observes that this is probably one of the Surahs from the early period when Mohammed was still powerless and under threat. (11) However, the Pope goes on to say, the Emperor also knew the instructions developed later and recorded in the Qur'an concerning holy war. (12) Then comes the most controversial part, which I will quote in full:

> Without descending to the details, such as the difference in treatment accorded to those who have the "Book" and the "infidels," he addresses his interlocutor with a startling brusqueness, a brusqueness that we find unacceptable, on the central question about the relationship between religion and violence in general, saying: "Show me just what Mohammed brought that was new, and there you will find things only evil and inhuman, such as his command to spread by the sword the faith he preached." (12)

> The emperor, after having expressed himself so forcefully, goes on to explain in detail the reasons why spreading the faith through violence is something unreasonable. Violence is incompatible with the nature of God and the nature of the soul. "God," he says, "is not pleased by blood—and not acting reasonably (*sun logo*) is contrary to God's nature. Faith is born of the soul, not of the body. Whoever would lead someone to faith needs the ability to speak will and to reason properly, without violence and threats...to convince a reasonable soul, one does not need a strong arm, or weapons of any kind, or any other means of threatening a person with death...." (13)

Now there is no doubt that the Emperor's comments about Mohammed were insulting, and the Pope himself says, in introducing them, that they are "unacceptable." But the issue the Pope raises here is one that members of all faiths, including Christians, as well as those who put their faith in secularism, and not just Muslims, should ponder. Violence has been perpetrated by members of all faiths, and some of the worst violence in human history has been perpetrated in the name of atheistic ideologies in the twentieth century. So we all have reason to regret the past actions of those who followed the belief system that we may follow.

It is unfortunate that this passage, cited in isolation and out of context, has led so many to conclude that the Pope was singling out Islam alone in this regard, but there can be no doubt that Muslim armies did sweep over North Africa, Asia and the Middle East during the centuries following the birth of Islam, and that violence was sometimes justified by the fact that it resulted in religious conversion, just as the recent invasion of Iraq by America was justified by some in terms of making converts to political democracy, individual freedom and other Enlightenment ideals. The initial reaction in Islamic countries was, as has been suggested, often based on misinformation, biased summaries and selective quotation of the Pope's words, and certainly the outbreaks of violence that ensued were certainly not an effective way to convince the world that Islam is a peaceful religion. Fortunately many Muslim scholars and intellectuals have now taken up the task of actually reading and debating with the Pope and other Christians and a serious inter-faith dialogue is now occurring. So in that sense, some good came out of this situation.

However, to think that the speech was primarily concerned to criticize Islam is to fail to engage with what the Pope actually said in the rest of the speech, that is, in paragraphs 15-63. In paragraph 15, Benedict notes from a French Islamist, R. Arnaldez, that Ibn Hazm held that "God is not bound even by his own word and that nothing would oblige him to reveal the truth to us. Were it God's will, we would even have to practice idolatry." (15) This is the point the Pope really wanted to get at, in order to contrast it with his understanding of Christianity. He continues: "I believe that here we can see the profound harmony between what is Greek in the best sense of the word and the Biblical understanding of faith in God." (16) Both Greek philosophy at its best and the Bible teach that God acts with reason—that is, according to *logos*—and here Pope Benedict quotes John 1:1. Clearly, what the Pope is doing is claiming that the Biblical tradition and the Greek tradition can come together to form a creative synthesis in which reason and religion are joined. This harmony of reason and religion is the key to avoiding violence in the name of religion, and is, therefore, key to the future of world peace. This is Pope Benedict's real concern in this lecture—to affirm that he way to peace is to join religion and reason together and not to let them come apart at the seams. We must not let religion become unreasonable, because that way leads to violence.

It is crucial to reiterate at this point that Pope Benedict does not think that the danger of severing the link between reason and religion is a purely Islamic one. Benedict lived through the madness of the Nazi era. He saw his homeland destroyed in the conflagration caused by that descent into irrationality, as a political movement was turned into a religion, and as technological reason drove forward an irrational hatred fuelled by an irrational ideology. The burden of the lecture, indeed, is devoted to an analysis of the history of Western thought that will show that the role of reason is being systematically denigrated in a very dangerous manner in the modern West. Benedict is calling here for reason and religion to come together; yet in doing so he must discuss what reason is and how the concept of reason has been debased in the contemporary West.

The argument begins with the vision of Paul, who saw a Macedonian man pleading "Come over to Macedonia and help us!" (Acts 16:6-10) Finding his path to Asia blocked, Paul took this as Divine Providence— and so does the Pope. For Benedict, indeed, the rapprochement between Greek and Biblical thought did not begin with this incident, but long before in Exodus 3 when Moses asked the God of his fathers what his name was. Benedict comments: "The mysterious name of God, revealed from the burning bush, a name which separates this God from all other divinities with their many names and simply asserts being, "I am," already presents a challenge to the notion of myth, to which Socrates' attempts to vanquish and transcend myth stands in close analogy." (20) For Benedict, something similar is going on in Greek philosophy and in the Old Testament long before the New Testament was written. The Old Testament wisdom literature display the results of a fruitful encounter between Greek and Biblical faith in the Hellenistic period and when the Old Testament was translated into Greek—the Septuagint—it furthered this synthesis of Biblical thought and Greek philosophical language. (23) Benedict comments:

> A profound encounter of faith and reason is taking place here, an encounter between genuine enlightenment and religion. From the very heart of Christian faith and, at the same time, the heart of Greek thought now joined to faith, Manuel II was able to say: Not to act with *logos* is contrary to God's nature. (24)

Now, Benedict turns to the Middle Ages and observes that the Biblical-Patristic synthesis, which came to a climax in the thought of St. Augustine and St. Thomas Aquinas, began to experience tension with the rise of the voluntarism of Duns Scotus. Of course, the Pope could have mentioned William of Occam or Thomas Hobbes. The voluntarism here is of the kind that that emphasized God's freedom to the point where it is thought that God could act in the opposite way to the way he has acted at any point and still be God. Here, Benedict draws a parallel between the positions of Ibn

Hazm, as he understands it, and that of late medieval/ early modern voluntarism. Clearly, in the Pope's mind, this sort of thinking appears in both Christianity and Islam and when it is allowed to progress to the point where it severs the harmonious link between religion and reason, it can lead to violence done in God's name. The suicide bomber who acts in the name of Allah is a spiritual and intellectual descendent of that strand of Islamic theology that upholds a voluntarist view of God. And, as we shall see, similar pernicious effects can be observed in the post-Nietzschean West when it does the same thing. It is very important to note that the Pope does not necessarily impugn Islam as a whole when he points to the problem of voluntarism in certain strands of its theology, any more than he impugns Christianity as a whole. His vision is for those from both traditions who hold to a view of God in which God and *logos* cannot be separated to come together in fruitful dialogue.

Benedict's case can, in fact, be located within a wider stream of recent theological scholarship, and is far from being an idiosyncratic approach. In a recent study, *The Theological Origins of Modernity,* for instance, Michael Allen Gillespie makes a book-length argument for the thesis that modernity should not be understood as an era that leaves religion behind, but as having been shaped decisively by the late medieval nominalist view of God as sheer, unpredictable will.[4] Gillespie's argument parallels Benedict's argument here and confirms that what Benedict is attacking in the theology of Ibn Hazm is indeed also identifiable in the nominalism stemming from Duns Scotus and William of Occam. Both Christianity and Islam, then, have had to contend with strands of their theological traditions that lead to a fearful image of God as arbitrary and irrational. Like Benedict, however, Gillespie argues that modernity has been shaped decisively by this strand of Western theology and that the elevation of human will to the level of God in modernity is in response to the crisis of nominalism.[5]

Pope Benedict XVI, for his part, proposes that the alternative to voluntarism and so the solution to the problem lies in a rediscovery of the analogical thinking that has characterized the faith of the Church from its beginning. To say that there is a real analogy between our mind and the mind of God is not to make God over into our image. A principle of analogical thinking enunciated by the Fourth Lateran Council is that in any similarity

---

[4] Michael Allen Gillespie, *The Theological Origins of Modernity* (Chicago: University of Chicago Press, 2008).

[5] It is strange that Gillespie does not refer either to Benedict XVI or to John Milbank in his book even though both of them may be construed as making remarkably similar arguments concerning the origins of modernity within late medieval nominalism.

between God and the creature, the dissimilarity is always infinitely greater than the likeness. (27) Yet, even so, there can be analogies between the mind of God and the mind of God's creature made in God's image. As Benedict cautions:

> God does not become more divine when we push him away from us in a sheer, impenetrable voluntarism; rather the truly divine God is the God who has revealed himself as *logos* and, as *logos*, has acted and continues to act lovingly on our behalf. (27)

This is why Christian worship is called by Paul "our reasonable service." (Romans 12:1-2) All Christian theology is rooted in and based on analogical thinking that bases itself on revelation.

Now, in the next major section of the lecture, Benedict XVI begins to discuss three stages of what he calls the "dehellenization" of the faith. Medieval voluntarism was the seedbed of the rise of the modern world, which took place, he suggests, in three stages. What Benedict XVI is doing here is arguing for a certain understanding of what modernity is; it is the culture that comes into existence through the dehellenization of Christianity. In other words, that is, in my words and not the Pope's words, modernity is a Christian heresy. Although Benedict XVI does not use the word "heresy" I find it the most accurate way to explain what he is talking about. Modernity is viewed by some as a logical and inevitable development of Christianity,[6] while for others it is something new in history.[7] For the Roman Catholic Church between Vatican Council I and Vatican Council II, and for Protestant Fundamentalism, modernity is something evil and false and therefore to be rejected *in toto*. For Liberal Protestantism, modernity is something to be embraced as it is, that is, something to which the Christian faith must be accommodated and adjusted. For Vatican Council II and for Evangelicals at their best, however, modernity is a complex phenomenon which calls for great discernment because it includes within it much that is of value, as well as much that can destroy the soul and the faith. Benedict XVI, like his great predecessor, John Paul II, is a Pope of the Council who has argued consistently over several decades for an understanding of the Council as neither a simple rejection of modernity, nor a simple embrace of modernity, but primarily as an encounter with modernity. The only way a fruitful encounter between the Church and modernity

---

[6] For example, see Karl Lowith, *Meaning in History: The Theological Implications of the Philosophy of History* (Chicago: University of Chicago Press, 1949).
[7] For example, see Hans Blumenberg, The Legitimacy of the Modern Age (Cambridge: MIT Press, 1985).

can occur is if the true nature of modernity is understood. This is why I find the category of "heresy" to be helpful. A heresy is never all wrong; a heresy includes much that is true. Heresy also arises out of the faith and history of the Church; a totally foreign idea can never become a Christian heresy but can only be a non-Christian idea. For Benedict, modernity arises out of a strand of Christianity, but is not simply a legitimate development of Christianity. Yet it is not totally new and unrelated. Heresy arises out of the faith of the Church and includes truth but twist or distorts the truth or mixes error with truth in such a way as to lead people astray into destruction. If modernity is a heresy, it would explain why so many Christians see so much good in it and it would also explain how it could result in something as evil as what John Paul II called "the culture of death."

Benedict XVI says that the first stage of dehellenization occurs with the Sixteenth century Reformation. He writes:

> Looking at the tradition of scholastic theology, the Reformers thought they were confronted with a faith system totally conditioned by philosophy, that is to say an articulation of the faith based on an alien system of thought. As a result, faith no longer appeared as a living historical Word but as one element of an overarching philosophical system. (33)

The principle of *sola scriptura*, on the other hand, sought faith in the Biblical Word. Metaphysics appeared as a premise derived from another source, from which the faith had to be liberated in order to become once more fully itself. (34)The Pope undoubtedly could have said much more about the Reformers, but he moves quickly on to Kant, saying that Kant carried forward the program of "liberating" theology from metaphysics with "a radicalism that the Reformers never could have foreseen." (35) Kant, he argues, "anchored faith exclusively in the practical reason, denying it access to reality as a whole." (35)

The second stage of dehellenization comes with the rise of liberal theology in the nineteenth and twentieth centuries, with Adolf von Harnack as its leading representative, although Benedict notes that it also was influential in Catholic theology in his younger years. The Pope sees Harnack as having the goal to "bring Christianity back into harmony with modern reason, liberating it...from seemingly philosophical and theological elements, such as faith in Christ's divinity and the triune God." (39) Benedict also sees the rise of historical-critical exegesis of the Bible as part of this project. By limiting theology in a Kantian fashion to what is "essentially historical and therefore strictly scientific," Harnack was able to make a case for theology fitting into the modern university.

It is important to recognize that Benedict is now qualifying the term "reason." Unlike earlier in the lecture when he referred to "reason," he now speaks consistently of "modern reason," and says that this modern reason limits itself in a Kantian manner to the realm of the empirical. Yet, modern reason, the Pope says, is a synthesis of Platonism, in a Cartesian form, and of empiricism. The resulting synthesis is confirmed by the success of technology. The Platonic element, the Pope points out, "is the mathematical structure of matter, its intrinsic rationality, which makes it possible to understand how matter works and use it efficiently." (40) By applying mathematical description to reality and combining it with the experimental method, modern science advances by means of verification and falsification. Now, the Pope says, we need to note two points about modern science. First, many modern thinkers hold that the only kind of certainty that can be considered scientific arises from the interplay of the mathematical and empirical elements. This is why the human or social sciences (psychology, sociology, history etc.) try to conform to this understanding of what it means to be "scientific." (45) Secondly, this method (which is the basis of the new "modern" understanding of reason) by its very nature excludes the question of God. Benedict calls this a "reduction of the radius of science and reason" and says that it needs to be questioned. To use this kind of reason in the study of Christianity, he points out, would reduce Christianity to "a mere fragment of its former self." (47)

However, rather than simply call for a revised definition of reason that is more hospitable to Christianity, the Pope instead points out that the problem with defining science (and reason) in this way is that to do so is to end up reducing humanity itself, for "the specifically human questions about our origin and destiny, the questions raised by religion and ethics, then have no place within the purview of collective reason as defined by 'science', so understood, and must thus be relegated to the realm of the subjective." (48) The result is that ethics and religion lose their ability to create community and become instead purely personal matters. I would venture to say that a better translation here would be "an individual matter." The implications are clear, as it leads to "the disturbing pathologies of religion and reason which necessarily erupt when reason is so reduced that questions of religion and ethics no longer concern it." (49) Note that the Pope says here that these pathologies "necessarily erupt." He is deadly serious in warning that a concept of scientific reason that excludes questions of God and ethics is a seedbed of pathologies. He is not talking about Islam here, but the modern, scientific West.

Briefly, the Pope refers to the third stage of dehellenization, which he calls the rise of cultural pluralism. This stage is only conceivable after the consolidation of the second stage. What is said in the latter is that the synthesis of Biblical faith with Hellenism in the older Christian tradition was incidental and accidental—it is but one instance of a process of inculturation that is not binding on other times and places. So we today do not have to take into account the dogmas of the early church, such as the dogma of the Trinity or the Chalcedonian formula as if they were in any sense binding on other cultures. (52) The problem with this idea is that it ignores the fact that "the New Testament itself was written in Greek and bears the imprint of the Greek spirit, which had come to maturity as the Old Testament had developed." (52) While the Pope recognizes that, of course, not every element in the evolution of the early Church has to be integrated into all cultures, "the fundamental decisions made about the relationship between faith and the use of human reason are part of the faith itself." (54)

With that, the Pope comes to his conclusion. He does not want to turn back the clock to the pre-modern era and reject all of modern science. He understands the scientific ethos as "the will to be obedient to the truth" (55) and views this as a completely Christian attitude. Rather than retrenchment, Pope Benedict XVI calls for a broadening of the concept of reason and an overcoming of the "self-imposed limitation of reason to the empirically falsifiable." (56) To drive home the point, he argues that theological inquiry into the rationality of faith is the only way that we can enable "that genuine dialogue of cultures and religions so urgently needed today." (57) The Pope, in a truly astonishing reversal of roles, here even speaks on behalf of non-Western cultures and criticizes the West by pointing out that "the world's profoundly religious cultures see this exclusion of the divine from the universality of reason as an attack on their most profound convictions." He then drives home the point by saying: "A reason which is deaf to the divine and which relegates religion into the realm of subcultures is incapable of entering into the dialogue of cultures." (58) Is it possible, then, that it is the West and not Islam, which is the real obstacle to the dialogue of reason?

Many secular Westerners view Islam as in need of its Reformation. But what do they mean by this? As one wag put it, "They don't so much think that Islam needs a Martin Luther as that they think it needs a John Spong." This witticism is probably close to the truth of what some mean when they call for an Islamic Reformation. What they really want is an Islamic Enlightenment. But Pope Benedict does not want either a Reformation or an Enlightenment for Islam; he wants the modern, scientific West to broaden its concept of reason in recognition that the Platonic element in the scientific method "bears within itself a question which points beyond itself and beyond the possibilities of its methodology." (59) Modern science, in order to achieve the experimental and technological success it has enjoyed simply has to presuppose what the Pope calls "the rational structure of matter and the correspondence between our spirit and the prevailing rational structures of nature as a given, on which its methodology has to be based." (59) Yet the obvious question is "Why?" Why is the material world structured rationally and why is our mind so structured as to be able to grasp that structure? Only philosophy and theology can address such questions, which is precisely the reason why they cannot be banished from the university.

Then, Pope Benedict XVI brings up something Socrates says to Phaedo in Plato's dialogue of that name. After discussing many false opinions, Socrates says:

> It would be easily understandable if someone became so annoyed at all these false notions that for the rest of his life he despised and mocked all talk about being—but in this way he would be deprived of the truth of existence and would suffer a great loss. (61)

One objection to the presence of theology and philosophy in the university is that they do not "progress" and achieve increasing certainty over time. But if Socrates was right, the difficulty of the inquiry must not discourage us from continuing on with it. Socrates drank the poison and died later on the day he said this and it may well be that not all disputes and questions can be settled in our lifetimes, yet for this professor-Pope the ongoing search is not only worthwhile but necessary. As Manuel II said seven centuries ago, "Not to act reasonably, not to act with *logos*, is contrary to the nature of God." This conviction should be the basis of a dialogue of cultures, says Benedict XVI: "It is to this great *logos*, to this breadth of reason, that we invite our partners in the dialogue of cultures." (63)

Concluding Observations

In conclusion let me make three brief observations. First, in order to appreciate the subversive nature of the Pope's argument, we need to be clear in our minds that he is saying that the problem with modern, Western science in its positivist form is that it is *not scientific enough*. Faith has nothing to fear from true science. Only an unduly narrow concept of science excludes faith. The exclusion of the question of God from scientific inquiry just because empirical methods are inadequate for the task is arbitrary and, in itself, unscientific. As Aristotle pointed out long ago near the beginning of his *Ethics*, "It is the mark of an educated man to look for precision in each class of things just so far as the nature of the subject admits."[8] So to expect to find God with telescopes is not reasonable and the fact that one cannot do so is no reason to dismiss the idea of God altogether. Theology will not operate with the same methods as physics, yet it need not be unscientific as long as it deploys reason in its work.

Secondly, a clear implication of what Pope Benedict XVI is saying is that just as there is a mathematical structure to the physical universe of which we are a part, there may well also be a moral order, which the human reason is capable of discovering if it does not refuse to open its eyes and look for it. If the universe is not just booming, buzzing confusion, but an ordered universe governed by mathematical laws, why would it be thought unreasonable to suppose that this same universe might be governed by moral laws as well? Whatever the source of the mathematical rationality of the universe could also be the source of the moral rationality of the universe. Of course, Christians and Muslims call this source "God," but much of modern, Western culture seems bent on denying that there is either a giver of moral order or even a moral order at all. But Benedict's challenge to the modern West is profound: how can you deny the moral structure of the universe while affirming its mathematical order as if it were obvious that we should accept the one and reject the other? It is ultimately arbitrary to do so. The sooner this is acknowledged, the sooner a common search for moral agreement can get underway as the basis for an agreed protocol of peaceful co-existence between cultures. And this search will need to include theology in the dialogue between cultures. I suspect that Pope Benedict XVI would be quite open to Michael Allen Gillespie's thesis that the West is not so much a totally secular culture as a culture that *pretends* to be secular in order to conceal its own theological presuppositions. If the West were to enter into real dialogue, Gillespie contends, it would be forced to confront these assumptions as it compares its thought to that of Islam, and that would be a real advance.[9] Once it became clear that all parties in the debate have theological assumptions, the real dialogue that is needed could begin.

Thirdly, I want to reiterate that it is on the basis of a common commitment to reason that the Pope is saying that this dialogue must occur. Benedict is not saying that the Islamic world must become rational in exactly the same way as the West, with its vaunted technological and scientific prowess. Remarkably enough, his position is quite the reverse. He

---

[8] Aristotle, *Nicomachean Ethics*, translated by W. D. Ross in *The Basic Works of Aristotle,* edited by Richard McKeon (New York: Random House, 1941), Book I, Chapter 3, Line 24-26.
[9] Gillespie, "Epilogue," 289-94.

does not want Islamic philosophy and theology to go away as if they had nothing to contribute to the dialogue and he does not demand that Islam accept modern (or heaven forbid) postmodern Western philosophy in order to enter the dialogue. He does not demand that Islam give up its fervent desire to live under the law of God in order to achieve the good life. On the contrary, all he asks is that Islam live up to its own best traditions concerning the commitment to reasoned discourse in order to enter into a dialogue of equals with a broadened and deepened Western philosophy and theology that is open to the question of why order exists in the world and why the human mind can grasp that order. This kind of debate, which requires that there should be movement on both sides, is the kind of debate the Pope wishes to foster and it will require no preconditions except a common openness to reason and rational discussion.

CHRISTIAN REALISM AND ITS LIMITS

GARY D. BADCOCK

War and Christian Theology

Although the twin themes of the critique of and justification for war have been absent from large sectors of Christian theology for some years, war has in fact been one of the major preoccupations of Christian theologians during the past century. This is scarcely surprising, given the two World Wars and the threat of a third that punctuated the period. In so perilous a time, theologians had no alternative than to attempt in some manner to come to terms with the great fact of their lives, lived as they were under the shadow of violence. That we have arrived at a similar position today, and that we need a theological response to the threat of war in our own lifetime, is not something anomalous or unusual. It has always been the human lot to be threatened with violence, and though one might protest the fact, one can scarcely ever escape it over the span of even a single generation.

For a Christian theologian in the contemporary Canadian context, however, the situation is massively complicated by the inter-faith questions posed by the Afghanistan conflict in particular, and by the general "war on terror." Al-Qaeda has made no secret of the fact that it intends to target Canada, and it is folly for any of us to suppose that a terrorist atrocity is impossible in this country. Canadian troops, meantime, have now been in active combat in Afghanistan as part of an internationally authorized military campaign for longer than they served in either of the two World Wars of the past century. The military campaign has been waged first against a radical Islamist (Taliban) government in that country, on account of its harbouring of and evident support for Osama bin Laden and the al-Qaeda network prior to the 11 September, 2001 attacks. It is currently being conducted against an apparently well-financed and certainly well-motivated radical Islamist guerrilla or "insurgency" force, much of which is certainly still broadly in the al-Qaeda fold. The cost to Canada of combating these movements has been significant, both in financial and in human terms, and yet, on the domestic scene, there has been relatively little explicitly theological engagement to date with the challenges posed by this very difficult situation.

Theology, however—or something very like it—has always been and perhaps must always be integral both to the justification and criticism of war. Since, in war, the state or other "legitimate authority" seeks to authorize a particular use of violence that otherwise contradicts both moral principle and the ordinary civil law, the state in the situation of war must look *beyond itself* for justification. Appeal is accordingly made to ultimate principle, to what is foundational even to the state and the law. Whether this be the will of God or some idealized principle of justice such as is asserted in the modern doctrine of human rights, or more minimally, some sense of the historical destiny of a people or a class, the claim is always that since the ultimate right is what is at stake, the ordinary conventions both of ethics and of law must be suspended. It is in this way that the state authorizes its military to do battle. Even the critique of war, wherever it is found, falls back on these same "ultimate" principles. When conscientious objectors, for instance, refuse to enlist, or when enlisted personnel refuse to fight, they generally do so in the name of precisely the same ideals that the state claims in its war polity. The question of ultimate principle is thus the question at stake in war. As this question is not only a political one, but implicitly *the* theological question, there will in the final analysis be no adequate account given of a nation's involvement in war, or indeed of its refusal to engage in it, which entirely by-passes the theological question. We should therefore take care to ensure that those properly "theological" questions are not handled dishonestly or disgracefully. Quite apart from the several explicitly theological questions opened up by the claim of al-Qaeda and the Taliban to be resisting a godless enemy in the name of God, a theology of war is needed in our time.

Now this, of course, raises an interesting range of issues concerning the justification of the war in Afghanistan given by the secular Canadian state and by secular western states generally. Shortly after the attacks of 9/11, in an interview broadcast on the Al-Jazeera network, Osama bin Laden repeatedly noted that use of the word "Crusade" had not only been made by George W. Bush in reference to the American response to the attacks, but also, and much more significantly, that it had been used extensively and repeatedly in the rulings or "fatwas" issued by a range of Islamic jurists concerning the interference of western nations in the Islamic world over many decades. On the strength of these fatwas, bin Laden went so far as to claim that Bush "carries the cross" in a global Christian Crusade, against which it is imperative for all Muslims to rise up and fight. Though it is not the primary theme of what follows, it is worth pointing out that the official policy of religious impartiality in the Canadian view of the Afghanistan conflict involves at least as much posture as it does substance, since, given the explicitly religious claim of the enemy, it is actually not logically possible for those battling against them to be religiously impartial. We must reject any language of "Crusade," though we might laugh at the suggestion that the war policy in Afghanistan represents some renewal of that dark medieval strategy—as if this were even conceivable today—but to the extent that the al-Qaeda network or the Taliban believe themselves to represent the cause of Islam, to fight against them is to fight against what that claim represents. In other words, the government of Canada and indeed all the national contributors to NATO's International Security Assistance Force, are either at war with Islam, or else *with some corruption of it*. It is not at war with a religiously neutral insurgency. To say this is merely to acknowledge something that perhaps hundreds of millions of Muslims globally already know full well, so for a Christian theologian to make the point in the present instance is only to state the obvious.

The theological dimension of the conflict cannot finally be avoided. This is least of all the case within Islam itself, of course—though it has to date shown remarkably little ability to tackle the question.[1] Ultimately, Islamic thinkers will have to face the grave problems posed by the grotesque claims of al-Qaeda and the Taliban, and of all those like them, for the simple reason that—as the case of Afghanistan amply demonstrates—their religious claims constitute a threat, not primarily to the West and its inhabitants, but to the Islamic world itself and to the individual welfare of millions of Muslims themselves. To the West, the likes of al-Qaeda and the Taliban are an irritant; to the Muslim world and indeed, *to Islam itself*, they are a genuinely present threat. From the theological perspective, furthermore, not only do they imperil the welfare of Muslims, but they also bring the name of God into public disrepute. One has to ask, as a Christian, why it is that it has been Danish cartoons that have provoked riots in the streets, and not the actions of al-Qaeda and the Taliban? Though it pains me to say it, this is a question that cannot be avoided.

---

[1] The exception to this, the importance of which I do not by any means want to minimize, is the appeal to global Christian leaders of 138 Muslim scholars from all over the world, and representing every major branch of Islamic religious scholarship, "A Common Word Between Us and You," dated October 13, 2007. The document is most readily available at http://www.divinity.cam.ac.uk/cip/documents/commonwordfinal091007.pdf. I will turn to this text in what follows. It is, however, patent that there remains a great deal of work to be done within Islam on the question of Islamic radicalism and violence.

It is neither possible nor desirable to pre-empt this necessary task, which it is the proper responsibility of Muslims themselves to undertake, rather than for someone in my position. Nevertheless, I can in what follows at least reflect on what a *Christian* theology can bring to this debate, partly in the hope of stimulating *discussion*, partly in the hope of *bearing witness* from the Christian to the Muslim world, and partly, as we shall see, in order to *learn* from the Muslim world as well. To begin this task, however, I want first to refer to the work of the two Christian theologians of recent times who, more than any other single sources, redefined the Christian response to armed conflict for the late twentieth century, moving beyond generic jurisprudential considerations in their treatment of war to a more strictly theological account of the question. The two theologians in question are the American, Reinhold Niebuhr (1892-1971), and the Swiss-German, Karl Barth (1886-1968). Though very different thinkers, each in his own way lent massive support to the development during the middle decades of the last century of that strand of just war theology known as "Christian realism."[2] Realism is perhaps best known as a rather hard-nosed political polity, but it was in fact founded on thoroughly theological principles. From a discussion of these principles, I wish to suggest, we can still glean important things.

Christian Realism and the Problem of War

The initial setting for the development of the distinctive approaches to war taken in the theologies of Niebuhr and Barth is in fact the horror of war itself, and in particular World War I. As the great "cause" of the youth of both men, it is scarcely surprising that the War shaped much of their thinking. Both became pacifists in the immediate context of World War I, but in both cases, the rise of Fascism in the 1930s meant that a very different position on war finally emerged from their theologies.

The early pacifism of Niebuhr and Barth was not especially unusual. Both in the European and the North American contexts, the experience of modern mechanized war led after the Armistice of 1918 to a widespread impatience towards classical just war theory within Christian circles. In

---

[2] Barth is not always seen as a "Christian realist," though in a recent study by Robin W. Lovin, *Christian Realism and the New Realities* (Cambridge: Cambridge University Press, 2008), the argument is that Barth's colleague and disciple, Dietrich Bonhoeffer, belongs with Reinhold Niebuhr in the Christian realist camp. I will use the concept of Christian realism loosely in this essay to refer mainly to the mid-twentieth century attempt to argue the cause of World War II in particular as a "Christian cause," drawing on aspects of that argument for today.

the case of Niebuhr's America, for instance, the heyday of the "social gospel" movement is found in the two decades punctuating the two World Wars. Mainstream American religion committed itself to building an equitable and just society during these years, explicitly endorsing a pacific and isolationist rejection of the option of re-armament in face of the rise of European Fascism. Ultimately, and in the light of the danger that Fascism represented for the world as a whole, Niebuhr was to break ranks with Christians in his time, not only arguing that the Christian Church is not pacifist, but daring to claim much more bluntly that the pacifist policy endorsed by American mainline Christianity in face of the rise of Fascism amounted to "heresy."[3]

On the European side of the Atlantic, it is equally important for us to recognize that respectable church leaders in western Europe were at the forefront in maintaining after 1933 that Hitler needed to be given a "chance." They further welcomed the act of appeasement represented by the Munich Agreement of 1938.[4] In 1940, by contrast, Karl Barth excoriated the churches of Britain and France not only for accepting the pact with the devil that Munich represented, but for permitting church bells to be rung throughout the land to celebrate it when announced.[5] He also ridiculed the nascent ecumenical movement of the time for its theologically spineless fence-sitting in the 1930s, and for being committed to peace at any cost—including the cost of the persecution of the Jews, toleration of the generic racism of Nazi Germany (which they had established versions of themselves) and of Germany's bizarre ambitions, the betrayal of the Confessing Church, and, not least, the abandonment of the Czechoslovaks in 1938. Barth wrote of its work, or its lack of work, in the following terms:

> Not in 1933 (the start of the German church struggle), nor in the summer and fall of 1938, when the political storm was gathering, nor in 1939, when it broke loose, neither at the time of the catastrophe of 1940 nor since then, was there directed to Christendom and to mankind a witnessing, clarifying,

---

[3] Reinhold Niebuhr, "Why the Christian Church is Not Pacifist," in Robert McAfee Brown, ed., *The Essential Reinhold Niebuhr* (New Haven and London: Yale University Press, 1986), 102-119.

[4] The Munich Agreement, of course, which was signed by the leaders of Germany, Great Britain, France and Italy, "permitted" the Nazi annexation of the Sudetenland of Czechoslovakia. The Agreement was followed immediately by a peace treaty between Great Britain and Nazi Germany—the basis of P.M. Chamberlain's infamous "peace for our time" speech on his arrival home.

[5] Karl Barth, *Letter to Great Britain from Switzerland* (London: The Sheldon Press, 1941), 24.

encouraging and comforting word from the ecumenical center. Why did I and do I have to send out such letters simply as a private individual after all the beautiful words which have been spoken and written again and again about the new unity of the Church of Jesus Christ discovered in the Ecumenical Movement? Why did "Geneva" always leave it to me to speak out?...[W]hy is the "one" church not in the arena with its message...?[6]

Like Niebuhr, then, Barth also appeared profoundly out of step with the church in his time. Since the church had rejected the necessity of war too woodenly as irreconcilable with the will of God, it had little to offer beyond public hand-wringing and private pastoral counsel in response to the crisis when it came. By contrast, Barth insisted that engagement in the war against Nazism *was* the will of God, and that as such, the war was both just and good, so that it became the Christian's obligation to wage it.

Niebuhr, for his part, is especially associated with the tradition of Christian realism. His formulation of the position, indeed, arguably represents the single most influential strand of Christian theology in America in the middle decades of the twentieth century, and certainly ranks among the most important contributions of American Christianity to modern theology in general. It is probable that without the reality of the War, the revelation of the horror of the Nazi death camps in 1945, and the continuing threat of Stalinism and the particular barbarism it represented in the decades following, Niebuhr's theology would have been left to wither. However, the reality is that, given these facts, it was the theoretical framework provided by Niebuhr that provided vast numbers of Americans with the spiritual resources to understand the situation that they faced.

Niebuhr's political theology is complex and subtle—vastly more subtle, certainly, than those recent simplistic adaptations of it attempting to legitimate the invasion of Iraq.[7] Developed for the most part in a lengthy series of occasional essays spanning decades, it is difficult to speak of it as a whole or to do justice to it within present limits. For our purposes, however, the key claim made by Niebuhr relates to the need for pastors and theologians (and indeed, politicians and political theorists generally) to take the Christian doctrine of original sin seriously, over against the revolutionary idealism of modernity. In his theology, Niebuhr contrasts what he sometimes speaks of as the "Renaissance faith in man" with "Reforma-

---

[6] Karl Barth, "Letter to American Christians," in Karl Barth, *The Church and the War*, trans. Antonia H. Froendt (New York: The Macmillan Company, 1944), 46. The document dates from late 1942.

[7] For a helpful overview, see Andrew Bacevich, "Prophets and Poseurs: Niebuhr and Our Times," *World Affairs* (Winter, 2008), http://www.worldaffairsjournal.org/2008%20-%20Winter/full-prophets.html.

tion realism," arguing that Western civilization is a synthesis of these paradoxical themes, and that both of them are required for a healthy political order. Without idealism, in short, there would be little to strive for in the political sphere, and there would certainly be no possibility of democratic government. Without realism concerning the pervasiveness of sin, however, there would be little to check the pride of those wielding power, and democratic freedom would lapse into tyranny.

In Niebuhr's hands, however, the understanding of sin results not from the story narrated in the Genesis myth but instead emerges from a broadly existentialist and often overtly psychological analysis of individual human existence.[8] This understanding, developed at length in the great work of Niebuhr's middle age, *The Nature and Destiny of Man*, dates from precisely the same period as the basic political position associated with the mature Niebuhr, as represented, for example, in the seminal essay from 1940, "Why the Christian Church is Not Pacifist."[9] The argument concerning sin that Niebuhr constructs need not detain us, beyond observing that basic claim is that human existence is characterized by a certain existential

---

[8] Niebuhr does not, of course, endorse any literal reading of the doctrine of original sin as deriving from our "first parents" in a Garden of Eden, nor the strict Augustinian theory of original sin *per se*. Niebuhr's position on the Genesis story, as of much else in both scripture and theological tradition, is not literalist. Indeed, Niebuhr might justly be thought to be among the most "liberal" of all "classical" American theologians. He was a thinker who had little interest in ideas such as the divinity of Christ or the doctrine of the Trinity, who most likely did not believe that it mattered whether Jesus had physically risen from the dead, who almost wholly ignored such fundamental themes as the role of the sacraments in his understanding of the Christian life—and yet this theologian's influence was profound even in the American Bible Belt. Niebuhr is commonly associated with the wider "neo-orthodox" movement in twentieth century Christian theology. The reason for this, one senses, derives from the fact that what Niebuhr does is to focus for practical purposes on an extremely narrow range of classic Christian doctrine, concerning himself essentially with the question of sin and grace, as typically encountered in the dynamics of Protestant religious experience in the context of modernity. Among the several reasons that Niebuhr managed to survive and indeed thrive in what might otherwise have been the hostile environment of conservative American religion is that so much of that religion tends to be concerned with the same themes: experiential Protestant Christianity as encountered in a distinctively American idiom.

[9] Reinhold Niebuhr, *The Nature and Destiny of Man*, 2 vols. (New York: Scribners, 1941, 1943). The essay, "Why the Christian Church is Not Pacifist," cited above from Robert McAfee Brown's invaluable collection, *The Essential Reinhold Niebuhr*, was first published as a pamphlet in wartime Britain: Reinhold Niebuhr, *Why the Christian Church is Not Pacifist* (London: SCM Press, 1940).

"thrown-ness": humans are both nature and spirit, characterized alternately by the capacity for sensuality or self-transcendence; only faith in God, according to Niebuhr, allows them to negotiate their existences without fear, and so without sin. Being insecure in the world, humans inevitably tend without God in one of the two directions signalled by their paradoxical nature: either towards a purely physical mode of existence, in which possession or pleasure or power predominate; or towards the affirmation of human freedom of spirit and of the possibility of human perfection. From this perspective, according to Niebuhr, sin is inevitable and inescapable, since no one trusts God completely, and since the paradox of nature and spirit is universal, along with the anxiety that is its main effect. In consequence, all humans sin in some way, in the characteristic Niebuhrian sins of sensuality on the one hand or of pride on the other. The questions that remain are to what extent we sin, how such sin is to be alternately restrained and forgiven, and above all, in view of sin's inevitability, how we are to live in the world.

In its political application, Niebuhr's theology implies first and foremost that there is no such thing as a perfect political order, and indeed, that there is no possible or actual political system in which the will of God can be fully realized. There is only ever the state as a mixed body, mired by and finally compromised by evil.[10] It is for this general reason that Niebuhr maintains that the western democratic model of government is neither sacrosanct nor dispensable: it is preferable to other models of government simply because in it, the capacity of an electorate to replace one government with another on a regular basis serves as a check on sin.[11] Sin can, of

---

[10] This insight, which is of course one of the great themes of St. Augustine's, *City of God*, Niebuhr appears to have arrived at independently of close study of Augustine, of whose work he apparently knew relatively little.

[11] On the whole, Christianity has historically not tied itself to any single political position or tradition, and though for some two hundred years it has tended to support the democratic institutions of modernity, the truth of the matter is that even as venerable an institution as the Roman Catholic Church has toyed over the past fifty years alone with political systems as varied as liberal democracy, social democracy, communism (as, for instance, in Cuba), and variegated forms of dictatorship, some more benevolent and some more brutal. Furthermore, Christianity in terms of its demographics has changed radically in the past century. If one were to ask the question what an average Christian looks like in the world of today, the answer might surprise: she is black, she probably lives somewhere in West-central Africa, is astonishingly poor, and she is not old but young. She is certainly not one of George W. Bush's "Crusaders" against terror. In a mere generation, by 2050 according to some projections, there will not be a single European nation in the ten most populous Christian nations on earth. Among the surprising new facts of life,

course, find expression at the social level as well as the individual level as sensuality and pride; indeed, the two tend to be woven together empirically. Nazism, for instance, though generally presented in Niebuhr's theology as the product of a monstrous pride, also exhibited, because of the nature of the social organism, manifold sins of sensuality. What Niebuhr does not suggest, however, is that the United States during the years of Nazism was in any sense sinless over against the evils of Fascism. Sinlessness, in political as in individual life, is an illusion. The question of sin is one of degree, or a question of where on the continuum one stands. But there is never an escape from sin's power.

The position on war that finally emerged from Niebuhr's theology is that the pacifism of the American and so many of the European churches during the 1920s and 1930s was "heretical" because it did not reckon seriously with the pervasiveness of sin. Opting instead to focus one-sidedly on the possibility of human perfection, it counselled that resources be allocated to the alleviation of economic hardship at home, and that rearmament represented a morally irresponsible, "unchristian" choice for the times. It is important also to recognize that the option of building an empire founded on military might, in parallel with the European empires, was condemned by these same religious leaders on grounds of principle. This is worth noting, not least in view of polemics against American expansionism that are commonplace in Canada and in the Islamic world alike. There is no doubt that there is a charge to be answered here, and that the problem goes back a very long way.[12] However, it is also important to recognize the fact that it was Niebuhr rather than the social gospellers who was proven right, and proven right in spectacular fashion, after 1939. Isolationism had led to America's complicity in the rise of Fascism, and given what had become common knowledge concerning the horrors of the death

---

however, is that communist China *will* rank among the top ten. There are today millions and millions of fervent Chinese Christians, much of it dating from a largely underground house church movement which thrived during the Maoist period, and who tend to regret the easier days that have arrived in the contemporary politics of China as more hindrance than help to the gospel. Whether one looks at the average Christian emerging from global Christian demographics, or to these new (and to our eyes, very strange) versions of Christianity emerging in nations like China, the sort of politics that corresponds with the new, great Christian centres in the population of the planet is not what we have in the West. Our days as the keepers and guardians of Christianity will have ended, and so will the association of Christianity with liberal democratic pluralism. See Philip Jenkins, *The Next Christendom* (Oxford: Oxford University Press, 2002), 90.

[12] Gary Dorrien, *Imperial Designs* (New York and London: Routledge, 2004), 223-258, provides a useful perspective on the history of American expansionism.

camps by 1945, Americans were ill-disposed to see it take place again in the form of a Stalinism that they perceived to be just as bad. Those who think, indeed, that Western Europe would not have been over-run by Soviet tanks in the decades following the War had American troops not been stationed in Europe in massive numbers are fooling themselves.

Insofar as it was a religious revaluation of values that changed attitudes, responsibility has to be laid at the door of one religious leader above all others: Reinhold Niebuhr. Niebuhr's distinctive political claim, which begins to emerge from the mid-1930s and that continued to preoccupy him to the end, was that in the mixed environment of actual social life, the way in which individual Christians, churches and whole societies fulfil the obligation to love the neighbour takes paradoxical forms. In relation to the question of war, where the justice of the cause is clear at any rate, love of neighbour can legitimately take the form of military action—and of the industrial and social preparations that make it possible. Clearly, there are for Niebuhr limits— limits that were clearly reached, in his estimation, in the American setting at the time of the Vietnam war[13] —but there are also times in which it is imperative to take action, to wage war for the sake of peace, and demonstrate love for the neighbour in defence of the defenceless.

Niebuhr's theology, however, is highly contextual and is generally characterized also by a highly sophisticated political and psychological analysis of human motives. It is a telling comment on some of those who today tend to appeal to the realist strands of his theology, some seventy years on, that such little awareness of the precariousness of human motives is in evidence. An uncritical supporter of American military action in Iraq, in the mode of a Paul Wolfowitz or even that lesser peril, John McCain, though perfectly capable of appealing to Niebuhrian realism as justification (though remember that President Obama is also said to be an admirer of Niebuhr), seem largely incapable of the self-examination that the theology equally demands, and indeed, presupposes. That is to say, they appear incapable of recognizing that all political motivation is mixed at best. Instead, what dominates is the idealization of political freedom and an all-too-modern "faith" in *American* humanity, and far too little of the "Reformation realism" that tempered Niebuhr's every political judgement.

When we turn to Karl Barth, by contrast, we enter a very different world. Barth is not associated directly with the version of "Christian realism" that has been so influential in American political life since the mid-1930s, partly because the latter is an entirely home-grown product, partly

---

[13] Reinhold Niebuhr, "Toward New Intra-Christian Endeavors," *The Christian Century* 86 (1969): 1662-1667.

because Barth was suspected to be a communist sympathizer in the McCarthy Era, and partly, one senses, because his version of the position proves to be theologically rather stronger meat than the American (and Canadian) religious constitution generally tolerates. Unlike Niebuhr, Barth rejected the adaptation to the Cold War situation of the anti-Nazi stance worked out in the context of the 1930s and 40s, famously maintaining (not without considerable protest from his contemporaries, Reinhold Niebuhr included) that Stalinism and Nazism simply did not belong together in the same theological discussion. The reason for this was that Stalinism was formally indifferent to the specific claims of the Christian gospel, whereas Nazism claimed explicit Christian warrant and made claims with clear biblical overtones. Its policy on the "Jewish question" was certainly its most sinister error, but it was by no means its only one. That in fact it stood explicitly against certain of the core claims of the Christian gospel, all the while pretending that its polity was a "true" Christianity, set it apart from Stalinism in Barth's understanding.

Whereas Niebuhr's theology is an application to particular, ever-shifting social and political contexts of a rather narrow range of Christian theological ideas, Karl Barth's theology is massively preoccupied with the entire structure and content of Christian faith, concerning which he is at once both a consummate commentator on tradition and among the most radical of innovators. In Niebuhr's theology, a rather overtly psycho-dynamic analysis of the structures of sin informs the application of the Christian gospel to practical and political problems. In Barth's theology, by contrast, the source of everything in creation is the love of God in Jesus Christ, and so this great Christian theme stands at the core of his approach to the problem of war as well. When answering the question of why it is that Christian theology and the Christian church should stand opposed to Hitler, Barth's position is unambiguous: the resurrection of Jesus Christ from the dead.[14] On account of this, Barth maintains, the world has not been given up by God to fate or chance, nor has it been abandoned to the sinister powers that roamed the earth between 1933 and 1945. Rather, as Barth puts it, citing the Pauline epistles, the "principalities and powers" have been overthrown, and the kingly rule of Christ extended to "the whole universe in all its heights and depths."[15] The creation, as he puts it, has already been consecrated through the resurrection of Jesus Christ, and we would be denying that fact if, owing to sloth or disobedience or fear, we were to permit the chaos that Christ has defeated to masquerade as the

---

[14] Barth, *Letter to Great Britain from Switzerland*, 9-15.
[15] Ibid., 10.

victor, as if it had had the final say and spoken the definitive word instead in raising Jesus Christ from the dead.

What is most notable about Barth's theological approach, in other words, is that he rejects the view that the war could be theologically justified by appeal to such ideals as "Western civilization," "the liberty of the individual," or "social justice," for the simple reason that these are not the grounds by which Christians can, on the basis of faith, decide on their attitude to anything, least of all to something as serious as war.[16] The fundamental loyalty of the Christian is, after all, not to the state but to God, and only to the state insofar as it is the instrument and servant of God. Later in life, Barth was so bold as to argue on these terms that only the Christian church has good reason to believe in the humanistic ideals of modernity, as summarized in the principles of liberty, equality and solidarity, or as formulated in the modern doctrine of human rights. For, apart from their theological ground in the wise patience and gentle love of God for the creature, above all as seen in the assumption by God of human nature in Jesus of Nazareth, these rights and freedoms are suspended in mid-air, without foundation.[17] Only on explicitly theological terms, Barth argues, can we make common cause with secular fictions such as "the liberty of the individual," and all the rest—only these must not be permitted to take the place of God and of the acts of God in the Christian theology of the state, or else we have merely substituted another idolatry for that of Nazism.

A Theology for Canada's Role in Afghanistan

In critical dialogue with these two theologies, let me conclude with some theological observations on the difficult question of Canadian military involvement in the Afghanistan conflict.

It should be observed at the outset that there are clearly massive differences between the theologies of the state and the problem of war in these Christian theologians, and the political theologies of the Islamic world. What is idealized in a good part of the latter is the idea of a divinely ordered politics, in which such human legislation as exists is subject to divine law; indeed, on a strict reading, there might be said to be no such thing as human law in Islam, as the concept of law in its true sense is a

---

[16] Ibid., 15-16.
[17] The source is Karl Barth, "The Humanity of God," in Barth, *The Humanity of God*, trans. John N. Thomas and Thomas Wieser (Richmond, VA: John Knox Press, 1960), 37-68. The theme of the goodness and dignity of humanity is, however, pervasive in Barth's late theology in particular.

theological one. Though the myriad traditions of interpretation of divine law by jurists in Islam means that, in practice, divine law can mean a multitude of things, and is woven together inextricably with human interpretation, the ideal is of a sacred state. Though for reasons of historical exigency, such a state may be unrealizable in a given epoch or in a given region, or even in any historical era, the ideal is important, as it tends, like all ideals, to regulate what people do in relation to the real.

Christianity, of course, has reasons to be suspicious of the idea of a sacred state, since it was in such a state that Jesus of Nazareth was handed over to death; this fact is literally written into the central texts of the New Testament canon. Beyond this, a Niebuhrian might want to say that the Islamic ideal of the state is fatally flawed because of its lack of a "realistic" sense of the pervasiveness and inevitability of sin, which infects even religious leaders (perhaps one might say, "especially" religious leaders). All human power is not only corruptible, but it is already and always corrupt. Therefore you do not want to trust it so far as to make it something that cannot be checked. This is, one might say, the bottom line in political Niebuhrianism.

Among the crucial points that one needs to make about this, however, is that the fiction of perfection exists on both sides. This has already been encountered, of course, in the tendency seen among major figures who have employed a broadly Niebuhrian analysis of the world in the years since 9/11. Is it not striking that in these analyses, the problem is always said to lie with *someone else* rather than with the West in general or the United States in particular? What would be the truly Niebuhrian move, in fact, would be to begin with a rigorous self-examination, to identify those features of the Western world's polity that are, let us say, instances of sensuality on the one hand or of pride on the other, and only then to turn to the question of the enemy. Had this step been taken long ago, indeed, there might have been less reason for war, less of the frustration that helps to explain, though it could never *excuse* the events of 9/11, and considerably less suspicion of the West among hundreds of millions of Muslims globally. A Niebuhrian analysis of the contemporary West might point to the fact that our principle of freedom of speech and of conscience, for instance, on the basis of which freedom of religion stands or falls, is precisely also and by an identical logic the basis for the existence of pornography on virtually every magazine rack. That Christians accept the former, while not typically endorsing the latter, does not excuse them from complicity in the sins of our culture, call it the commodification of women or what you may.

One of the more arresting illustrations of the difficulty that we face can be found in a missiological study by Timothy Tennent, who tells the story of a Kuwaiti who, when asked what he knew about Christians, replied that "a Christian is someone who promotes immorality, pornography, and sexually oriented television programs like *Sex in the City, Desperate Housewives*, and so on ...."[18] In short, the Christian world (identified still as the Western world) is widely seen in the Muslim world as a morally bankrupt, apostate community. Though this distortion is akin to the prejudiced Western view that Islam is inherently violent and so on, since that is almost all that a good many Westerners ever encounter of it in the news or in popular culture, perceptions on the ground matter, and they need to be understood.

The idea that so many Western Christians have that there is nothing religiously problematic—or to use good Niebuhrian language, sinful—with and in the political and social worlds that they help to prop up is among the great sources of the tensions in the world between Islam and what is perceived as "Christianity." You and I may know that good Christian people are not sexually promiscuous and the like; what seems likely, however, is that the average local jihadists on the borders of Afghanistan and Pakistan, whom Canadian troops are at this moment attempting to root out, cannot in all honesty make the distinction between the typical Western Christian and this stereotype. Most likely they would find the distinction so fine as to be meaningless in the context of their particular rural, impoverished and in many ways pre-modern *Realpolitik*. However distorted the perception, furthermore, it is not without point. To cite but one example, the sexualization of children at an outrageously young age in the West is scandalous, and in the eyes of much of the world, it refutes all our fine words about human dignity and freedom. For is such a freedom worth having? Does it not, rather, tend to a kind of slavery, and is it not much to the credit of global Muslims that they can see this so clearly from such a distance?

Whether democratic liberalism can survive without the ethical foundations that religion alone can provide is an open question, concerning which our grandchildren, perhaps, may one day have critical words to say. In the meantime, there is, I wish to suggest, something that diasporic Islam might be able to help us Christians in the West to do in the present situation, and that is to critique liberal democratic society as we presently know it as religiously and morally inadequate, and therefore as ultimately dehuman-

---

[18] Timothy Tennant, *Theology in the Context of World Christianity* (Grand Rapids: Zondervan, 2007), 195, citing R. Butler, "Unlocking Islam," *Mission Frontiers* 13 (1991): 24.

izing. Among the several things needful is a rather Niebuhrian analysis that points to our "heresy" of the moment, which, like the churches of the 1930s, denies or ignores the problem of evil in our midst and for that very reason falls prey to it. There are, after all, barbarisms other than Fascism. There is arguably no greater service that Christians and Muslims living in a nation like Canada could do together to ameliorate the global tensions between Islam and Christianity in the West than to address such questions with "a common word," and there would in the final analysis be no greater memorial that they could construct to those who have died in Afghanistan resisting a very different evil in the form of the rule of the Taliban.

Beyond such social and political questions, there are pressing and pertinent and overtly theological questions that Muslims and Christians in the West might helpfully face together. To make this more concrete, I would suggest that we can put the basic theological problem that Western Christianity faces in one word: that word is God. But it is also the case that there is a correlative problem that Muslims globally face, and that Christians in the West might help them to address through a dialogue that can probably only take place here. Once again, the problem can be put in a word: that word is humanity. In fact, these are ultimately the questions that underlie the point just made: the question is, how can a political or social order rightly reflect the dignity of humanity on the one side and the claim of God on humanity on the other?

It is not possible to develop these claims at any length within the limits of this paper, but let me begin, at least, by sketching the general shape of the argument that I wish to make before concluding with a more general observation. I will begin with an historical parallel. After the Holocaust of the Jews under Nazism, a movement of massive importance took place within Christianity and within Judaism alike, in which each for the first time in 2000 years recognized that it had become essential to reach mutual understanding and, in a way, to learn to speak the language of the other. In Christian scholarship, this took the basic form of an exploration of the Jewish matrix of the earliest Christianity, and to some extent of the Judaism of the post-biblical period, as the framework for understanding anew the figure of Jesus of Nazareth. The obscenity of anti-Judaism within Christian thought has been largely overtaken by an awareness of the importance of Judaism *for Christianity itself*. On the other side of the coin, it is highly significant that Jewish biblical scholars since the War down to today have worked and work actively on the documents of the New Testament and on the historical figure of Jesus, even owning the New Testament for the first time ever for what it is: a Jewish document.

Christianity in the Western world today, however, faces another problem, which is not the shame that it bears in relation to the Jews historically and in the mid-twentieth century in particular, and which must never be allowed to be forgotten, but something else again: a difficulty in grasping what is at stake in talk of *one God*. For some two centuries, the whole question of the meaningfulness of our words about God have been placed in doubt, owing to the anti-religious thought of the Enlightenment in the first instance and of the culture of nineteenth and twentieth century modernity in general that followed. To put the point as concisely as possible, the problem is that we do not, in our culture, know what to do with transcendence. In a manner of speaking, even where transcendence is acknowledged *formally*, Western Christianity has, broadly speaking, forgotten what such transcendence might entail *materially*. How does acknowledgement of one God impact upon human life? In what ways does it critique the desire to "serve" other so-gods, whether these be the Nazi gods of blood and soil, or other purely human gods and goals closer to our culture? It interests me, for instance, that the document, "A Common Word Between Us and You," issued in the Autumn of 2007, signed by 138 global Islamic scholars and addressed to the leaders of the Christian churches of the world, speaks of the necessity not only of recognizing the love of God, along with the love of neighbour, as central to the problems of our time, but also the theme of *the unity of God*. It also recognizes the fact that at this moment in time, the future of the world depends on how well or how poorly Muslims and Christians together come to recognize these things.

Western Christians are today, in many respects, largely uncommitted to what essentially counts as belief in one God. An index of the problem can be seen in their dubiety in relation to the one who is, in the distinctively Christian form of monotheism, known as "Father." The God who is spoken of in the pages of the New Testament as the one whom "no one has ever seen" (Jn. 1:18), and who "alone...has immortality and dwells in unapproachable light" (1 Tim. 6:16) has largely been collapsed into the immanence of either incarnation, presence, or even purely humanistic "religious experience." Elsewhere, I have argued that the problem we face is nothing less than the loss of the one whom we call God "the Father."[19] Perhaps we can be reminded by the witness of others, and at this historical juncture by the witness of Islam to the unity of God, of the theoretical and practical importance of this central religious question.

---

[19] Gary D. Badcock, "Whatever Happened to God the Father?" *Crux* 36 (2000): 2-12.

It was part of the service of Karl Barth to the theology of the twentieth century to remind the Christian church in Europe and ultimately the world that it takes its stand on God or else it falls. I would like to observe publicly once again in the present context that I do not judge Barth's otherwise utterly remarkable theological achievement be have been equal to this task, but this does not mean that the theocentric thrust of his position was entirely misguided.[20] But I will leave this aside. For there is another service that Karl Barth performs for us very well indeed, and that is to highlight the importance of the theme of the goodness and dignity of humanity in the Christian theological tradition, which is grounded, not primarily in generic talk of being made in the image of God (not least as "images of God" are a distinctly problematic theme in the Hebraic thought from which the phrase derives), but in what Christians say about Jesus Christ. To put the point in a nutshell, the astonishing depth of the love of God for the creature in Christian theology involves nothing less than the proposition that there is, by God's sovereign choice and grace, *a human nature in God*—and this, to say the least, changes absolutely *everything* that we are obliged to say about humanity.

There are a number of ways in which the importance of this claim can be illustrated, from the vast differences seen in the handling of scripture in Christianity over against Islam, and the unwillingness of the latter to allow for the kind of historical criticism that Christians employ in relation to it; to the clear tendency to political despotism in Muslim countries that attempt to develop "secular" government on the Western model; to the status of women in the strictest Muslim polity; to the differences in approaches to the figure of Jesus in Christianity and Islam. On this last question, which is a matter of the utmost importance, one might have thought that Christian faith in Jesus as Son of God would produce a man whose human nature is more diminished, and that Islam, which insists that Jesus is purely a prophet, would allow for additional emphasis on his humanity. In fact, the converse is true: Christians insist on the authenticity of Jesus' humanity, for the simple reason that the humanity of the incarnate one actually has key theological importance; Islam, by contrast, presents us with a shadowy figure who talks as an infant in his cradle, who turns clay birds into real ones as an adult, and who does not experience the death of

---

[20] My own objection would be that because of the lack of a philosophical theism, Barth is unable to give full content to the Christian doctrine of God, and transcendence is finally collapsed into immanence. To put this in plain English, to say that "God is revealed in Jesus Christ" assumes that the word "God" already means something. On this question, see John McIntyre, *The Shape of Christology*, 2nd ed. (Edinburgh: T & T Clark, 1998), 173.

the cross. To say this is not to *invent* a criticism: Christians have long been struck by the "Gnostic" character of the Islamic treatment of Jesus, and so by the relative unreality of his humanity, which, of course, need not be asserted in any depth because it is of no real theological importance: what matters is that he is "but a slave of Allah."[21]

But for our purposes the test case is Afghanistan, in which we are faced with the prospect of an inhuman theocracy, in what is undoubtedly a distortion of Islamic theology, presenting a religious outlook that appears to be without humanity, which seeks to set itself up in service to a God who is distant and authoritarian, justifying the dictates of a cruel and unimaginably narrow vision of human life. Certainly the love of God for the human creature and the creation is missing from it. A Christian can only call the God who is defined as such in the outlook of the Taliban an *idol*, since such assumptions about God cannot be accepted as adequately representing the truth about God. That this harsh and alien God presents us with a caricature of the best in Islam is obvious; but what is not at all obvious to the Christian eye is that it does not represent the particular *danger* within Islamic thought that needs to be identified and criticized—not in the name of this or that culture, but above all else in the name of God himself, who for all of us is "the Compassionate" and "the Merciful." Permit me to say these things, because this must be part of any Christian voice that speaks honestly of the "common word" that is needed in our time.

More generally, of course, all this may seem little use in the context of a disastrous war that has raged in several phases for decades, or in relation to the small part that Canada has played in the immense sufferings of the people of Afghanistan, and our costly attempt to try to heal them. However, we have entered—some might say, "blundered"—into this situation owing to NATO commitments after 9/11, and now, finding ourselves embroiled in the war, we see and hear the cry of the people and cannot escape the question of justice, which comes to us through the sheer need for hope and a future. I believe, however, as a Christian theologian and in view of what has been said, that it is possible to justify Canadian military engagement in the Afghanistan conflict on the basis of the common humanity that we share, and share with Jesus Christ, in the name of which surely, in the final analysis, this war is waged.

It may be that our all-too-secular Western "faith" in humanity requires correction, first by a Niebuhrian recognition of our own failings, and second by a reminder from Islam that, just as a God without humanity is not worth having, so also, the situation of a humanity without God is empty

---

[21] I am inclined to say at this point that "Christology," to use the Christian word, is key to understanding Islam.

and precarious. Nevertheless, there is justification within the Christian tradition for our involvement in the lot of the Afghan people. The risk, of course, is that we should be misunderstood to stand in support of the same policy that was pursued in Iraq, or to stand in principle against an Islamic constitutional government, which might, after all, even for the Christian West come closer to the will of God and the human good than some of us yet realize. This possibility, however, we certainly do not yet see in its application in the hinterlands of Pakistan and Afghanistan where the Taliban exercise their grim rule. Thus, we are obliged to pray that God will save the people of Afghanistan from such evils. And, as our actions in this case must follow our prayers, we find ourselves at war, in an operation not intended to impose Western values—for if this were the case, there is no theological justification for it at all—but much more humbly, to keep madmen from power, to preserve the rule of law in the service of the needs of our neighbour, and to affirm the dignity of human life in the service of God. The point at which such humble—and *therefore* great and true—goals cease to be in view in our policy is the point at which a Christian theology would need to criticize our own idolatry and inhumanity, our pride and our faithlessness, which would then have become of a piece with what we must for the present oppose in Afghanistan.

RECONCILIATION AND THE "WAR" ON TERROR: CANADIAN CHURCHES RESPOND TO 9/11 AND THE WAR IN AFGHANISTAN

ERNIE REGEHR

Framing the Question: Canadian Churches and 9/11

That the American psyche and America's relations with the rest of the world, including Canada, would be profoundly affected by the attacks of 11 September, 2001 was readily recognized by everyone on that dark day. What the immediate future held, however, was at the time anything but clear. The specific form of the American reaction had yet to unfold, as clearly, no policy had been formulated. In the broad international affairs community in Canada too, there was no uniform sense of how best to respond. The Canadian churches were certainly no exception. The attack on North America, including on the twenty-four Canadians who were killed at the World Trade Center, was genuinely unprecedented. The accused perpetrators were largely unknown outside the professional intelligence community. American shock and anger were palpable, however, and the demand for a "payback" mounted by the day.

In the immediate aftermath of 9/11, informal conversations within the ecumenical community linked to the Canadian Council of Churches recognized that the churches generally lacked well-developed policies on effective responses to terrorism. They had virtually no association with Afghanistan, where early claims said the attacks had been planned, and they did not yet have the information and context needed to develop a coherent and common public witness. But as conversations continued, a growing sense emerged that in fact the churches did have the benefit of a rich and collective body of experience and policy engagement on questions of war and sustainable peace that were relevant to the circumstances. Project Ploughshares, the ecumenical peace agency of the Canadian Council of Churches, offered to prepare a discussion document for the purpose of bringing together some immediately discernable and relevant learning from the churches' responses to armed conflict and other human and natural disasters.[1] The objective was to identify some of the basic principles that should guide the churches, and which the churches would convey to the Canadian Government to help it shape a constructive response.

This discussion paper, in turn, helped to inform an ecumenical letter to the Prime Minister, coming jointly from the Canadian Council of Churches and Project Ploughshares. It was sent on September 21, 2001, only 10 days after the attacks.[2] A separate version of the letter was sent by several denominations—Anglican, Baptist (Convention), Lutheran, Presbyterian, and United Church—to their congregations about appropriate Canadian Christian responses to 9/11.[3] Then, on October 12, five days after the launch of the US war on Afghanistan a larger group of national church leaders wrote to all Members of Parliament in advance of a Parliamentary debate called to hear responses to the 9/11 attacks.[4]

Together, the discussion paper and ecumenical communications with the churches and government drew attention to a series of basic principles that could helpfully guide a Canadian response to the crisis. These are briefly outlined in what follows.

1. A Call for Reliance on Proven Values During Times of Crisis

A central message of the churches in those initial documents was to remind their own constituencies, as well as the Government, that in times

---

[1] Ernie Regehr, "Responding to terror," *The Ploughshares Monitor* 22, no. 3 (September, 2001), http://www.ploughshares.ca/libraries/monitor/mons01b.html.

[2] Canadian Council of Churches to Jean Chrétien, September 21, 2001, http://www.ploughshares.ca/libraries/Statements/CCC%20Letter%20to%20PM%209-11.pdf.

[3] Rev. Dr. Ken Bellous, Executive Minister, Baptist Convention of Ontario and Quebec; The Rev. Stephen Kendall, Principal Clerk, Presbyterian Church in Canada; The Right Rev. Dr. Marion Pardy, Moderator, United Church of Canada; The Most Rev. Michael G. Peers, Primate, Anglican Church of Canada; and Bishop Raymond L. Schultz, National Bishop, Evangelical Lutheran Church in Canada, to the members of our churches after the tragedy in the United States, 21 September, 2001, http://www.ploughshares.ca/libraries/Statements/Church%20Leaders%20Letter%20to%20Churches%209-11.

[4] Rev. Dr. David Pfrimmer, Chair, Commission on Justice and Peace, Canadian Council of Churches [and fourteen other national church leaders], "Canada's Response to Terrorism: An Ecumenical Appeal to Parliament," October 12, 2001, http://www.ploughshares.ca/libraries/Statements/MPletter.Eng%209-11.pdf.

of crisis it is doubly important to remember and to focus on the social and political values that we claim when we are at our best:

> In the face of the grief and rage that tempt many to yield to vengeful retaliation, the appeal to enduring values and principles helps to steer us toward more measured and, in the end, more effective action. (21 September, 2001)[5]

While those values, several of which are discussed in the eight additional principles which follow, might not produce formulaic responses in particular circumstances, they can serve as a brake on the tempting claim, prominent at the time, that because these were "extraordinary times," extraordinary measures were required.

A prominent feature of public advocacy at the time, for example, was the assertion that the American President should not be constrained or inhibited by the practices that guide America in normal times. The mantra of the day was that on 11 September, 2001, "everything changed"—and because everything changed, because we were in a whole new context, facing unprecedented realities and threats, America and its allies could not rely on the familiar moral and political rudders or navigational aids. Over time, of course, the idea that new dangers must lead to the abandonment of old principles and restraints came to be known by other names—like "waterboarding," or "enhanced interrogation techniques," or what the name of the Iraqi prison "Abu Ghraib" represents. Traditional values and principles had been so persuasively jettisoned that President Barack Obama was later driven to conclude that these practices and places were a reflection of the US "losing [its] moral bearings."[6]

2. A Call for Accountability and Rejecting Impunity

> The perpetrators of these heinous crimes must be brought to justice. This imperative is unambiguous and it is not rooted in revenge but in the principle of accountability....The obligation to bring terrorists to justice is a broad obligation to bring to justice all those who commit terror and other crimes against humanity, regardless of where the victims are. (21 September, 2001)

---

[5] This and subsequent references to the four church documents listed are given parenthetically, by document date or title, in the text.
[6] "Bush-era interrogation may have worked, Obama official says," 24 April 2009, CNN, http://edition.cnn.com/2009/POLITICS/04/21/obama.memos/index.html?eref =edition.

The obligations of justice, however, are always broad and inclusive. Campaigns against "terrorists" must obviously be based upon impartial laws and be pursued with equal vigour against *all* who commit acts of terror, and not just some. The churches emphasized that rejecting impunity means holding perpetrators of such acts accountable wherever the crimes are committed, whether in the cities of North America or the bushlands of Africa. Drawing attention to this point was a way for the churches to make the case for a vigorous, unrelenting response to those guilty of terrorism, thereby also removing any sense that the call for careful and measured responses was in effect playing down or failing to recognize the fully heinous dimension of the acts of 9/11.

3. A Call to Prevent Further Acts of Terrorism

The churches insisted that "efforts toward the reduction and eradication of terrorism must be immediate, as well as long-term and multi-dimensional." Prevention, they said, requires a two-fold effort:

> …to enhance security measures in the interests of reliable public protection and safety, and to address the social, political and economic conditions that promote or are conducive to terrorism. (21 September, 2001)

They also acknowledged that while a "war" on terror can be understood as a metaphor—in the sense that protecting our societies from acts of terrorism requires a more total commitment, perseverance, and sacrifice that we associate with countries at war—they pointed out that the post-9/11 rhetoric soon lost the metaphorical character of the "war on terror" to become mobilization for a real war. The Canadian churches recognized early the inappropriateness of that "war" framework for preventing further acts of terror and emphasized instead that the perpetrators of acts of terror must be held accountable through proven processes of crime detection and accountability:

> It is highly regrettable, therefore, that states have allowed attention to shift prominently to military measures. The essential non-military character of the struggle against terrorism must be restored. (12 October, 2001)

4. A call for Due Process

By emphasizing that times of crisis require strict adherence to long-standing and proven values and procedures, the churches insisted on what was for them the obvious requirement that response to 9/11 conform to international and national laws. This call for due process applied to the full range of responses to crises—including diplomacy, intelligence-gathering and sharing, co-operation among law enforcement agencies, economic pressures, and military/police actions. The churches' warnings were notably prescient in anticipating the predilections of the Bush Administration. The churches acknowledged "that in international relations due process is not always clear, but we remind you," they wrote to Prime Minister Chrétien:

> that the United Nations and its Security Council are the essential custodians of international due process, and along with the affected national governments are central to ensuring that those being pursued, and the societies in which they are pursued, have the protection of law and just practice. (21 September, 2001)

Hence, the obligation to respect due process was unambiguous—for reasons of justice as well as political and moral legitimacy, even if in international relations due process is under construction and its requirements are still far from clear. The International Criminal Court had only recently become operative, there was no ongoing global tribunal before which accused terrorists could be brought, and the United Nations Security Council has not proven itself to be an unfailingly reliable forum for the disinterested pursuit of justice or international peace and security. Effectiveness requires measured action, supported by thorough investigation. There was and still is a need to develop reliable confidence in the effectiveness and appropriateness of whatever action is chosen. Internationalization of responses can be part of the legitimizing process.

5. A Call for Examination of Potential Grievances Behind 9/11

The churches reminded the Government of Canada that:

> ...it is important for Canada to assert that it is possible to hear and address the grievances that are linked to acts of terror without thereby in any way condoning such terrorism....[A] serious campaign against terrorism needs to address the social, economic and political conditions that tend to nurture the emergence of terrorism." (21 September, 2001)

Acknowledging that terrorism has root causes does not excuse it any more than acknowledging that higher than average crime rates tend to be linked to adverse social and economic conditions excuses individual crimes. The clear implication that the churches were drawing is that any serious crime reduction effort cannot be confined to more intensified police work; it must also address the economic and social conditions that tend to produce increased rates of crime. Similarly, any serious campaign against terrorism needs to address the social, economic and political conditions that nurture the emergence of terrorism. To argue that terrorism has roots and that some contexts are more conducive to producing terrorism than others, also is not to say that adverse social and economic conditions inevitably spawn terrorists, or that terrorists never come from conditions of relative prosperity and openness. It is to say, nonetheless, as NGOs insisted at the time, that global disparity is fundamentally incompatible with global security.

6. A Call to Realize that the World is Interdependent

Because the world is interdependent, "we know that if the world itself is an unsafe, hostile place" (21 September, 2001) there is no reliable means of insulating any part of the world from threatening global realities—whether they be climate change, nuclear arsenals, or terror networks. Security is mutual and must ultimately be advanced through co-operation. Even the major powers will finally have to embrace inter-dependence—and to see it as a source of strength rather than as a sign of weakness. The churches argued that the United States in particular would have to actively re-engage with the world. It would have to negotiate the foundations of mutual co-operation, which in turn would mean rethinking its approaches to issues like the International Criminal Court, the Kyoto Environmental Protocol, the Comprehensive (nuclear) Test-Ban Treaty, the Anti-Ballistic Missile Treaty, and so on. The churches, in other words, anticipated the changes that would finally come, almost a decade later, to at least begin the necessary process of essential rethinking.

7. A Call For Clear Constraints on Military Force

The very least that could be said about perpetrators of the 11 September, 2001 attacks on the United States and other acts of terror around the world was that they were fugitives from justice—fugitives who had to be pursued and apprehended if they were to be held to account and brought to justice. The churches acknowledged the difficulties involved. The fugitives might be spread among any number of countries, so that their capture would involve the police and intelligence forces of all those countries. It was possible that not all the states involved would fully cooperate in the pursuit of those responsible, and in some instances might even choose to harbour rather than to pursue them. Therein lay a major challenge to the international community, but the churches noted at the time of 9/11 that the early characterization of the response to the terrorist attacks on the United States as "war" misrepresented the nature of that challenge. Furthermore, they noted:

> the pursuit of fugitives across international borders without the consent of states involved requires authorization from a responsible body, which we understand to be the Security Council; but it does not require, and must not include, broad military attacks (21 September, 2001).

Police forces in the United States and beyond, with cooperation among them being facilitated through diplomacy, were before the Autumn of 2001 the primary focus of the pursuit of the fugitive terrorists. But the concurrent mobilization of a broad spectrum of United States military forces, from strategic bombers to cruise and ballistic missiles and special forces for possible assassination missions, signalled a virtually inevitable turn to a use of military force that would go well beyond police or police-support actions—and, sadly, well beyond the limits of international and humanitarian law.

Punitive military strikes against civilian populations and infrastructure would themselves, in short, be heinous violations of international law, and to human decency, and would be politically and militarily counter-productive. They would inevitably spawn new generations of terrorists and aggravate, in Afghanistan for example, the humanitarian crisis which was then already well advanced among one of the most vulnerable civilian populations in the world—one from which all international humanitarian workers had by then fled. The churches added that, if military force would be counter-productive or of limited utility in bringing the fugitives of 9/11 to justice, its role in the wider campaign against terrorism would be even more marginal. Terrorism is not amenable to military defeat. The defeat of terrorism requires a broad range of domestic security measures, effective national and international law enforcement capacity, and urgent attention to the political and social conditions that nurture it.

8. A Call Regarding the Danger of Losing Perspective

The churches emphasized that while an active response to terrorism and other crimes against vulnerable people was urgent and necessary, it was not to be pursued at all costs:

> A campaign against terrorism is required, but not at all costs…. We urge you to resist the growing pressures to permit increased invasion of privacy,

reduced access to information, reduced immigration, reduced access to safe havens for refugees, increased military spending at the expense of social programs, and any number of other measures that would erode fundamental rights and freedoms, all in the name of combating terrorism. (21 September, 2001)

Indeed, Afghanistan already offered a notable example of the extraordinary damage that can be incurred to a society through intense, single-minded campaigns that in their zeal ignore the inevitable negative consequences. In the 1980s the United States committed itself to support the war against the Soviet Union's war in Afghanistan, in the name of standing against the spread of communism, but without apparent regard for any outcome other than the defeat of Soviet policy. It was a spectacularly successful campaign, but at what cost? The cost was, among other things, a ready supply of huge quantities of small arms and light weapons through Pakistan, which only continued to fuel an unending civil war in Afghanistan, and to help generate social chaos and escalating violence in Pakistan. Uncritical support for the *mujahadeen* "freedom fighters" in the 1980s spawned the Taliban, which made common cause with the same bin Laden who is now the leading fugitive being pursued.

Now, years later, attacks on the new set of villains in Afghanistan has once again spawned another kind of violence and suffering, and the nurturing of a new round of terrorist activities, with international forces among those paying a price, but with the local population once again carrying the lion's share of the burden. In fact, the churches can now confirm what they then warned, that a single-minded and simple-minded military campaign against terrorism must have profoundly damaging consequences when it is not guided by due process and actions that honour the very laws, values and freedoms that terrorism threatens.

9 A Final Call for Demilitarization

The emphasis on demilitarizing the international response was accompanied by strong encouragement for a return to multilateralism. Of the American attack:

We fear…that the military attacks on Afghanistan…could seriously undermine the international community's efforts, both to bring those responsible for the September 11 attacks to justice and to reduce the incidence of terrorism in the future. (12 October, 2001)

Again, they write:

We fear that relying on military attacks, some of which are already resulting in the displacement and deaths of civilians, will erode essential regional support and cooperation for the pursuit of the accused, and that a predictable result will be the infliction of widespread damage on an already mutilated Afghanistan, without the successful apprehension of the accused. (12 October, 2001)

On multilateralism the churches observed that "…safety for any people or nation is inseparable from the collective safety of the international community itself," and quoted then UN Sec-Gen Kofi Annan to the effect that it is only the UN that "can ensure global legitimacy for the long term response to terrorism." (12 October, 2001)

Following the Initial Response

This broad ninefold call, issued in close proximity to the events of 9/11, represented the basic concerns of the Canadian churches represented by the ecumenical movement. In the years to follow, the churches would build on these foundational concerns.

The Canadian Council of Churches next wrote, in 2002, to Parliamentarians regarding both the treatment of detainees and questions about Canadian support for the Bush "doctrine" that had declared, "if you're not with us, then you're with the terrorists."[7] This, the Council pointed out, 'seems to fall far short of the best traditions of diplomacy, the careful standards of good international law, and very far short of the traditional "just war doctrine" historically held by many churches.' Responding to the plan at that point to deploy Canadian Forces with US Forces, rather than with the UN authorized International Security Assistance Force (ISAF), the letter asked whether Canada had accepted the Bush doctrine, and how the Canadian Government was showing 'its opposition to the elements of ruthlessness and of disregard for "collateral damage"' in American operations in Afghanistan.

The churches' public witness on Afghanistan was not based, as noted earlier, on either direct involvement in that country or on cooperation with counterparts or partners there. Instead it was based on broad and still evolving approaches to protracted conflict, peacebuilding, and solidarity with the victims of chronically failing states. Inasmuch as the churches'

---

[7] Janet Somerville, General Secretary, Canadian Council of Churches, A Letter to the Standing Committees on Foreign Affairs & International Trade and National Defence & Veterans' Affairs, 16 January 2002,
http://www.ccc-cce.ca/english/justice/afghanistan.htm.

engagement on Afghanistan is informed by these broader approaches, the following two sections review elements of ecumenical understanding of two particularly relevant issues—the protection of vulnerable people in extreme peril, and the limits to the utility of force in coming to the aid of people and states in peril.

Protecting the Vulnerable

The Canadian churches' response to 9/11 and to the subsequent attack on Afghanistan were set in the context of ecumenical discussions of the most effective and appropriate ways to meet the broader challenge of responding to chronic and extreme human suffering within what are regarded as failed or failing states. Afghanistan, of course, is now and was then only one of the current locations of advanced state failure and consequent human suffering. Sudan, the Democratic Republic of Congo, Iraq, Pakistan, Somalia, and Zimbabwe all belong on a list that could be much longer. For the churches, the obligation to respond to those crises includes but goes beyond the most basic recognition of people everywhere as part of one interdependent humanity. In an important sense, it is also a function of culpability. The churches' engagement with counterparts and the most vulnerable in many affected societies, as well as their attention to issues of global economic justice, has of course taught them that state failure is not simply about the internal behaviour or will of troubled states. It is also heavily driven by external factors. These include international economic pressures, practices, and rules; the legacy of historic and more recent imperial adventures emanating from northern states where churches of the ecumenical movement are prominent; complex regional dynamics; and external support for tyrannical regimes—all of these are at play. It is also true that all states fail to some degree, our own included. All lack in some measure the capacity or the will adequately to serve the well-being of all their citizens. The churches are also keenly aware that one of the key characteristics of advanced state failure is a state's loss of its monopoly over the exercise of lethal force. That failure is reflected not only in faltering law enforcement and escalating criminal violence, but also in the inability to prevent political violence linked to particular communities or political movements and to specific political objectives.

Church concern is obviously heightened by the fact that the international community has generally not responded well to the growing instances of advanced state failure, indifference being perhaps the most prominent posture. And it is self-interest rather than compassion that is most often the spur to action. In his introduction to the 2002 US National

Security Strategy, President Bush declared that "America is now threatened less by conquering states than...by failing ones."[8] In other words, powerful states have to defend themselves against the impact of powerless ones. Similarly, the Failed States Index produced by *Foreign Policy* journal and the Fund for Peace is not really focused on the plight of the vulnerable within those failing states. Instead, the journal adopts a tone of alarm to explain that "the threats of weak states...ripple far beyond their borders and endanger the development and security of nations that are their political and economic opposites."[9]

In Canada, the debate over Afghanistan frequently adopts a similar tone: we are in Afghanistan to protect Canada's national interest, to fight them there so we won't have to fight them here. Canada's defence policy currently goes under the theme: "Canada first" and is intended to "...enable the [Canadian Forces] to maintain the ability to deliver excellence at home, be a strong and reliable partner in the defence of North America, and project leadership abroad by making meaningful contributions to operations overseas."[10] This approach that leaves little doubt as to whose interest intervention is intended to serve. If the primary assumption about failing states is that they threaten the security of distant, powerful, and stable states, it follows that international action is likely to be filtered through the perceived security needs of the powerful rather than the welfare of the most vulnerable.

At the same time, the post-Cold War era has seen some new and welcome efforts, including doctrines of "human security" also encouraged by the ecumenical community, to formalize more constructive responses to people imperilled by extreme state failure. In Africa, when the Organization of African Unity (OAU) became the African Union (AU), African diplomats talked about a transition from a policy of non-interference to one of non-indifference. The primacy of sovereignty was to give way to a commitment to solidarity with the most vulnerable. The Canadian-sponsored International Commission on Intervention and State Sovereignty was at work at roughly the same time articulating the doctrine of the "responsibility to protect" (R2P)—making the same point that protecting vulnerable people should ultimately trump sovereignty and the princi-

---

[8] President George W. Bush, "The National Security Strategy of the United States of America," September 2002, http://www.globalsecurity.org/military/library/policy/national/nss-020920.pdf.
[9] The Fund for Peace and Foreign Policy, "The Failed States Index 2007," *Foreign Policy* 161 (July/August 2007): 55.
[10] Department of National Defence website:
http://www.forces.gc.ca/site/focus/first-premier/index-eng.asp.

ple of non-interference. In 2005, the UN Summit formally accepted a responsibility "to help to protect populations from genocide, war crimes, ethnic cleansing and crimes against humanity." It included a reference to Chapter VII and the resort to non-military and military coercion in extreme circumstances.[11]

A few months after this statement was issued, the February 2006 Ninth Assembly of the World Council of Churches (WCC)—culminating a long process of study and consultation that began well before 9/11—endorsed the R2P principle. The WCC decision was not easily taken, but its constructive balance is based on the careful commitment to take seriously two prominent traditions within the ecumenical community: the deeply rooted wariness of militarism and the bold global ethic of solidarity with the suffering and imperilled within a common humanity. The WCC Ninth Assembly Statement on the Responsibility to Protect, "Vulnerable populations at risk," also struck a careful balance on the question of force—acknowledging the need, under extraordinary circumstances, to resort to force to protect people in extreme peril, but also recognizing the very real limits to the utility of force. On the one hand the churches conclude that:

> In calling on the international community to come to the aid of vulnerable people in extraordinary suffering and peril, the fellowship of churches is not prepared to say that it is never appropriate or never necessary to resort to the use of force for the protection of the vulnerable.

And, at the same time:

> Just as individuals and communities in stable and affluent societies are able in emergencies to call on armed police to come to their aid when they experience unusual or extraordinary threats of violence, churches recognize that people in much more perilous circumstances should have the right to call for and have access to protection.[12]

On the other hand, the statement insists that "this refusal in principle to preclude the use of force is not based on a naïve belief that force can be

---

[11] 2005 World Summit Outcome, General Assembly Resolution 60/1, 24 October 2005, paras 138-140, http://daccessdds.un.org/doc/UNDOC/GEN/N05/487/60/PDF/N0548760.pdf?OpenElement.
[12] Adopted at the Porto Alegre, Brazil Assembly, 14-23 February, 2006, http://www.oikoumene.org/gr/resources/documents/wcc-commissions/international-affairs/responsability-to-protect/vulnerable-populations-at-risk-the-responsibility-to-protect.html.

relied on to solve intractable problems." It then goes on to elaborate at some length on the limits to force:

> The churches do not, however, believe in the exercise of lethal force to bring in a new order of peace and safety. By limiting the resort to force quite specifically to immediate protection objectives, the churches insist that the kinds of long-term solutions that are required—that is, the restoration of societies to conditions in which people are for the most part physically safe, in which basic economic, social, and health needs are met, where fundamental rights and freedoms are respected, where the instruments of violence are controlled, and in which the dignity and worth of all people are affirmed—cannot be delivered by force. Indeed, the limiting of legitimate force to protection operations is the recognition that the distresses of deeply troubled societies cannot be quickly alleviated by either military means or diplomacy; and that in the long and painstakingly slow process of rebuilding the conditions for sustainable peace, those that are most vulnerable are entitled to protection from at least the most egregious of threats.
>
> The use of force for humanitarian purposes can never be an attempt to find military solutions to social and political problems, to militarily engineer new social and political realities. Rather, it is intended to mitigate imminent threats and to alleviate immediate suffering while long-term solutions are sought by other means.

In effect, the Churches in the WCC have collectively said that in some circumstances, the introduction of foreign military force is part of the process of advancing well-being, but in others it is destined to make things worse. That being the case, it is important for the ecumenical community to become part of the process of political discernment to understand when multilateral force is likely to be effective and when it is not. The Ninth Assembly statement said clearly that when force is used the context is critical and that the resort to force "…for humanitarian purposes must therefore be carried out in the context of a broad spectrum of economic, social, political, and diplomatic efforts to address the direct and long-term conditions that underlie the crisis." The context is central to the question of when the resort to force is most likely to contribute to the safety and well-being of the vulnerable.

Precisely this question was central to Canadian ecumenical approaches to Afghanistan. The churches recognized that if military intervention was undertaken in the interests of the security and well-being of the people of Afghanistan, it should be a resort to force conditioned by clear political and economic measures to resolve conflict and improve lives.

Conditioning the Resort to Force

The international ecumenical community, born out of the devastation of World War II, has a built-in suspicion of militarism and the resort to force. While most churches in that tradition have well-developed doctrines about the just use of force in extreme circumstances, there is nevertheless a wariness of the resort to force, and that wariness was certainly present in the responses of Canadian churches to Canadian military involvement in Afghanistan. While there has been basic support for Canadian involvement, it is also based on the understanding that for force to be effective in bringing security to vulnerable people, attention needs to be given to a range of accompanying social, economic, and diplomatic initiatives.

Indeed, the growing failure in Afghanistan to recover the state's monopoly on the resort to force is instructive about the limits to force—a demonstration that military force itself depends on particular political and social conditions to make a positive contribution to local security. In other words, force is not a *deus ex machina* or autonomous power that can transcend its context and simply cause a predetermined outcome, regardless of political and social conditions. Lessons learned from international engagement in conflict zones more broadly suggest there are at least six key factors[13] for setting a context in which an international force like ISAF can function as a peace support operation to end criminal and political violence and to bring stability and greater safety to the lives of affected populations. These six factors are as follows:

Political consensus and reconciliation

In the Afghanistan context, the churches have consistently identified the absence of diplomacy as a key failing. The refusal to mount energetic efforts toward a comprehensive political consensus or peace agreement arguably reflects one of the most neglected elements of the collective international effort in Afghanistan. Without a negotiated settlement—that is, without a broad political consensus to support a new national order—inserting international military forces into any ongoing armed conflict risks prolonging and intensifying that conflict and puts the international community on one side of a civil war. As the security situation continues to deteriorate in Afghanistan there is growing recognition, at least among some, that contemporary Afghanistan has yet to go through the transfor-

---

[13] Ernie Regehr, "Failed States and the Limits to Force: The Challenge of Afghanistan," in Lois L. Ross, ed., *Fragile States or Failing Development? Canadian Development Report 2008* (Ottawa: North South Institute, 2008), 1-20.

mative experience of a national peace and reconciliation process—and without it, there is no foundation on which to base an effective security assistance or peace support force.

Legitimacy

There is also a primary requirement for any new order or government being assisted by foreign security forces to conduct itself in ways that continually, and not only through elections, earn the trust of the local population. This is a *governance* issue and speaks to the legitimacy of the Karzai government—which continues to be bedevilled by charges of corruption and a lack of capacity to meet basic expectations. Unless there are determined and observable efforts to deal with those failings, the foreign military forces deployed in support of that government will also be regarded as illegitimate—helping to entrench leaders that are not trusted and to strengthen a regime regarded by many as antithetical to the interests of their community.

Disarmament

A visible effort at gun control is also essential. There has been some disarmament in Afghanistan, especially the collection of some surplus larger weapons, but small arms obviously continue to be ubiquitous and the objective of disarming non-state groups, particularly in the North (the only part of the country where it might currently be possible), has made little progress—and is unlikely to do so in the face of ongoing war.

Regional cooperation

The cooperation of neighbours is obviously necessary and much has been written about regional dynamics and the importance of Pakistan. It is of course the testimony of experts that the instability in the region is interconnected, and given current events in Pakistan, that is not a promising reality.

Development

Active peace-building and reconstruction are obviously central and also, in the case of Afghanistan, chronically underfunded (although Canada is making a substantial investment). In the absence of measurable improvement in the daily lives of people, the presence of foreign military forces becomes yet another adversity, the scourge of increased violence on a social and economic landscape that is already overwhelmed by trial and hardship.

Force methodology

The constructive resort to force also depends on it being appropriate to the circumstance—demonstrating high respect for, and with the highest priority assigned to, the safety of the people. The way in which force has been used in Afghanistan has of course come in for widespread criticism by Afghans and other observers. Foreign forces that abandon restraint, or that do not respect the safety of civilians caught in the crossfire, not only undermine support for those foreign security forces, but also jeopardize support for the leadership and institutions that those forces are there to bolster.

Reversing failure in Afghanistan

Such broad learnings from international intervention experience thus informed the Canadian churches' initial assessment of Canada's military mission in Afghanistan, as well as subsequent ecumenical communications with Government.

Following their active intervention in the Afghanistan debate in the aftermath of 9/11, however, the churches did not issue another formal collective statement until the summer of 2007, when the Canadian Council of Churches wrote twice to the Prime Minister—the first letter came from the Officers of the Council and the second from twelve member churches. In the intervening years, especially when Canadian Forces were deployed in Kabul in a role with the international forces that was perceived by Canadians to be within the scope of Canada's peacekeeping tradition, Afghanistan had a considerably lower profile among Canadians and the Canadian churches. But in 2005, when planning began for deployment of Canadian troops to the active war zone of Kandahar province, Afghanistan was back on the agenda.

The 2007 letters from the ecumenical community emphasized three policy points.[14] First, the churches called for Canadian objectives to be

---

[14] The Rev. Dr. James Christie, President, and the Rev. Dr. Karen Hamilton, General Secretary, Canadian Council of Churches, to Prime Minister Stephen Harper, 25 June, 2007; and His Grace Bishop Bagrat Galstanian, Primate, Armenian Holy Apostolic Church, Canadian Diocese [with eleven other leaders of member

focused on the pursuit of peace specifically for the people of Afghanistan, not on advancing a generalized "war on terror." Second, the Council called for a political solution, including negotiations and the pursuit of a comprehensive peace agreement, and redoubled diplomacy in support of that end. And, finally, the Council said that the role of Canadian troops in Afghanistan should be to protect the people of Afghanistan, as well as the civilian infrastructure, "in the manner prescribed by the Responsibility to Protect doctrine."

These letters were sent in the context of a steady stream of reporting on the deteriorating security situation in Afghanistan—reports that have continued in the same vein to the present and removed any doubt that Afghan and international military and police forces are failing in their primary mission. The churches were well aware that the failure to deliver basic security was especially acute in those parts of the country that were demonstrably outside the fragile political arrangement that was achieved in Bonn in late 2001 and early 2002. Moreover, they understood peacekeeping and counter-insurgency experience to caution that even a combination of foreign military reinforcements and significantly accelerated training and expansion of the Afghan National Army or the Afghan National Police was unlikely to sustainably improve security conditions as long as the country continued to suffer a deep and enduring political deficit—that is, as long as particular (and prominent) communities regarded themselves as excluded from the national agreement.

The August 2007 letter by 12 national church leaders therefore called on the Prime Minister to focus Canadian efforts on reconciliation, noting that

> With all that has happened in Afghanistan since 2001, but also in the decades preceding Canada' direct military role there, the internal wounds are deep and the prospects for reconciliation are uncertain.

The leaders welcomed the 2004 Afghanistan Compact's "Peace, Justice, and Reconciliation Action Plan," encouraged Canadian support for it, and called for "culturally appropriate" processes for reconciliation. They "urged that every possible effort be made to seek negotiated solutions." In urging the pursuit of negotiated solutions, the letter specifically called for an openness to talk to "Taliban insurgents willing to participate in peaceful negotiations." It called on Canada "to dedicate more of its efforts and fi-

---

churches of the Canadian Council of Churches], 16 August, 2007, to Prime Minister Stephen Harper, both at: http://www.ploughshares.ca/libraries/ Statements/ AfghanChurchDocsJunAug07.htm.

nancial resources to diplomacy in Afghanistan and the surrounding region (such as Pakistan)."

Calls for negotiations with the Taliban and other insurgent and militia forces with extraordinarily dismal records on human rights necessarily raise concerns. So the churches reaffirmed that "human rights resonate with the Christian belief that all people are made in God's image and, therefore, deserve respect and protection." They emphasized human rights as foundational to the building of just, participatory, and sustainable peace. They also called on Canada to adhere strictly to international human rights standards in its handling of detainees.

The church leaders pointed to the failures in governance in Afghanistan, including the failure to fully include the country's Pashtun communities, and urged Canada to seek out new opportunities "for good and inclusive governance in partnership with Afghan civil society." They went on to say that "the longer term imperative is to strengthen the fragile state apparatus in Afghanistan so that it can better provide security and public services and meaningful democratic representation." They also called on greater attention to development: "To be more effective in building peace, we believe a significant shift in Canada's concentration of financial resources toward long-term human development is necessary." Concerns were also raised about the militarization of aid—that is, the close identification of military operations with assistance—and thus a call was made for strict adherence to universal humanitarian principles.

On the security question, the church leaders reiterated the 2001 call for accountability and due process in the pursuit of perpetrators of terrorist acts, emphasizing again that the response to terrorism is not primarily a military challenge. The Canadian military "should focus on enhancing protection of vulnerable Afghans rather than on aggressive engagement with insurgents in areas where the local population is suspicious or alienated from the central government." Their concerns were set clearly within the context of a global responsibility to protect the most vulnerable as articulated in the R2P doctrine: "Canada has an obligation not to abandon the people of Afghanistan. The vulnerable must be protected. As Scripture instructs us, we are to care for and respect our neighbour, especially the poor, the voiceless and the defenceless."

In October 2007 the Prime Minister of Canada appointed the Independent Advisory Panel on Afghanistan (the "Manley Panel") and the churches responded to the report through a brief joint communiqué by the Canadian Council of Churches and Project Ploughshares in January

2008.[15] The churches were forthright in their criticism of the Manley Report, saying that "sadly, [it] has missed the opportunity to guide Canada towards a truly constructive role in securing a long term sustainable peace in Afghanistan." The statement went on to reject the Manley Report's focus on continuing and expanding the counter-insurgency war and noted the failure of the report "to recommend that Canadian diplomatic support be focused on assisting Afghans and the international community in building a comprehensive peace negotiation that includes those elements of Afghan society that were excluded from the Bonn Compact." The communiqué thus insisted that the best hope for peace in Afghanistan rests in "a comprehensive peace building, reconciliation and diplomatic approach." It pointed out that "Canada, with its NATO/ISAF partners, is a party to a civil war in supporting one side in an internal conflict that precedes 9/11. A way must be found for the largely excluded Pashtun from the south and east of the country to join in the political process."

Though the churches might be criticized here for a failure to specify how such laudable goals are to be achieved, at a deeper level, they were also pointing to the basic truth that the current security failures in Afghanistan cannot be overcome simply by applying more and more force. The story of successful peacekeeping is that to build stability and protect vulnerable people, security forces must be accompanied by a range of processes and measures, identified earlier as basic political (diplomacy), governance (legitimacy), economic (development), and social (peacebuilding) commitments. If those measures are not actively pursued, the escalation of force inevitably leads to the escalation of violence without advancing the strategic or over-riding objectives. Discussions within the ecumenical community recognized a parallel to domestic law enforcement—after all, the combat operations in Afghanistan are, at their best, substantially about upholding the rule of law or domestic law enforcement. Even in stable societies, the threat and use of police force is clearly a factor in generating the confident expectation that those who violate laws will be caught and that the rule of law can be relied upon. But it is also true that law *enforcement* is most successful when it is bolstered by a high degree of consensus on the rightness or justness of the laws, confidence in and support for the institutions of the justice system, and acceptance of the legitimacy of the governance system that manages public affairs. In other words, a society based on the rule of law functions largely according to the law because the people overwhelmingly give their consent and voluntarily comply with

---

[15] Canadian Council of Churches, "We Believe God Desires Peace in their Land as in Ours," 24 January, 2008, http://www.ploughshares.ca/libraries/Statements/Manley%20Report%20CCC%20ENG.pdf.

laws because they believe that to do so is better for everyone, including themselves. The resort to force is thus reserved for the exception, for the spoilers.

Take away the consensus and the confidence in public institutions and the voluntary consent soon follows—leaving a society that is largely ungovernable. When genuine grievance and utter distrust of the authorities are combined with ready access to guns, the inevitable result is the escalation of violence, well beyond isolated spoilers, and the disintegration of public order. In the absence of a concerted focus on political and social measures designed to gradually build a collective trust, it is genuinely naïve to assume that military forces, no matter how robust, will be able to force consent and thus compliance. Afghanistan is in the process of demonstrating, once again, that any effort to substitute political engagement with intensified militarily action to defeat those outside the consensus is doomed to failure and entrenched warfare.

The churches were therefore highlighting the unfortunate fact that the international community has to date not tried hard enough to encourage the pursuit of a more inclusive political order that would enjoy the support of the broad majority of Afghans. Instead, the international community has tried to make up for the absence of political consensus and the pursuit of reconciliation with expanded military enforcement efforts.

In December of 2007, KAIROS, a Canadian inter-church group on justice issues, prepared a discussion paper that raised additional basic questions about the role and interests of the United States in its Afghanistan operation, about Canada's adjunct role, and about human rights and humanitarian relief.[16] In exploring the geo-political framework of Western military involvement in Afghanistan, the paper concluded:

> If, as this paper suggests, those objectives relate at least in part to the commercial and energy interests of the US, then the Canadian role may need to be understood quite differently. The fact that both OEF [the US Operation Enduring Freedom] and ISAF bear the heavy imprint of the US government and military suggests that even if Canada's role is focused on "good governance" and "stability," we need to ask some questions about how this role relates to the US objectives over and above the Canadian public's interests and Afghan ones.

---

[16] "Canada, Afghanistan and Human Rights: A KAIROS Discussion Paper," December 2007, http://www.kairoscanada.org/fileadmin/fe/files/PDF/HRTrade/ SubmissionsEtc/Discussion_paper_Afghanistan_fulltext_and_front_page _Dec07.pdf.

The paper suggested that the international community's predilection, at least for some, to turn to military action regardless of the circumstances is linked more to the over-riding interests of the major powers, in this case the United States, than to the objective pursuit of the well being of the Afghans on whose behalf intervention is ostensibly undertaken.

In mid-2009 the ecumenical community was in the process of developing a further appeal to the Government of Canada to focus Canadian resources in Afghanistan on reconciliation and support for negotiations toward a new comprehensive agreement on which a more durable stability can be built. Gen. Stanley McChrystal, the new US Commander in Afghanistan at that time, raised the prospect of ending the war through reconciliation with insurgents in his initial assessment of Afghan security:[17]

> Insurgencies of this nature typically conclude through military operations and political efforts driving some degree of host-nation reconciliation with elements of the insurgency. In the Afghan conflict, reconciliation may involve [Government of Afghanistan]-led, high-level political settlements.

The "high-level political settlement" to which McChrystal refers was in fact supposed to have been negotiated, as the churches have argued, in Bonn in late 2001 and was to be the foundation on which the International Security Assistance Force was originally mounted in 2002.[18] The war that ensued was not a consequence of some parties to that agreement defecting from it, but rather, of the fact that it never was a comprehensive, inclusive agreement involving all the key stakeholders to begin with. Michael Semple, the European Union's special representative in Afghanistan in 2004-2007, put it this way in a report for the United States Institute of Peace:

> It is now widely understood that the Bonn Accords did not constitute a peace agreement. They needed to be supplemented by a strategic pursuit of reconciliation in order to bring all Afghan parties to the conflict into the peaceful political process.[19]

---

[17] Gen. Stanley McChrystal "Commander's Initial Assessment," 30 August 2009, http://media.washingtonpost.com/wp-srv/politics/documents/Assessment_Redacted_092109.pdf.

[18] Originally approved by UN Security Council Resolution 1386 (2001), http://www.daccessdds.un.org/doc/UNDOC/GEN/N01/708/55/PDF/N0170855.pdf?OpenElement.

[19] Michael Semple, *Reconciliation in Afghanistan* (Washington: United States Institute of Peace Press, 2009), 89.

Eight years later, the "strategic pursuit of reconciliation" still has not happened. A core message of the churches during that time has been that the strategic pursuit of reconstruction must become the central focus of the Canadian mission in Afghanistan.

The reconciliation imperative

The Canadian Churches have been especially critical of Canada and of the international community for the persistent failure to launch new political and diplomatic efforts to negotiate a basic national political consensus to undergird Afghanistan's fledgling public institutions; instead, the focus has been on militarily defeating those outside the current but partial consensus. But that military effort has neither defeated the opposition nor delivered the promised security to the people of Afghanistan.

The churches anticipated the failure that an overweening focus on military counterinsurgency operations would bring, and the churches now anticipate that negotiations and diplomacy will have to become the central focus in Afghanistan—because that is how the vast majority of insurgencies end. The churches also realize that political consensus in Afghanistan, as in Canada or any other nation, does not mean enduring political harmony. Like Canada, Afghanistan is a place of enormous regional, geographic, and ethnic diversity in which broad political agreement will always be fragile and elusive—perhaps at best cobbled together through informal, temporary, and often issue-specific coalitions. That means that the objective should be to rebuild basic mechanisms or institutions and power-sharing arrangements capable of mediating, without resort to violence, the myriad of political conflicts that are endemic to any contemporary state. That is why the churches continue to insist that reconciliation efforts in Afghanistan are imperative, and urgently so, and that just as much international support and encouragement as is now reserved for assistance to military and police forces must in future be focused on the reconciliation agenda.

Many Faiths, One Planet: The Perils and Possibilities of Religion in a Fragile World

Douglas John Hall

The Ambiguity of Religion in the New World-Consciousness

The concern that underlies the argument of this paper was articulated in the starkest manner conceivable in two words scrawled, a few years ago, on the graffiti-inviting outer wall of the Presbyterian College in the city in which I live, Montreal. These words, written in large, black, angry letters appeared in the immediate wake of the events of 11 September, 2001, and they were obviously intended as a challenge to all of us in the region of McGill University's Faculty of Religious Studies, with which the Presbyterian College is affiliated. The two words were: "Religion Kills!" I am sure that all of us who taught or studied in the Faculty of Religious Studies at that time felt the sting of this accusation. I know that, as a Christian, I did; and I suspect that the same sense of judgement was felt by my colleagues and students who were Jewish, Hindu, Buddhist, Muslim, or members of other faith traditions.

"Religion Kills!" The same sentiment was expressed more gently, and at greater length, in a letter to the editor of *The International Herald Tribune*, and it seemed important enough to the Moderator of the Central Committee of the World Council of Churches to be cited early in his official "Report," delivered in Geneva in the Autumn of 2003. "The fundamental problems we are facing today," the letter declared, "derive from religion. Most of the terrorism and counter-terrorism in the world are based on religious fanaticism and extreme belief systems."[1]

These sentences are not the ravings of secular exhibitionists or disgruntled atheists. The accusation they level at religion is representative of

---

[1] Aram I, Catholicos of Cilicia, *The Ecumenical Review* 55, iss. 4 (2003): 378.

thoughts entertained by significant numbers of our civilization's most concerned citizens. And do they not represent, also, the spoken and unspoken anxieties (perhaps even the shame) of those of us who, to a greater or lesser degree, regard ourselves, and are regarded by society at large, as being "religious?" Few thinking persons would be ready to consider religion wholly detrimental to the life of the world. Yet it would be difficult indeed, in today's global village, to ignore the role of human religious fervour in the many and various threats to planetary existence that shout at us from every news broadcast and look out at us through the eyes of many who are the most obvious and immediate victims of those threats.

The threats of which I am thinking include not only terrorism and counter-terrorism but economic injustice and the maldistribution of global resources, environmental degradation, the oppression of women and children, globe-encircling diseases, and many other impediments to creaturely well-being that use and misuse the religious impulse for their inspiration. The day is over when religion could be thought an unambiguously "good thing," as many in the past believed it to be. Informed and sensitive members of every faith tradition today are likely to think twice, if not explicitly to demur, when they hear themselves described as "religious" persons.

It may be that the human being is by nature religious: Dietrich Bonhoeffer's well-known remarks notwithstanding,[2] *homo religiosus* may still be a more accurate generalization about humankind than is the rather pretentious designation, *homo sapiens*. But it is no more self-evident that our religious impulse will actualize itself in ways that are recognizably good and life-giving than that our human instinct to self-preservation or sexual expression will actualize themselves in a benevolent manner. At very least, religion, like sexuality and self-preservation, seems to be an ambiguous quality in the human. Its actualization will depend upon many influences, internal and external, that are not necessarily implicit in the impulse to religion as such.

Among those influences is what might be termed the "world-consciousness" that pertains in given historical settings. In the relatively small and homogeneous geographic units that were dominant in pre-modern periods, and, in varying degrees, until very recent times even in the so-called "developed" world, there was little—relatively speaking—to challenge a religion that assumed the right to pursue its own interests without considering the implications of its beliefs and pursuits for the larger community of human and extra-human life. I am old enough to remember a time when most Canadians and Americans lived their lives and

---

[2] Dietrich Bonhoeffer, *Letters and Papers from Prison* (London: SCM Press Ltd, 1953), 124.

thought their thoughts almost entirely within the confines of their villages, towns, or townships. The great world (Asia, Africa, Latin America, even Europe) was of course there—"out there"—for them, for us; but with few exceptions it was not part of our immediate and involuntary consciousness. Most people not only "acted locally," they also "thought locally."

The realities of the past half-century have changed all that. Not only the communications revolution but frequent travel, the mobility of entire populations, the presence in our midst of large numbers of non-European peoples, the fact that the vast majority of our population now lives in sizable multicultural cities, the swiftness with which communicable diseases in human and animal life affect us all, and many other factors have produced in most of us a degree of world-consciousness unheard of in my childhood and youth. As many have pointed out, the most important consequence of post-War space exploration has probably been the subtle but entirely effective manner in which it has engendered in all of us an awareness of our common and unalterable location within the biosphere of a small blue-green planet, beautiful and fragile, floating in an unbounded sea of space. I do not for a moment suggest that everyone has fully absorbed the ontological and ethical implications of this new world-consciousness—hardly! But I do believe that it affects all of us at an appreciable level of awareness, and—more importantly for our present topic—I feel sure that the extent to which it has entered one's consciousness will inevitably be reflected in one's understanding of and attitude towards religion. In a manner that was simply not true of western societies prior to the mid-twentieth century, most people today are apt to regard religion from the perspective of its actual performance on the global stage. There can be no doubt, I think, that for many of those who in the most recent surveys declared "no religious affiliation"[3], a prominent factor in their thinking is the suspicion that religion is inherently divisive if not inimical to world peace and order.

Can Religion also Contribute to Planetary Well-Being?

The question that this new world-consciousness raises for those of us who are in some meaningful sense of the word "religious" is whether religion—and specifically our own religion—is, or has the potentiality for being, also a positive contributor to the well-being of the planet; and of course, beyond mere speculation, whether such a potentiality, if it is pre-

---

[3] In the 2001 Canadian census 20% of Canadians, as compared with 13% in 1991.

sent, can be more fully realized in the actual living-out of faith in the tradition in question.

The answer to this question is bound up with religious plurality and the readiness of the religions to engage in dialogue aimed at greater mutuality. No specific religious faith may be pursued seriously today in isolation from the lived awareness of a multitude of religions other than, and perhaps at odds with, one's own. Part and parcel of our expanded world-consciousness is our increasingly existential awareness of the plurality of religions. In the very—indeed the exclusively!—White Anglo-Saxon Protestant village in southwestern Ontario in which I grew up, one could be "Christian," Protestant Christian, in a nonchalantly isolated way. That kind of innocence (which was never guiltless!) has been impossible now for decades. As Wilfred Cantwell Smith put it in his 1962 CBC lectures published under the title, *The Faith of Other Men*:

> The religious life of mankind from now on, if it is to be lived at all, will be lived in a context of religious pluralism....It will become increasingly apparent...that to be a Christian in the modern world, or a Jew, or an agnostic, is to be so in a society in which other [people], intelligent, devout, and righteous, are Buddhists, Muslims, Hindus.[4]

The more conscious we become of the physical unity and the vulnerability of the one planet, the more pressing is our need to come to terms with earth's many religions. While ordinary (or perhaps one should say extraordinary) human tolerance and liberality, where it exists, can provide a reprieve from intellectual and spiritual struggle with the reality of religious plurality, serious faith of whatever specific brand cannot for long avoid the need for understanding where this multiplicity is concerned. And in significant portions of the globe, by which nonetheless the whole is affected, such tolerance and liberality cannot be counted upon.

There is an urgency, therefore, about inter-faith understanding and dialogue, and this is widely felt. Yet the actual experience of such dialogue is still severely limited. By comparison, dialogue within the divided and once-militantly-independent faith-communities of Christendom has by now accumulated a century's worth of encounter and struggle towards greater unity—and I refer only to the modern ecumenical movement, which should be dated from the Edinburgh Missionary Conference in 1910, which led to the establishment of the International Missionary Council in 1925. The World Council of Churches grew out of these delib-

---

[4] Wilfred Cantwell Smith, *The Faith of Other Men* (New York: Harper Torchbooks, 1972), 11.

erations, and was actually conceived in 1937, though on account of the Second World War, its inauguration was delayed until 1948. Despite the acknowledged fact that ecumenism has never been able to overcome the entrenched and stubborn divisions of the churches, and despite the fact that still today its course is characterized by an alternating "ebb and flow" (as the recently-published *Encyclopaedia of Protestantism* puts it), no-one can gainsay the extent and depth of a hundred years of concrete experience in the quest for Christian unity. All who are able personally to remember the ecclesiastical situation that pertained prior to (let us say) 1950 can only marvel at the distance we have come, in fifty or sixty years, from that kind of non-communication between the churches. With the Second Vatican Council in 1962 and beyond, a whole new era in Christian life opened up almost overnight, and those of us who experienced it at close range are still, many of us, in a state of happy astonishment.

The question, therefore, to which I should like to address myself in what follows can be stated thus: Is there in this extended Christian experience of ecumenical dialogue any wisdom to be gained that is applicable to the larger diversity of religious faiths? In putting the question that way, I am assuming (and of course not everyone assumes this) that Christians ought to be committed to a serious quest for understanding and mutuality between the religions of the world. Personally, I find myself in wholehearted agreement with the great Jewish thinker, the late Abraham Heschel, who in his address before the Congress on the Theology of the Renewal of the Church convened by Roman Catholics during Canada's Centennial year, 1967, announced: "I believe that one of the achievements of this age will be the realization that in our age religious pluralism is the will of God."[5]

How Can Christian Ecumenical Experience Facilitate Inter-faith Dialogue?

Christianity can I believe make an enormous contribution to the "realization" of such an "achievement." It is in fact the central conviction of this essay that Christian ecumenical experience has provided a background of both theoretical and practical wisdom from which it is possible to derive certain principles that could prove invaluable in inter-faith encounter and dialogue.

---

[5] Abraham Heschel, "The Jewish Notion of God and Christian Renewal," in Laurence K. Shook, ed., *Theology of Renewal*, vol. 1 (Montreal: Palm Publishers, 1968), 110

More to illustrate than to exhaust the possibilities, I will describe four areas of ecumenical Christian experience from which such principles may (I repeat may) be deduced. If I speak tentatively here it is of course because Christians themselves have by no means *fully* accepted or exemplified any of these principles; yet, in the most profound expressions of Christian ecumenism in all branches of the universal church, these principles have been present both clearly and centrally. Thus they represent what may at least be termed "tried and true" guidelines for any discourse between persons and communities of diverse religious conviction.

1. The Well-Being of the World as the Foundational Rationale of Ecumenical Endeavour

This first principle (and therefore I have put it first) speaks directly to the background concern with which I have begun this address, namely, the fear that religion is inherently divisive and prone to violence. One may readily draw such a conclusion about religion, alas, even about religions, like Christianity, that emphasize such virtues as peace and justice and love, when religion is driven exclusively or chiefly by its own internal dynamism and quest for survival and enhancement. But what may occur when a faith-community embraces a *raison d'être* larger than itself?— when it comes to regard as the primary rationale for its existence, its mission, its struggle for integrity, a world that vastly transcends its own existence and is deemed by its own authoritative scriptures to be the chief object of the sacrificial love of God? Obviously, such a vision will exercise both a self-limiting and an expanding influence upon its entire life and outreach.

And that, I suggest, is precisely what the Christian ecumenical movement of the twentieth century came to realize as it gradually worked its way into its task. It discovered that, so long as the churches were concerned chiefly for their own security and influence, dialogue between them was bound to flounder. But when they felt themselves led by the divine Spirit and by the gospel itself to discern and develop a genuine regard for the fate of the earth, they experienced what I would like to call the grace of a sufficient self-forgetfulness to be in dialogue with one another as participants in a common task: namely, the peace, prosperity and flowering of God's beloved world. While ecumenical deliberations over the past century have frequently degenerated into preoccupation with narrowly-conceived ecclesiastical relationships, the great exponents of Christian ecumenism (like W.A. Visser t'Hooft and Karl Rahner) have always reminded the churches that the fundamental rationale of the movement towards unity is not the well-being of the church but the well-being of God's beloved world. I suppose that the biblical text most frequently quoted in ecumenical discussions over the past decades has been John 17: 20-21. There, in his so-called "High Priestly Prayer," the Christ is represented as praying for the unity of his little band of followers to the end "that the world may believe." The one-ness of the church, said the great ecumenists, is not and must not become an end-in-itself; it is only a means—for Christians the most pressing means—to a right and credible communication to the world of the truth and trustworthiness of God's abiding love for and commitment to creation. A gospel of reconciling love proclaimed by a church notoriously divided within itself is a contradiction in terms. If the world is to take seriously the message that it is greatly loved, and that the lived experience of its Creator's love effects a wondrous new mutuality among creatures who hear and believe that message, then the apostolic messenger must at least approximate such "new creaturehood" in its own life.

While John's account of Jesus' Gethsemane prayer can be read to support Christian exclusivity (as seems to be the case in Christian fundamentalism), and while authentic Christian concern for the world has always been tainted by a lingering Constantinian expansionism that wants to conquer the world, the programs and pronouncements of the main ecumenical bodies of the churches manifest a genuine and consistent world-orientation that is not marred by excessive self-interest. Personally, I feel that this kind of world-orientation was most concretely articulated in the decision of the Vancouver Assembly of the World Council of Churches in 1983 to adopt as its working theme for the next seven years, "Justice, Peace and the Integrity of Creation."

There is, it seems to me, a principle here that can be applied in both theoretical and practical ways to inter-faith discourse; for while, like Christianity, every religion no doubt manifests a certain all-too-human desire for pre-eminence, it is also true of most great world religions (and therefore they may be thought great!) that they contain dimensions of generosity and vigilance for universal peace and justice which, when stimulated by awareness of the great need and vulnerability of the world as a whole, are able to exercise a countervailing influence in the face of religious isolationism, exclusivity, and chauvinism. With its long and studied experience of the manner in which world-orientation modifies and guides religious discourse between historically divided faith communities, Christianity could help to make such commitment to the well-being of the planet more effectively present in other religious bodies and in our encounter with one another.

2. Particularity as Entrée to Universality

At the centre of the Christian confession of faith there stands the figure of an historical person, entirely human, yet representing in the very fullness of his humanity a transcendence that has prevented the church, even in its more humanistic expressions, from describing him in human terms alone. This "Christocentric" concentration is not optional for Christians. What would Christianity mean without Jesus as the Christ at its centre and core? As Paul Tillich affirms in the Christological section of his influential Systematic Theology:

> Christianity is what it is through the affirmation that Jesus of Nazareth, who has been called 'the Christ', is actually the Christ, namely, he who brings the new state of things, the New Being. Wherever the assertion that Jesus is the Christ is maintained, there is the Christian message; wherever this assertion is denied, the Christian message is not affirmed. Christianity was born, not with the birth of the man who is called 'Jesus', but in the moment in which one of his followers was driven to say to him, 'Thou art the Christ'.[6]

There can be no "Christianity," then, that is not bound up with this particular person and event. That realization led theologians in the first half of the twentieth century to introduce the phrase, "the scandal of particularity." The term "scandal" in this usage of course derives from St. Paul, who in First Corinthians speaks of the *skandalon* of the gospel of the crucified Christ (1 Cor. 1:23).

For many Christians both yesterday and today, belief in and about the Christ, often defined in very explicit and doctrinaire forms, is treated as the great test of authenticity. Many of those who have refused membership in the World Council of Churches, for instance, have done so on the basis of the Council's alleged failure to be sufficiently centred in Christ. And even within the World Council itself there has been a never-ending debate between those who stress a strong, definitive Christology, to the point of suspecting all who do not embrace their definitions, and others who are vigilant against the substitution of "Christomonism" for "Christocentrism."

Among the latter group there has emerged what I would like to call a new awareness of the role of particularity in religious faith. There is no entrée to the universal (and faith is ultimately bound up with universals, including the understanding of deity) that does not pass through the particular. I only encounter "childhood" or "womanhood" through my meet-

---

[6] Paul Tillich, *Systematic Theology*, vol. 2 (Chicago: University of Chicago Press, 1957), 97.

ing with particular children and particular women. I only encounter deity, or transcendence, or "the holy" through particular beings, symbols, events, texts or oral testimonies that authenticate themselves to me as being bearers of ultimacy.

The question that must be asked of all particulars is how they function for us. Attachment to a particular child could (and often does) produce indifference—or worse!—towards other children. On the other hand, profound knowledge of and love for one child may so enlarge the imagination and compassion of the knower that he finds himself introduced in a new way to the whole world of children—and thus to a concern for "the future," a future that surpasses his own futurity. The question about the particulars that are always present in religion is, surely, how they function for believers. Do they function to exclude and circumscribe, or do they function to include and enlarge the range of human awareness and care?

It has been the discovery of those most deeply involved in Christian ecumenism, I believe, that the particular called "Jesus"—if he remains person; if he is not reduced to mere dogma; if the ineffability of his historic personhood is sustained; if he is encountered as the Word incarnate who defies retranslation into mere words!—that this particular "particularity," while "scandalous" in terms of the usual presuppositions about deity, nevertheless does not function for true faith as an excluding factor but rather opens faith to the other, to difference, to the mystery of the whole, and in a manner that is both new and, often, radical. The greatest symbolic representations of Christian faith in our time (including that of Martin Luther King, Mother Theresa, Bishop Romero, Dietrich Bonhoeffer, Jean Vanier and others) are the symbols that they are precisely because their Christian faith has expressed itself in exceptionally non-partisan and inclusive ways.

Now, every religion—even those which assume direct access to the absolute—is involved with particularity, whether that be the particularity of a person (Mohammed or Moses or Baha Ullah), the particularity of a text, particular historical events or experiences, or whatever. And what one may ask, out of Christian ecumenical experience, is whether the particularities associated with other religious traditions do not also contain or suggest openness to the other that Christian ecumenists, in their internal debates, have found to be the case in a Christology that is pursued at depth. Perhaps no religion has been so intensely focused on its particularity as has Christianity upon Jesus Christ—and often, to be sure, with dire consequences for others. Yet in the most searching Christological contemplation in and around the modern ecumenical movement, precisely Jesus the Christ—the "scandal of particularity"—has proven the very doorway of many Christians of all persuasions to a universality that, otherwise, they would not have known. It is therefore possible for Christians to encourage representatives of other religious traditions to explore as fully as possible the potentiality of their particularities to give birth to similar expressions of inclusivity. It is, in short, not a matter of abandoning the particular foci of our traditions, but of allowing them to deepen our awareness of their grounding in a universal transcendence that cannot be possessed exclusively by any one religion, or even by all religions.

3. The Quest for Power Always Impairs Ecumenical Discourse

It has been the experience of Christians involved in inter-church dialogue that there can be no dialogue when the bodies represented approach the ecumenical task with a prior and adamant commitment to the maintenance of their own pre-eminence. This refers not only to the determination to control discourse and to exercise political power in all decision-making; it refers also, and more importantly, to the assumption that a particular doctrinal tradition has captured truth and must therefore maintain itself intact over against all alternative perceptions. Ecumenical dialogue comes to a standstill whenever its participants act on the assumption that they alone are in possession of ultimate verity.

The actual experience of the breakdown of dialogue whenever that assumption is present, either openly or (which is more often the case) covertly, has led in ecumenical circles to a more modest—and I would say a more profound and biblically-informed—understanding of the nature of theological truth. It has done so, not as a triumph of Christian humility or bourgeois niceness, but for the very practical reason that, without such a critique of truth and of the human and institutional relation to truth, ecumenical dialogue could not have proceeded. In the meeting of ecclesiastical bodies that had for centuries been almost totally isolated from one another, and in their isolation could pursue their various "orthodoxies" without reference to or challenge from other versions of Christian truth—in the actual meeting of these long-separated groupings it was necessary to rediscover an understanding of the nature of truth which, though never wholly neglected by theological scholarship, could remain a pious sentiment without exercising its innately critical function with respect to the truth-claims of the churches.

I am referring to the biblical conception of Truth as a living reality. "No one," wrote Paul Tillich, "not even a believer or a church, can boast of possessing the truth, just as no one can boast of possessing love."[7] Jesus did not offer his disciples a systematic theology; he offered them himself. "I am...the truth," St. John's Gospel has him declare (John 14:6), thus capturing the livingness of truth as it is understood to be throughout the older and newer Testaments. Whoever hears this "I" knows that the entire assumption is false and idolatrous that theological truth can be possessed, owned, and used to confound every rival claim. At most, we may be oriented towards truth; and insofar as we are so oriented we shall be open to others in whom we may perceive the same orientation. In specifically Christian parlance: Those who are turned towards the truth that Jesus "is" will be able to recognize others who also look beyond themselves for what is ultimate, even when these others are not looking specifically towards Jesus.

Christian ecumenicity has been able to function—not, often or consistently, to flourish, but at least to function!—for a hundred years only insofar as it has been capable of realizing the modesty-factor inherent in this principle. Cynicism might write such modesty off as being nothing more than the influence of modern humanism and liberalism; but it is in fact the consequence—I would say the absolutely necessary and self-evident consequence—of a faith that is founded, not on propositional truth, but the truth of encounter with Person, with "the eternal Thou" (Buber). Under the impact of diverse and sometimes antithetical testimonies to the meaning of that encounter, Christians in ecumenical conversation had once more to realize that their doctrine can only point to ultimate reality, and therefore cannot and must not be regarded as a source of power over others. This realization is plainly present in the concluding words of the report of the Moderator of the World Council of Church's 2003 address, from which I quoted briefly at the outset: "Any religion that aims for power loses its *raison d'être*. God is the owner, protector, sustainer and reconciler of the whole humanity and creation. Religion is the servant and agent of God's universal plan."[8]

Again we may ask: Is there not in other religious traditions also, and perhaps in the religious impulse as such, something comparable to this recognition of the transcendence of ultimate power, especially the power of *truth*? And may not Christians, on the basis of their own experience of the ways that such a recognition, stimulated by diversity, exercises a qualifying effect on religious discourse, exemplify and encourage members of other faiths to explore their own traditions for such insight? If the assumption of power, its possession and retention, has proven a sure barrier to

---

[7] Paul Tillich, *On the Boundary* (New York: Charles Scribner's Sons, 1966), 51.
[8] Aram I, *op.cit.*, 391.

inter-church discourse, it will certainly prove a barrier to serious attempts at inter-faith discourse. Can the concrete ecumenical Christian experience of the transcendence of power, especially the power of truth, find an echo in all religions as they seek to enter into new relationships with one another?

4. Dialogue with Other Traditions Can Enhance Knowledge and Appreciation of One's Own

It has been a source of hesitation on the part of many Christians and ecclesiastical groupings that the prospect of ecumenical encounter, if entered into earnestly, could have the effect of distancing them from their own tradition, by somehow incorporating them into a kind of globalized spirituality, a super-church, in which the familiar comforts and challenges of their own established tradition had been absorbed and, for all practical purposes, forgotten. There are still Christian denominations and elements within all of our denominations that fear and distrust ecumenism, especially at the local level, for precisely that sort of reason.

Yet most of us who have actually been involved in ecumenical discourse for several decades realize, I believe, that such fear is unfounded. In fact, with few exceptions (in my experience at least), the exact opposite is the case. Not only do we become more knowledgeable of our own ecclesial tradition when we enter into dialogue with persons of other heritages, we frequently find ourselves appreciating aspects of our own tradition that had eluded us heretofore. The presence and testimony of the others has illumined both positive and negative qualities in our own received faith. We change, in consequence of such illumination; but we do not feel that we lose what is essential to our own historic faith. Rather, we find ways of sharing that essence with the others, and of being enriched by what they bring. Thus, as countless Christians of all historic persuasions have found over the past hundred years, while ecumenical discourse introduces something new to all who undertake it sincerely, it does not destroy but puts into wider circulation emphases and concerns that are the treasures of the whole, varied testimony of the ages.

In quite practical terms, ecumenical Christian experience throughout these decades has helped immensely to overcome the forgetfulness, not to say the plain ignorance, of many with respect to their own ecclesial traditions. You cannot sit in theological or ethical discussions that are representative of many doctrinal and moral traditions without sooner or later being brought to the point of asking yourself, "What does my church teach on that subject?" In the post-Christendom era that is now the social and cultural context of all Christian groupings, there is a growing awareness of the often appalling lack of knowledge (scriptural, doctrinal, historical) that characterizes most of our churches. Yet without such knowledge faith itself will not survive, to say nothing of specific communities of faith. Churches will not be kept going by sentiment, or ritual, or hereditary custom. Anselm's dictum, *fides quaerens intellectum*, has a new currency and urgency among us now. In churches that face the demise of automatic religiosity, there is among those who remain a felt need to understand what they believe. And that need is nowhere more in evidence than in the meeting with one another of once-separated Christian bodies.

This experience of Christian ecumenicity, namely that hospitality towards and discourse with "the other" does not diminish but can enhance knowledge of one's own, has immediate applicability—*a fortiori!*—to inter-faith encounter. Conscientious Christians often tell themselves and one another that their knowledge of other world religions is appallingly slight. But whenever inter-religious dialogue is attempted, especially though not exclusively at the congregational level, Christian participants have realized, often to their chagrin, that their knowledge of their own tradition is almost as minimal as their knowledge of other faiths. Heretofore, they have been satisfied with generalities and pious clichés and "favourite Bible verses"; in inter-faith discourse they now find themselves incapable of articulating Christian belief in an informed and nuanced way. The presence and testimony of "the other," especially when "the other"— Muslim, Jewish, Hindu or whatever—is religiously informed and articulate, often goads Christians into deliberate and disciplined attempts to comprehend their own tradition in ways that might never have occurred apart from this encounter with religious difference.

I must conclude therefore that another contribution that ecumenical Christian experience can make to inter-faith dialogue is the confidence that opening oneself to the faith of others, far from risking the loss or relativization of one's own tradition, much more consistently results in a deepening of understanding of one's own, while at the same time being the occasion for greater knowledge of and compassion for other faith-traditions.

This is perhaps the most important lesson to be learned by all of us, especially, who live in conspicuously multi-religious cultures. For the great fear of those most committed to a particular religious tradition, I think, is that close encounter with religious diversity will rob them of their assumption, nurtured in more homogeneous contexts, that their own religion is the best, the truest, the ultimately approved. Genuine and sustained inter-faith dialogue, which surely must include those most committed to their specific religion and not only persons of a liberal frame of mind, will only be feasible where there is some assurance that the encounter with difference will not result in such loss of the faith one has known and loved. Christian ecumenical experience can contribute much to the building of such assurance.

Conclusion

My contention, then, to sum up, has been that there are numerous ways in which the ecumenical experience of Christians over the past century particularly can facilitate dialogue between the various religions that are present in our world and, especially, in multicultural and religiously pluralistic cultures. By way of illustration, I have described briefly four of these ways: (1) that the well-being of the world is the foundational rationale of ecumenical endeavour; (2) that particularity profoundly appreciated is our entrée to a deeper universality, (3) that the quest for power always impairs ecumenical discourse, and (4) that hospitality towards and dialogue with other traditions does not diminish but can in fact enhance one's knowledge and appreciation of one's own tradition. There are of course many other principles that could be derived from a century of Christian ecumenical experience.

Now, it would be false and misleading to exaggerate the potential Christian contribution to inter-faith relationships, for not only have Christians themselves failed to appropriate fully or consistently any of the principles I have named, but in addition to that there are of course barriers to inter-faith dialogue that are not present in inter-church dialogue. But we must not wait to be perfect before we attempt to apply whatever wisdom we have learned about seeking understanding and unity between religious communities. For the alternative to such a quest is a world that is already, and will increasingly be, victimized by religions that refuse dialogue and court the kind of intransigence that is inherently belligerent and, ultimately, violent. The quest for harmony and trust between religions, even if it can only hope for approximation, is no longer an option for serious persons of every faith posture. For the one planet cannot for long contain the human suspicion, envy, competition and revenge that are augmented and emboldened by a religious fervour that lives exclusively within its own "dividing walls of hostility." While keeping our eyes wide open to the conflicts that religion inspires or is caused to sanction, we should never lose sight of the blessings that all humankind's great faiths, at their best, wish to bestow upon the world.

CONTRIBUTORS

Howard Adelman

Howard Adelman is a Professor Emeritus at York University in Toronto. He was previously a Professor of Philosophy there from 1966-2003, where he founded and was the first Director of the Centre for Refugee Studies and served as Editor of *Refuge* until the end of 1993. Professor Adelman recently completed a three year term as Research Professor at the Key Centre for Ethics, Law, Justice and Governance at Griffith University in Brisbane, Australia, along with a three-year appointment as Deputy Convenor for the governance research network in Australia. In that role, he helped create an international consortium of governance researchers and co-founded the International Consortium for Research on the Global Health Workforce (ICR-GHW), HealthNet Australia, and the Canadian Consortium for Research on the Health Workforce.

Gary D. Badcock

Gary D. Badcock studied philosophy at Memorial University and theology at the University of Edinburgh. He taught Systematic Theology at the Universities of Aberdeen (1991-92) and Edinburgh (1993-99) before being appointed to the Peache Chair of Divinity at Huron University College (1999-). His teaching and publications span the areas of Christian doctrine, philosophical theology, and ethics. He is currently writing a book on Christian monotheism and the doctrine of the Trinity.

Craig A. Carter

Craig A. Carter is a Professor of Religious Studies at Tyndale University College and Seminary, Toronto, where he teaches Systematic Theology, Moral Theology, and Christianity and Culture. He received his Ph.D. from the University of St. Michael's College at the Toronto School of Theology. He is currently working on a volume on the doctrine of God and human personhood.

Rashed Chowdhury

Rashed Chowdhury is a PhD Candidate in the Department of History at McGill University in Montreal, Quebec. A Belarusian-Bengali-Canadian Muslim, he holds degrees in international relations from Grinnell College, Iowa, and in Islamic Studies from McGill University. He is active in interfaith dialogue in Canada and writes regularly for the pro-democracy Belarusian magazine *Arche*.

Walter Dorn

Walter Dorn is Associate Professor of Defence Studies at the Canadian Forces College and the Royal Military College of Canada. He is a consultant to the UN's Department of Peacekeeping Operations and has served in various UN missions in Africa, Asia and Central America.

Douglas John Hall

Douglas John Hall is Professor Emeritus of Theology, McGill University, Montréal, Québec, and among the foremost Christian theologians in North America. His many publications include major works in Political Theology as well as in Systematic Theology.

Christopher Hrynkow

Christopher Hrynkow holds degrees in theology and in the social foundations of education. He is currently a Doctoral student in Peace and Conflict Studies at the Arthur V. Mauro Centre for Peace and Justice, St. Paul's College, University of Manitoba, teaches Conflict Studies at Menno Simons College, University of Winnipeg, and leads a seminar, "Cultures of Violence, Cultures of Peace" at the Canadian Mennonite University.

Remmelt C. Hummelen

Dr. Hummelen has worked in Afghanistan on three occasions, first in 1994 (pre-Taliban) to 1995 (with Taliban) with the United Nations (UNDCP, now UNODCC); second, in 2004 with as Programme Advisor for Law and Order Trust Fund under the United Nations Development Program, based in the Ministry of the Interior, Kabul; and, third, in 2007 based in Jalalabad as Conflict Mitigation Specialist, part of the Local Governance and

Community Development Project (funded by USAID). Has also worked and lived in Pakistan for 4 years, as well in Iraq and Somalia.

Darren Marks

Darren C. Marks holds degrees in science and theology from the University of Toronto and degrees in theology from the University of Oxford. He has also studied at the Friedrich Wilhelms Universität (Bonn). His primary research area is contemporary Systematic Theology. He has written extensively on Protestantism, global Theology and has a forthcoming work entitled *Justifying God: A Theology of Sin*.

Ernie Regehr

Ernie Regehr is the co-founder of Project Ploughshares, and an Adjunct Associate Professor in Peace and Conflict Studies at Conrad Grebel University College, University of Waterloo, Ontario. He is also a Fellow of the Centre for International Governance Innovation. In addition to publishing widely on peace and security issues, he has frequently visited conflict zones and engaged in Track II diplomacy efforts, particularly in southern Sudan with the Africa Peace Forum of Nairobi. In 2008 Ernie visited Kabul, Afghanistan, to conduct a series of interviews on approaches to political reconciliation. He has served as an NGO representative and expert advisor on a number of Government of Canada delegations to multilateral disarmament forums and is a former Commissioner of the World Council of Churches Commission on International Affairs. Ernie Regehr is an Officer of the Order of Canada.

Erika Simpson

Erika Simpson is an Associate Professor in the Department of Political Science at the University of Western Ontario in London, Ontario. She specializes in International Relations and International Security, and has written extensively on nuclear issues–mainly nuclear proliferation and disarmament and contemporary Canadian defence and foreign policy issues. She is also the vice chair of the Canadian Pugwash Group, an affiliate of the Pugwash International Conferences, and for seven years served as one of its Executive Directors.